Dagestan – History, Culture, Identity

Dagestan – History, Culture, Identity provides an up-to-date and comprehensive overview of Dagestan, a strategically important republic of the Russian Federation which borders Chechnya, Georgia and Azerbaijan, and its people.

It outlines Dagestan's rich and complicated history, from 5th c ACE to post USSR, as seen from the viewpoint of the Dagestani people. Chapters feature the new age of social media, urban weddings, modern and traditional medicine, innovative food cultivation, the little-known history of Mountain Jews during the Soviet period, flourishing heroes of sport and finance, emerging opportunities in ethno-tourism and a recent Dagestani music revival. In doing so, the authors examine the large number of different ethnic groups in Dagestan, their languages and traditions, and assess how the people of Dagestan are coping and thriving despite the changes brought about by globalisation, new technology and the modern world: through which swirls an increasing sense of identity in an indigenous multi-ethnic society.

Robert Chenciner was a Visiting Academic at St Antony's College, University of Oxford. He was an honorary member of the Dagestan Scientific Centre of the Russian Academy of Sciences.

Magomedkhan Magomedkhanov is Head of the Ethnography Institute of the Dagestan Scientific Centre, Russian Academy of Sciences, Makhachkala, Republic of Dagestan, Russian Federation.

Routledge Contemporary Russia and Eastern Europe Series

102. Shamanism in Siberia
Sound and Turbulence in Cursing Practices in Tuva
Mally Stelmaszyk

103. Stalin and Soviet Early Cold War Policy
Southern Neighbours in the Shadow of Moscow, 1945–1947
Jamil Hasanli

104. Disinformation, Narratives and Memory Politics in Russia and Belarus
Edited by Agnieszka Legucka and Robert Kupiecki

105. The Nagorno-Karabakh Conflict
Historical and Political Perspectives
Edited by M. Hakan Yavuz and Michael Gunter

106. Innovation and Modernization in Contemporary Russia
Science Towns, Technology Parks and Very Limited Success
Imogen Sophie Kristin Wade

107. Ukraine, Russia and the West
When Value Promotion met Hard Power
Stefan Hedlund

108. Regional Leadership in Post-Soviet Eurasia
The Strategies of Russia, China, and the European Union
Edited by Irina Busygina and Svetlana Krivokhizh

109. Dagestan – History, Culture, Identity
Robert Chenciner and Magomedkhan Magomedkhanov

For more information about this series, please visit: www.routledge.com/Routledge-Contemporary-Russia-and-Eastern-Europe-Series/book-series/SE0766

Dagestan – History, Culture, Identity

Robert Chenciner and Magomedkhan Magomedkhanov

With contributions from, alphabetically:

Alexander Bakanov
Saida Garunova
Magomed-Rasul Ibragimov
Maysarat Musaeva
Zoya Ramazanova

Ethnography Department of The Institute of History, Archaeology and Ethnography of the Dagestan Scientific Centre of Russian Academy of Sciences

LONDON AND NEW YORK

First published 2024
by Routledge
4 Park Square, Milton Park, Abingdon, Oxon OX14 4RN

and by Routledge
605 Third Avenue, New York, NY 10158

Routledge is an imprint of the Taylor & Francis Group, an informa business

© 2024 Robert Chenciner and Magomedkhan Magomedkhanov

The right of Robert Chenciner and Magomedkhan Magomedkhanov to
be identified as authors of this work has been asserted in accordance with
sections 77 and 78 of the Copyright, Designs and Patents Act 1988.

All rights reserved. No part of this book may be reprinted or reproduced or
utilised in any form or by any electronic, mechanical, or other means, now
known or hereafter invented, including photocopying and recording, or in
any information storage or retrieval system, without permission in writing
from the publishers.

Trademark notice: Product or corporate names may be trademarks or
registered trademarks, and are used only for identification and explanation
without intent to infringe.

British Library Cataloguing-in-Publication Data
A catalogue record for this book is available from the British Library

Library of Congress Cataloging-in-Publication Data
Names: Chenciner, Robert, author. | Magomedkhanov, Magomedkhan,
    1951– author.
Title: Dagestan – history, culture, identity / Robert Chenciner &
    Magomedkhan Magomedkhanov.
Description: New York : Routledge, [2023] | Series: Routledge
    contemporary Russia and Eastern Europe series | Includes bibliographical
    references and index.
Identifiers: LCCN 2023000417 (print) | LCCN 2023000418 (ebook) |
    ISBN 9781032483429 (hardback) | ISBN 9781032483450 (paperback) |
    ISBN 9781003388579 (ebook)
Subjects: LCSH: Dagestan (Russia)—History. | Dagestan (Russia)—Ethnic
    relations. | Dagestan (Russia)—Social life and customs. | Ethnology—
    Russia (Federation)—Dagestan.
Classification: LCC DK511.D2 C478 2023 (print) | LCC DK511.D2
    (ebook) | DDC 947.5/2—dc23/eng/20230111
LC record available at https://lccn.loc.gov/2023000417
LC ebook record available at https://lccn.loc.gov/2023000418

ISBN: 978-1-032-48342-9 (hbk)
ISBN: 978-1-032-48345-0 (pbk)
ISBN: 978-1-003-38857-9 (ebk)

DOI: 10.4324/9781003388579

Typeset in Times New Roman
by Apex CoVantage, LLC

Contents

List of maps	*vii*
List of figures	*viii*
Preface	*ix*

1	Introduction – what is Dagestan?	1
2	Shaitans, monsters, magic places and substances	4
3	The Sasanian walls against the Huns	14
4	Trade with the Kievan Russ and the Golden Horde	18
5	Trade with the Moscow Tsardom XV–XVI centuries	26
6	Trade with Muscovy XVII–XVIII centuries	34
7	Under Russian governance 1801–1859	42
8	XIX Century historical consciousness	53
9	Shamil's Ethno-religious Imamate	60
10	Legal systems under the Russian government	73
11	Repression and Sovietization	80
12	Language policy of the USSR	93
13	Schools, literacy and publishing under the Tsar and Soviets	100

vi *Contents*

14	Poems written in Avar and Archi languages	108
15	Re-Islamization of public consciousness	118
16	Pre-Soviet and contemporary cultures	127
17	New traditions in urban weddings	132
18	Social media – the XXI century	144
19	Surviving Covid and traditional medicine	152
20	Traditional medicine of mountain Dagestan	164
21	Dagestan mountain-valley horticulture	174
22	About Mountain Jews	183
23	Meat and Fish of the Mountain Jews	188
24	Heroes of sport and finance	192
25	Monetizing the Mountains	201
26	A virtual tour to Archi	206
27	In Dagestan, as they say, everyone sings and everyone dances	221
	Index	*227*

Maps

3.1	Derbent Walls	15
4.1	The Great Silk Roads from China	22
5.1	The Volga route from the Caspian to and from Moscow	27
5.2	Trading routes between Moscow and Europe	31
6.1	Locating Tersky	35
7.1	Ethnic lands of Dagestan c. 1900	47
26.1	Getting to Archi	206
26.2	Archi's villages, mountains and rivers	208

Figures

	Robert in the mountains	x
2.1	Stylized dragon	9
2.2	Another dragon	9
8.1	Shamil	57
12.1	Kultsansturm 1928	96
17.1	Inside a wedding banquet hall	138
19.1	Covid-19 as of 7 December 2020	154
21.1	Terracing in Dagestan	176
21.2	Avar Kolkhoz woman	181
24.1	Magomedov	195
24.2	Suleiman Kerimov	196
24.3	Khabib Nurmagomedov alongside his father	198
24.4	Tagir Gadzhiev	199
26.1	A view of Archi from the north	214
26.2	Archi village at the confluence of the Bidi and Klala rivers	214
26.3	The sacred mount Bedeku	215
26.4	Sheep and shepherd on summer pasture	215
26.5	The author (MM) checking wool	216
26.6	Tasty dried meat and sausage	216
26.7	Archi felt mosaic carpets	217
26.8	Highland dancers	217
26.9	Highland singers	218
26.10	Men cooking the wedding feast	218
26.11	Khvatli is a dish of oat flour	219
26.12	Showing gifts to the bride	219
26.13	Flowers from Archi	220
27.1	Lezginka dancers	225

Preface

Robert first obtained permission to visit Dagestan in 1986. Dagestan – a remote and mountainous region of the Caucasus – a place visited by few. His intention was to study closely related flatwoven rugs, but Dagestan and the eastern Caucasus provoked an interest far beyond this. Through years of ethnographic fieldwork, and with the help of Dr Magomedkhan Magomedkhanov and local scholars, Robert – known to many as Bob or Chence – visited hundreds of Dagestani villages.

He became a senior associate member of St Antony's College, Oxford, in 1987, and was similarly honoured as a fellow of the Royal Geographic Society, in 1989, and later as an honorary member of the Dagestan Scientific Centre of the Russian Academy of Sciences in 1990.

Robert would talk of how his heart should return to the Dagestan mountains as he loved them so dearly. This book is his last work and confirms this ethnographic legacy. It is dedicated to the people, lands and traditions of Dagestan.

Robert was sadly overtaken by cancer as he was writing this book, and he died in London on 30th October 2021. As a result, parts of this text have had to be edited, revised and even in places reshaped without oversight from Robert, as he would have otherwise liked. The authors must be excused for any remaining flaws and delays arising from these difficult circumstances. We would like to thank and commend James Waterfield who has been dedicated, kind and unendingly committed to this scholarly and editorial process, and to whom we are very much indebted.

We, the readers, would do well to remember Robert's prescient words reverberating from 1997, in the preface to his first text on Dagestan:

'. . . the future for neighbouring Dagestan – at the whim of a hostile, lurching Russia – is bleak and uncertain. The only response is to build a monument to a rich and varied culture in celebration of the perseverance and diversity of the Dagestanis. Please join them in a wry laugh and forget nothing . . .'

We shall not forget.

Marian Chenciner
Louisa Chenciner
Isabel Chenciner
June 2022

x *Preface*

Robert in the mountains

Note to readers

Please note

- 'Dagestan' is used throughout the text as a more modern version of the name, except when referring to previous publications that used the older form 'Daghestan'
- centuries are in Roman numbers as cardinals, thus 'XV century'
- referencing system: numbers are in brackets rather than superscripts and the numbers are not always sequential: if item 1 is referred to a second time we get [1] a second time, even if the sequence has got to [2] or higher
- italics are used in the first instance of foreign words but then not; similarly the meaning is indicated in the first instance but not subsequently; with exceptions to both these where there has been a long gap since previous use.

1 Introduction – what is Dagestan?

History teaches even those who do not learn from it: it makes them study.
VOK, below.

Chenciner met Magomedkhanov about 1984, and we have been working on Dagestan together ever since, said to be the longest friendship ever between a Caucasian and a European, strong after 37 years.

The subjects covered here are wide and we are grateful for essential contributions from the following Dagestani scholars from the Dagestan Scientific Centre Russian Academy of Sciences: Murtazali Gadzhiev (chapter 3), Alexander Bakanov (chapters 4, 5, 6, 7, 8, 15, 25), Saida Garunova (chapters 4, 5, 6, 7, 8, 17, 25, 26), Maysarat Musaeva (chapters 17, 19), Zoya Ramazanova (chapter 22), A. N. Sadovoy (chapter 25) and Magomed-Rasul Ibragimov (chapter 17); and Novoe Delo Makhachkala's reports on Covid (chapter 19).

From outside Dagestan, further essential contributions were made by Stefan Williamson-Fa (chapter 27), B. H. Rodrigue (chapter 26), and the late missed Moshe Gammer obm (chapter 14).

We also acknowledge a welcome debt to Academician Vasily Osipovich Klyuchevsky (1841–1911) [1] the Russian scholar and teacher, called the Pushkin of Russian historiography, whose ideas have influenced this book. He was the first and leading Russian historian of material, economic and demographic history, not the history of victors, rulers and strong-men [2, 3, 4].

This book opens into two sections, the first a chronological review from 5th c ACE to post USSR times seen from the point of view of Dagestani people rather than Russia. We begin with a chapter on the unrecorded history of *Shaitans* and mythical monsters (chapter 2), then the material history of the Sassanian walls (chapter 3) and history of the growth of Russian power in the region from the Kievan Rus (chapter 4) to today (chapter 15).

DOI: 10.4324/9781003388579-1

2   Dagestan – History, Culture, Identity

The second section explores Dagestani culture, starting with pre-Soviet to contemporary culture (chapter 16), continuing with chapters on modern urban weddings, social media, clinical and traditional medicine, food cultivation, a little-known history of Mountain Jews during the Soviet period, heroes of sport and finance, new business opportunities, ethno-tourism and a music revival.

From all of these swirl an increasing sense of identity in an indigenous multi-ethnic society.

What is Dagestan?

Fragmentary information about the tribes of the present territory of Dagestan from c.1000 BCE is known from ancient authors. Arabographic writing existed in Dagestan for a millennium in numerous manuscripts and epigrams (chapter 14). Early medieval Dagestan was described in IX-XIV centuries Arabic and Persian writings [5] but it is not known for how long Dagestan was perceived by the 'external' or 'internal' worlds as a single social entity. Historically, the name described a country of multilingual peoples, known to neighbouring nations as 'Laks', 'Leks', and 'Lezgins', which are unifying exoethnonyms. 'Dagestan' has been used since 1861 as the name of the Russian Empire administrative region [6–9]. *Tarih* (History of Dagestan) by Muhammad Rafi, 1312–3 [10], gives the earliest description of a common consciousness: "Know that Dagestan was a beautiful country, vast for its inhabitants, strong [to] a stranger, pleasing to the eye, abundant in the wealth of [the inhabitants] because of justice. It [had] many villages, a large number of cities and three regions (*nahiya*): Avar, Plain (*Sahl*) and Zirichgeran. The inhabitants of Dagestan were [formerly] infidels, vicious people from the war region (*dar al-harb*). They worshiped idols, were endowed with courage and wealth, [and at the same time] were more disgusting than dogs. In each village there were rulers who were unfit, vicious (*fajiruna*), and gripped by unbelief and sin. In every city there were criminal and sinful emirs who 'command the unapproved and avoid the approved.' The tyrant (*malik*) Suraka of at-Tanus city in Avaria, the strongest of Dagestan on account of his pagan power was worthless, a bearer of evil, violence and misfortune. He had the title *nusal* – it's their custom to give their rulers nicknames. His income came from [subject] lords, possessions (*vilayat*), lands (emirate), and he collected *haraj, jizya* and *ushr* (*al- ashar*) a tribute at a tenth, from the inhabitants of all Dagestan, from the vilayat Charcas to the city of Shamakh . . ."

"These lines came from an old, decrepit manuscript, dated 318AH/ 930ACE," so the perception of a territory of Dagestan likely existed before the XIV century. As indirect confirmation, in the XI century Leonty Mroveli recorded that Lekos (the fifth son of the forefather of the Caucasian peoples Targamos, grandson of Yaphet, great-grandson of Noah) received from his father "land with borders from the Derbent Sea to the Lomeki river and north, up to the great Khazaria river."

Amri Shikhsaidov drew attention to Rashid ad-Din's use of the term Lezistan for the first time, which contained a broad concept of Dagestan (1247–1318).

The Persian historian and geographer Hamdallah Qasvini (d. 1349), "describing the Caucasus Mountains (Elbrus), indicates that the western side of them, adjacent to the mountains of Gurzhistan, is called the Lekhi Mountains (Kuh-i Leksi) . . . They extended the term Leks to almost the whole of Dagestan . . . primarily intended to be territorial, rather than ethnic and political." He deduced that during the XIII-XIV centuries there were no authors from Dagestan with a clear idea of its political geography.

In later histories Dagestan – Mountain (*Dag*) Country (*stan*) – and its inhabitants are mentioned with certainty, as a matter of course, having developed "ideas of a common Dagestan meaning" in the XI–XV centuries. XVII century and later manuscripts confirm that the societies and peoples of Dagestan considered themselves part of a larger grouping and the outside world considered "the inhabitants as a unity" [11] (chapters 5 and 6).

In Russian translation 'people' usually means 'ethnicity.'

References

[1] Magomedkhanov M.M. Bakanov A.V. In memory of Vasily Osipovich Klyuchevsky. Klio. 2019. Nauk No. 6 (162). 2020.
[2] Klyuchevskij V.O. Composition in nine volumes. Special Courses. Vol. VI. 1989.
[3] Klyuchevskij V.O. Composition in nine volumes. Special Courses. Vol. VII. 1989.
[4] Klyuchevskij V.O. Composition in nine volumes. Articles. Vol. VIII. 1990.
[5] History of Shirvan and Derband. 1106.
[6] Mahmud from Khinalug. Events in Dagestan and Shirvan. 1456.
[7] Derbent-name V-X centuries. c. 1600.
[8] History of Karakaytag X-XV centuries.
[9] On the struggle of the Dagestanis against the Persian conquerors c. 1600. ND corresp. 1851.
[10] Mahammad-Rafi. History of Dagestan X–XIV century. 1312–3.
[11] Karpov. 2005. p. 119.

2 Shaitans, monsters, magic places and substances

Introduction

Pre-medieval and medieval Arab authors wrote about the beliefs of the inhabitants of Dagestan. Ibn-al Faqih al Hamadani recorded that in the X century that there were two revered graves in Derbent of white stone with images of lions, where "rain was requested". In the kingdom of Sarir/ Avaria, according to Ibn Rushd, his contemporary: "everyone . . . worships a dried head". Al-Garnati wrote in the XI-XII century about the ancient pagan burial rites and belief in the afterlife of the Zirehgerans/ Kubachis.

From 1861–1881 surviving pre-Islamic beliefs were gathered in the *Collection of information about the Caucasian mountaineers; the Collection of materials describing the tribes and localities of the Caucasus; and the newspaper Kavkaz.* The literature was added to during the Soviet and post-Soviet periods. G. F. Chursin (1874–1930) identified the ritual of ploughing to protect villages from evil forces, dangerous animals, and provided information about the petrification of people and animals. He also wrote about magical actions in wedding and birthing rituals, as well as beliefs associated with the cult of the dead and ancestors. He described the role of metal in wedding and birth rituals, to prevent evil forces "draining the source of the birth of the newly-weds, i.e. making them fruitless." Together with their talismans and amulets, these made up the armoury in the highlanders' fight against diseases and demons. Another Soviet, E. Schilling, described and analysed the fertility cult, rain rites, divination, sorcery and signs.

From the VIII century Dagestan joined the cultural orbit of the Muslim world. But its spread took several centuries. Pre-monotheistic beliefs and rituals were either forgotten or adapted to sharia. Ingrained Old-Testament superstitions that did not contradict Islam, such as rituals for invoking rain and the First Furrow gradually were perceived as Islamic. This nuanced fusion formed their ideology.

Dagestan is located at one of the busiest crossroads of Eurasia. From antiquity, a distinct Caucasian civilization evolved, on cultural washes from the Turkic, Iranian, Slavic, Jewish, and Greek worlds. As part of Caucasian Albania and the Sassanian Empire they developed relations with the Byzantine Empire, the Khazar

DOI: 10.4324/9781003388579-2

Shaitans, monsters, magic places and substances 5

Kaganate, and the ancient Russian state, absorbing their spiritual values, governance, and technology. Christianity, Judaism and to some extent Zoroastrianism exerted influence. Indigenous local animist and shamanist beliefs were blended with these newer ideas.

"The inhabitants of Dagestan were [previously] unfaithful, vicious people [who] worshipped idols" [1], and however much Islam rejected them, idols and cults predating monotheism lingered. The significance of heavenly bodies, mountains, springs, earthquakes and other natural phenomena persisted in the mountaineers' lives. The belief in the Shaitan (demon) in fact overlapped with Islam. Mentioned 88 times, the shaitan, together with the angels, are the most frequently mentioned supernatural entities in the Quran [2].

"In the mind of the people" [3], Shaitans are always negative spirits. They believed that everyone has a Shaitan, as an inseparable companion, penetrating even into his blood. According to legends, all the killings, outside quarrels, scandals and quarrels within the family came from Shaitans who would sow hostility between neighbours, turn everything upside down in the house, beat any person they came across, hide the necessary thing, throw it up after a while, and so on . . . They always tried to lead a person off the right path. They did this ostensibly most often with people who were unsure of themselves. Usually, if a person stumbled, they said that 'his Shaitan had beguiled him'.

Demons, associated spirits, magic and surroundings

The following demons, together with associated magic and surroundings, are taken from fieldwork since the 1860s. Professor Sir Harold Bailey thought that names were most important as historical identifiers. Also that if there was a name for something or a personage then either it existed or the concept of it existed where that language was spoken. In this chapter several unfamiliar names are given that could fruitfully be explored by philologists. The following examples are representatives of pre-monotheistic personages found in every village.

1. The Khvarshin spirits [4]

"All supernatural beings in Khvarshin are called *houbal*. A demon is visible to human eyes, commonly seen with the appearance of people or animals. A demon was recognisable, for example if a married woman's eyes were slightly downcast; or a squirrel was covered with blood; or their feet were turned backwards. Chadorol gorge about Zhenizhdagyand or the Devils' pit is a favourite home of all evil spirits.

"In one story a man named Pilma had the sheep farm of Kamilil Marku where he cooked his own food. A woman came and said: '*Va*, Pilma, let me prepare your food?' She took her time, and spilled water on all his flour. He got angry and hit her, took a closer look, and saw that it was his wife. She began to scream loudly. The house shook all over. Pilma was frightened by a strange noise and rushed to hide in the

6 Dagestan – History, Culture, Identity

sheep house. Suddenly the roof appeared to raise itself and was filled with a multitude of men and women, peeping-in but staying outside as if they were afraid of the sheep. Pilma sat quietly, but his wife made a noise and pushed the roof down and next day went to the *dibir* or local Islamic scholar, who wrote a talisman to protect them.

"Khvarshins believed in forest hunting spirits called *Budalla* who lived on rocky mountain tops in the Osokiah area, who ruled all the wildlife. When game is eaten by Budalla they then return the meat to local people. The hunter only eats what is left by the forest spirits. Someone called UlahIazhiyav could not get to Khvarsha by night-fall, so he had to spend the night in the mountains. He lit a small fire to keep warm. In the middle of the night, a voice addressed him: 'Hey, living being, since you are our guest, we are coming to you!' UlahIazhiyav understood that this was Budalla. They assumed the guise of ordinary people. First of all they prayed. Then one of them clapped his hands – a *tur* (great mountain goat) came running. Immediately the second one killed and skinned the tur, put it on a skewer and roasted it. They all sat down at the table and ate. One of them collected all the bones, clapped his hands again, and the tur came back to life.

UlahIazhiyav felt uncomfortable and unwell and could not hide his amazement, but Budalla told him that they would only offer humans animals which they revived."

2. The Kumyk demonic female character 'Albasty' is represented by an ugly woman with huge breasts draped over her shoulders, who usually harmed women in labour and in the three months before birth threatened to kidnap the baby from her womb. For protection, pregnant women left a piece of bread on the window sill at night and, if possible, did not stay at home alone. Among the peoples of Dagestan, she is also known as: Absally, Albasty, Kish Kaftar, Syutkatyn (the spirit of rain and fertility), Suv-anasy (Mother of Water, would drown bathers, later found transfixed by an axe or sword); Basdyryk (who in a dream can strangle people); Sulag (a voracious creature); Ayuli, Khal, Alpab, Budallaba, KhuduchI, (-*chI* represents an ejective) and GuduchI.

3. Habitats of evil spirits – In the forest, located on the east side of the village of Tindi, near GarachI farm there is a place called '*Bela Anchaba Tlo Gyini*'. Absolutely nothing may be taken from this place – grass or trees. The culprit would develop a fatal illness and his family or village will not escape misfortune.

On the way from Tindi to Angida there is a tree, and if someone breaks off its branch, he may die. In the same village, there is a place where if someone cuts grass to make hay, there would be trouble for him or his relatives. Even cutting a single tree from that forest caused the culprit's death. Belukatli, located on the way to Obatl farm, is another such deadly place to touch anything, or even attend to nature's call. It is the abode of devils who cause evil, called 'Gieri', 'Gjageri', meaning "full of blood". Near Guineici farm, they believe that a Shaitan can lure a person, cloud his mind, create illusions that he is at a wedding or surrounded by his friends, having fun, singing, or playing the *zurna* (reed instrument somewhat resembling an oboe) – only to find himself in dark places, on the edge of an abyss or in a gorge, beaten and ill.

4. Mental illness and sulphur

People believed that Shaitans and djinns caused memory disorder or mental illness. (In Islam a djinn was a spirit often capable of assuming human or animal form and exercising supernatural influence over people.) The causes of 'external' diseases such as abscesses, rashes or tumours were similarly attributed to Shaitans' machinations. A person with mental illness was said to be "detained by Shaitans," or "full of djinns." Fumigation with sulphur was the preferred treatment. For defence from Shaitans and djinns, one had to additionally light a fire, shoot a gun, draw a dagger from its scabbard and/or read a prayer. Djinns are represented as small dark humanoid creatures that always act together. They only harm people, but sometimes they can correctly punish a guilty person. A healer, "associated with the djinns," was able to cure the "disease of the djinns", free him from the harm caused by the djinns, drive them away by lamentations, manipulations, magic actions (fumigating with sulphur, burying black chicken bones in places frequented by djinns, or breaking flat stone tiles on the victim's back). People walking in the street in the evening or at night, especially to the mill, to the woods or to the cemetery, were advised to read a prayer, to bring matches, or a metal object such as a knife or scissors. They were forbidden to attend to nature in an unclean place, or to whistle. Any harmful effects of Shaitans and djinns were a consequence of the negligence of the victim.

Djinns were either harmful (*djin-kapura*, infidels) or harmless (*djin-muslims*). Nobody expected anything good from them. A person prone to lying was worse than a Shaitan; a good-hearted person 'does not have Shaitan in his heart.' Among fantastic achievements of Shaitans, it was said that in one day they could teach a person to play both the zurna and *pandur* (lyre).

5. The mythical Azhdaha (serpent or dragon, in the Iranian languages)

The Azhdaha is very popular and has multiple forms. Its habitats range from impassable forests, behind high mountains, on land, on or under water, in the underworld, in an iron lock, in a palace of gold and silver plates, to household *sunduk* (chests).

It takes various forms from a huge male and female monster, with one to 12 heads, two eyes and two ears on each head, noses and lips; two or four legs; or single-headed and one-eyed with snakes and lizards in its hair. Flames erupt from its eyes, the sky darkens in the smoke from its nostrils. It makes a scary squeak or "the whole village shakes from its cough, its sneezing is like thunder, its eyes sparkle like lightning". More reasonably it negotiates in human language and knows sayings such as "a brave man does not tease his enemy" and is grateful for politeness and values honesty.

It gets married, and has mock weddings and has siblings, parents, husbands and wives; it cooks and eats flour and meat dishes including pilaf, bread and people, and drinks milk and girls' blood; it can fly and hunt for several days and sleep as long; it has herds of cattle and horses; it protects rivers and lakes from people; it keeps treasures, captures people, and abducts girls.

8 *Dagestan – History, Culture, Identity*

The old mother of Azhdaha can save girls and boys from her sons and daughters for a weekly tribute of a jug of water for each house, carried by a village girl.

Special weapons are required to kill them. Birds tear off their feathers and throw them down in token of worship. Creatures crawl in front of them and beat their heads three times on the ground in subjugation. It hides in the womb to quicken the dead and can turn people into stone and revive them. It is capricious, superstitious and its soul is hidden. It overcomes difficulties. It can turn into an eagle or a horse, or a royal messenger. It fears evil old women.

6. The mythical 'Risis' in Tindi village.

Tindi villagers say that there is an invisible indescribable creature called 'Risis', which only attacks a sleeping person, whom it first paralyzed and then crushes and chokes with his weight. The victim may also experiences pain and aches, confusion and fear. Such domestic spirits are known by various names: *Kibishan, Ilbanhan, Kibiran, Chicabansan, Simagyad, Siigya* – in Dargin; *Kjegel, Gyshl, Tamiho, Risi-sa Kegilu* – in Avar; *Sukhasulu, Sukhalutu, Appalav Kharytsu* – in *Laki; Lutu, Kval. Khvarts* – in Lezgin; *Basdyryk* – in Kumyk and Nogai; *Kurchel* – in Kvarshi; *Khvars* – in Russian.

7. Textile symbols.

Apotropaic designs appear in Kaitag silk embroideries c1600–1900 have brightly-coloured cosmic/solar signs, anthropo- and zoo-morphic and vegeto-morphic motifs, as well as birds, animals and human hands [5]. The amulet symbols protected a baby from the evil eye and evil forces; granted the bride happiness and wealth; and were part of the funerary ritual.

Woollen-pile carpets usually XIX century featured stylized animals, birds, multi-legged creatures, pin-wheel swastikas (the sun), flowers, circles, crosses, and diamonds. Davaghin and *dum*, long woollen tapestries, are given Dagestani names, inter alia *ruklzal*, Avar for 'home'; *azhdaha*, dragon; *Gulyagdin kal*, Lezgin for 'serpent's lair'; *betler*, 'coil/snake/cat's head'; *gozo*, Avar for 'beak'.

Limbless snake/serpents are distinct from dragons. Snakes are endowed with both harmful and useful magical qualities, such as those with golden horns which protect homes and households. They live only in happy homes in the basement or in the main room facing the central pillar. It's impossible to see them, but if someone does, the household will be happy.

8. *Kizilov* (Cornelian cherry dogwood)

A bundle of cornelian twigs (*bilikly* in Avar) are used as an apotropaic charm against the evil eye. It was tied to the wrist, to a shepherd's crook, or to the horns of livestock. The cornel branch was favoured for the craftsman's hammer handle, to avoid any jinx on his skill. A child was protected if he or she was smeared with cornelian soot, as were animals. A cow with a swollen belly could be healed if it was struck there with a cornelian switch.

Shaitans, monsters, magic places and substances 9

Figure 2.1 Stylized dragon: Kaitag silk embroidery detail, XVIII century

Figure 2.2 Another dragon: woollen knotted carpet detail

9. Protection of children from the evil eye and diseases

His dried umbilical cord and first-cut hair, tied into a clean cloth were hung from the cradle until the baby outgrew it. Later the amulet was hidden under a roof or in a wall. If a snake touched a baby's first-cut hair, it would grow insane. Children were protected at night by a knife, matches, or other sulphureous items, as above.

10 Dagestan – History, Culture, Identity

Young children were barred from the flour mill. But if it was necessary, the child was taken into the mill head first, so it grew clever, fast and nimble. Against illness a raw chicken's egg was painted and put it into the fire or hot ash. If it burst, then the child will recover. If someone was suspected of hexing the child, they unnoticeably tore a piece of cloth from his clothes, made nine holes in it and burnt it with sulphur, reading *Alham* (the first sura of the Koran) nine times. Old magical women such as fortune-tellers also nullified the evil eye. Various amulets and talismans were used, even his clothes were a patchwork of cloth collected from nine different male relatives.

As well as the above narratives, personages, materials and surroundings there are the following magic customs around death, fire, rain, sacred trees, ceremonial bread, wedding rites, and wolves.

1. Death cult

In the X century Ibn Rushd strangely recounted about his journey from Khazar to Sarir that 'the inhabitants of Sarir all worship a dried head' [6]. To explain, "Avar the Christian king who ruled over 20,000 ravines, towns and cities, had a throne of gold and a throne of silver in his castle, but the inhabitants of his state were all infidels."

Ibn Rushd was told, "When someone dies, he is taken on a stretcher to the square and left there for three days; then the inhabitants of the city wearing helmets and steel mail ride out to the square, pointing their spears at the deceased and circling threaten the corpse but avoid striking him." They explained to their guest: "We had a man who died and was buried, and after three days he shouted from his grave. Therefore, we leave the dead man for three days, and on the fourth day we threaten him with a weapon, in case he will return back to his body." This custom was then about 300 years old.

2. Magic wedding rites

The main objective was to protect young people from 'spoilage,' possible harm from ill-disposed people; and, second, to ensure their prosperity, ability to continue their line . . . There were various measures to protect the bride from the evil eye and witchcraft caused by detractors [7].

"The captured bride had to avoid meetings with people who had been jinxed with childlessness. Danger increased during her transfer to the groom's house. Detractors could scatter charcoal, black beans, millet dipped in female urine, manure, sewage or smash a jug to break the couple's dream of a happy life. For protection, the bride covered her face with a red or white cloth, or wore a brightly decorated dress. Her young protectors walked ahead of the procession with torches and daggers. At the door of her father-in-law's house a ram's throat was cut at her feet. A protective mirror and a lighted lamp were both compulsory dowry gifts. To make her new life bright and long-lasting with many children, her lips and cheeks were smeared with honey or sugary water. Sweets, grains and coins were thrown at the door of the groom's house, and also on the groom's knees. A broom was put in his hands, to beget many children, especially sons. Talismans in the young friends' private room included a vessel filled with water with a chicken egg to protect the future children. At the door of her new house, the bride crushed a saucer underfoot, to break all evil thoughts of ill-wishers."

Our late lamented colleague Sergey Abdulkhalikovich Luguev, Doctor of Historical Sciences, observed that water rites with pitchers of water were used at traditional weddings to prevent evil. These would be deployed in the wedding procession leading the bride to the groom's house. Further rituals followed arrival: "In the private room of the young were containers filled with water. Persons performing the *maghar* rite and others present took a sip of water before the ceremony, and rinsed their hands. In the water rite for the newlyweds, one of the bride's girlfriends filled their ewer and emptied it at her feet. From the same ewer, all the women present sprinkled water on the bride, giving good wishes. The first ewer of water brought from the spring by the bride was offered to her father-in-law to drink" [8].

There were also mock weddings partly as rehearsals, partly as satire, partly as theatrical performance all of which had magical meaning connected to real weddings (*kyodoba*) [4, 7].

3. Ceremonial bread

Ceremonial breads also possessed apotropaic powers. As observed by an Abkaz ethnographer, "The image of a protective divine being or patron can be considered, first of all, in those ceremonial breads in the shape of a human figure," to be found in the Russian Ethnographic museum in St Petersburg [9]. In First Furrow celebrations we have also seen large sun-shaped loaves with *derkhap*, Dargin for 'good luck!', written in thin dough rolls on it and hard boiled eggs inserted around the perimeter.

4. Rain rituals [10]

Rain was vital in an arid zone. "A naked teenage boy, and sometimes a girl, was covered in branches and herbs, and a mask of dangling herbs was put on his/her head. Anonymous masked mummers were led through the village, accompanied by teenage youths. The procession stopped in front of each house and the mistress went out into the street, poured water over the mummers, and gave bread, cheese and eggs to the rest. After a progress around the village, the procession went to a sacred grave or walked around the cemetery, and then at the edge of the village or by the river shared out the food. The main character – a rain-donkey – was called *urtilunchov* by the Laks; by the Avars *cIadulhIam*, *cIdudiIma*, *cIudulhIam*; in Dargin – *myarkushi*; in Lezgin – *pepepai* or *peshepay*. On this day too ritual porridge was cooked from . . . cereals collected from all residents of the village . . . in the village of Akhar (present-day Laksky district) . . . a representative of one particular *tukkhum* (clan) had to clean the bottom of the man-made rain reservoir from silt, while praying and the women and children sang magical songs."

12   Dagestan – History, Culture, Identity

5. Fire and the spring festival [11]

"The most ancient mythological views go back to stories about the heroes who gave fire . . . they are women . . . the keepers of the hearth who taught people to bury embers in the ashes."

At *Yaransuvar* the spring festival [12], "On the first day one of the mullahs carried a bowl of water to the homes of every villager, offering a drink with his prayers against poison, in exchange for a painted egg. All people on the first night, 21st March, lit bonfires and torches . . . fire was the mighty healing and cleansing force, so everyone who could, including the sick and the old, wanted to jump over the fire. When they jumped Laks declared: 'My disease – fire – healthy body' and Lezgins addressed the fire: 'We have lived well all year until this spring, God grant that the next year should pass similarly.' These ceremonies acted as a symbolic purification before the start of the new agrarian economic year."

Also called *pervaya borozda*, the First Furrow [4] celebrated the vernal equinox, to cause rain. 'Seeing off winter' (*igbi*), a similar festival, was held by the Didoi of western Mountain Dagestan.

The First Furrow was not complete without the blessing of the imam. In the Soviet years of persecution of religion, red posters at the celebration proclaimed 'Glory to the CPSU!' Even Communist Party leaders took part in the festival. But the purpose of this holiday – to ensure a bountiful harvest and well-being – never changed. The Soviet repression of 'obsolete' customs and the introduction of new 'socialist' customs and rituals clumsily developed by the central and local ideological institutions turned out to be useless.

6. Sacred trees [1]

Ibn Rushd on his journey added: "At a distance of ten *farsangs* from Avar's city is Ranhas where there is a huge tree that does not bear fruit, where every Wednesday the city dwellers gather and hang all sorts of fruits on the tree, to venerate it and make sacrifices".

On expeditions we have seen sacred trees which are covered in coloured ribbons, each one supposedly tied to grant a wish or protect the owner.

7. Wolves

"The speed of a wolf – *batsI* in Avar, *bat* in Dargin, *bartz* in Lak – and courage in his raids were compared to a bold man. His gallbladder and fat were used as a healing agent for pulmonary diseases. His baked liver was given to a child to acquire his bravery, similarly domestic puppies were given wolf meat. In apiaries the pelt was hung as a talisman. A wolf's tooth was hung on a child's chest as a guard against the evil eye, and also on one sheep in the flock to divert the evil eye. For enhanced romance a husband had but to touch a shred of his fur on his beloved for her to reciprocate. Negatively if a piece of the neck of a dead wolf was attached to a malevolent's throat and, facing his foe's house, he cursed: 'Divorce your wife!', then that couple would soon break up. To stop people loving each other, it was sufficient to carry a wolf's eye between them" [7].

References

[1] Muhammad-Rafi, compiler of *Tarikh Dagestan*, XIV-XVI centuries.
[2] Teuma E. More on Qur'anic jinn. Melita Theologica. Vol. 39. 1984. pp1–2; 37–45. https://en.wikipedia.org/wiki/Shaitan.
[3] Alimova Bariat Magomedovna. Ms. RDAN (Republic of Dagestan Academy of Sciences).
[4] Musaeva Maysarat Kamilovna. Khvarshiny, XIX- early XX century. Ms. RDAN.
[5] Chenciner Robert. Kaitag textile art of Daghestan. 1993; Chenciner R., Magomedkhanov M. and Ismailov H. Tattooed Mountain women and Spoonboxes of Daghestan. 2006.
[6] Ibn Rushd (Abu-Ali Ahmed Ibn-Omar). Encyclopedia 'Dear Values.' 1st half X century.
[7] Gadzhiev Gailar Abdulvagidovich. Pre-Islamic beliefs and rites of the peoples of Nagorny Dagestan. 1991.
[8] Luguev S.A. Akhvakhs: Historical and ethnographic study, XIX- early XX century. 2008.
[9] Chursin Grigory Filippovich. Material on Abkaz ethnography. 1957.
[10] Ramazanova Zoya Butaevna, Ms. RDAN.
[11] Khalidova, Misay Rasulovna. Mythological and historical epos of the peoples of Dagestan. Ms. RDAN.
[12] Bulatova Angara Hamidovna Ms. RDAN.

3 The Sasanian walls against the Huns

The following comes from *The Ghilghilchay defensive long wall new investigations* [1].

The appearance of the Huns in modern-day Europe initiated the great period of the Migration of Peoples and the beginning of the Middle Ages. In 395–396 ACE the Huns made their first devastating whirlwind campaign through the Caucasus range to Transcaucasia and the Near East. Contemporaries recorded it, in particular from the extreme limits of Meotida, between the icy Tanais and the furious peoples of Massagetes, where Alexander's bolted locks constrain the wild tribes of the Caucasus. There the Hunnish hosts escaped [2] "along an unexpected way through the Caspian Gates and Armenian snows" [3]. The Huns' invasion had inflicted a significant blow on Persia and Byzantium and confirmed the power of the new nomads.

Thus, the protection of the Caucasian borders became important to the Sasanians, especially for Ctesiphon, since after 387 almost all of Transcaucasia was incorporated within the Sasanian empire. By 408, a Persia-Byzantium treaty had been signed. Shahanshah Yazdegerd I (399–421) entered into negotiation with the Byzantine court and, as a result, took up legal trusteeship of the young emperor Theodosius II (408–450) and signed a treaty regarding the shared responsibilities for the protection of the Caucasian routes. [4] As these passes were within the territory of the Persian state (or Iranshahr), their protection was carried out by the Sasanian Persian forces, and Constantinople undertook to pay half of the necessary expenses. Under the treaty, Byzantium's annual payment was 500 litres (160 kg) of gold [5].

About 424, a new treaty confirmed the charges for the protection of the Caucasian passes [6]. According to Priscus [7] and Egishe [8], in 441 the Huns, commanded by Basikh and Cursikh, and also by Attila's youngest son Ernah (in Egishe-Heran), conducted another devastating invasion of Transcaucasia and Asia Minor through the Daryal pass and Derbent Gate [9] In the same year, Ctesiphon and Constantinople agreed an armistice, and in 442 signed the long-term peace treaty confirming the obligation of the treaty of 424 [10].

After this, in the mid-440s, Shahanshah Yazdegerd II (439–457) began building a defensive system on the western Caspian coast. At first Persia erected a solid

DOI: 10.4324/9781003388579-3

The Sasanian walls against the Huns 15

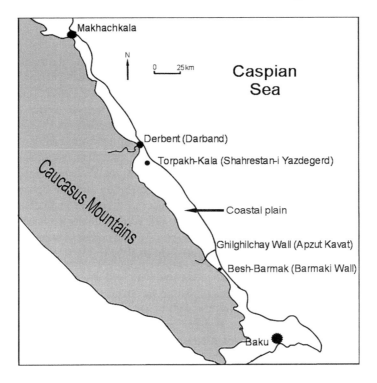

Map 3.1 Derbent Walls

In 2002 the Azerbaijani-Dagestani-American archaeological expedition carried out careful visual investigations and mapping of portions of the Ghilghilchay Sasanian fortification wall that was built in the VI century ACE on the Caspian coastal plain. There were identified inter alia over 300 tower buttresses spaced regularly along the wall, five towers with interior cultural deposits, three military garrisons or forts (two of which were unrecorded), and one apparently fortified Sasanian settlement.

mud-brick wall in the Derbent pass, which partitioned off a narrow 3.5 km seaside plain and the citadel on an elevated spur [11]. Between 447 and 450, a stronghold was constructed near Beliji, 20 km south of Derbent, which has been reliably identified as the city of Shahristan-i Yazdegerd [12] consisting of a huge fortified settlement (approximately 100 ha) called Torpakh-kala [13].

When the emperor Marcian (r. 450–457) ascended the throne he concluded the union with Shahanshah Yazdegerd II, confirming the bilateral treaty signed in 442. Byzantium regularly paid Persia a half share of the charges for the protection of the Caucasian passes; the Armenian writer of the VIII century, Ghevond [14], states that in 717 ('in the second year' of the caliph Sulayman) the Arabs, having seized Derbent, discovered a plate in the masonry of the wall inscribed: 'Marcianus, Autocrat, Caesar has constructed this city, this tower with a great quantity of talents from his own treasury.' Apparently, these expenses were connected with the restoration of the Chor fortification that was damaged during the revolt of 450–51. It is indirectly confirmed in Michael the Syrian's (XII century) reference to John of

16   Dagestan – History, Culture, Identity

Ephesus' (VI century) statement that 'the Gate of Turaie' (i.e. Derbent) is a city constructed by the Romans (i.e. Byzantines) [15].

Other contemporary written sources [15] reported that during the reigns of the Shahanshahs Peroz, Kavad I and Khusraw I Byzantium gave financial support under the treaty (only under pressure) to Sasanian Persia for the struggle against the nomads, including monies for the construction and service of the defensive structures. In addition to the mud-brick fortifications at Derbent and Torpakh-kala, they referred to the Ghilghilchay long wall, Besh-Barmak fortification, and other military camps and fortresses, fortified cities and settlements as shown on the sketch map. The Derbent stone defensive complex, of the VI century, replaced the mud-brick fortification and included the city fortification and a 40 km mountain wall (*Dagh bari*). This complex became a model of defensive architecture and a crowning achievement in the *Limes Caspius*. The cordoned long walls on the eastern and western shores of the Caspian Sea served as the border between the settled agricultural and the nomadic stockbreeding worlds.

The first mention of the Ghilghilchay defensive long wall was in VII century when Ananias of Shirak (Pseudo-Moses of Khorene) in his *Geography* (Armenian: *Ashkharatsuyts*) mentions not only 'the wall of Darband,' but also 'the long wall Apzut Kavat up to the Alminon marshes and to the sea' [16]. The now widely accepted identification of the Apzut Kavat wall (in translation from the Middle Persian, Kavat is 'exalted') with the Ghilghilchay wall was first made by S.T. Yeremian [17] who attributed its construction to the reign of Shahanshah Kavad.

References

[1] Aliev Asker A., Gadjiev Murtazali S., Gaye Gaither M., Kohl Philip L., Magomedov Rabadan M. and Aliev Idris N. The Ghilghilchay defensive long wall new investigations. TSETS. 2006. pp143–6.

[2] Eusebius Hieronymus. Letters. c.400. p8.

[3] Claudius Claudianus. Rau: 2. c.400. pp22–30.

[4] Kulakovskiy I. History of Byzantium. Vol. 3. 1913. pp227–8.

[5] Theophilos. Chron. c.840. pp13–26.

[6] Theophilos. Byz. c.840. F. 68.

[7] *idem* F. 8.

[8] Egishe: About Vardan and the Armenian war. Tr. I.A. Orbeli. Notes Yuzbashyan K.N. 1971. c. 450. p121.

[9] Semenov A. 2002. pp15–17.

[10] Marcian. Chron. 2. c. 450. p80.

[11] Kudryavtsev A. 1978. pp243–57; 1979. pp31–43; Gadjiev V.G. 1989. pp61–76.

[12] Hoffman. 1880. p50.

[13] Gadjiev V.G. The role of Russia in the history of Dagestan. 1980. pp144–52; 2001. pp32–40.

[14] Ghevond. History of the caliphs by archimandrite/vardapet Ghevond. VIII c. Tr. K. Patkhanov. 1862.

[15] 'Gate of Turaie' is a borrowed translation from Armenian. Durn Coray (gates of the Hun). Altheim F. and Stichl R. 1958. p110. On the identification of Chor and Derbent, see Kuznetsov. 1893; Marguart. 1903. pp96–100; Artamonov M. 1962. pp120–1; Kudryavtsev A. 1978; 1979; Gadjiev. 2002. pp10, 46–8.

[16] Moise Corene: Geography of Moise Corene after ptolemy. Ed. and tr. A. Soukry. 1881. p27; Ananias of Shirak: The Geography of Ananias of Shirak (Aaxaracoiz). Tr. and comm. Hewson R.H. 1992. pp12–13.

[17] Yeremian S.T. 1941. p35.

4 Trade with the Kievan Russ and the Golden Horde

"From time immemorial" the Caucasus occupied an exclusive place, connecting Europe and Asia, where roads converged "from almost all possible directions" [1]. The Great Silk Road (GSR) originating in China and India with its main route through Central Asia, Persia, the Middle East and Asia Minor towards the Mediterranean Sea and further into Europe, has always passed through the Caucasus. From mid-VI century it passed through coastal Dagestan, the Darial gorge, and the Klaukhorsky and Sapcharsky passes of modern Karachay-Cherkessia [2]. The route linked the Caspian, Baltic and Black Sea coasts, the steppes of the Ciscaucasia and the Caucasus, and the Volga, Don, Dvina, Neva and Dnieper river passages.

Until the 1860s construction of the Georgian Military Highway, the way through the Caucasus mainly consisted of tracks through mountain passes and gorges, traversable for only a few months a year. A year-round connection between Europe and Asia could be ensured only by the west Caspian coastal route, passing through modern Dagestan. Many states tried to exploit the riches of the GSR arriving at the west coast of the Caspian, and it was natural that Russia to the immediate north and west was one of them.

It appears that ties between Russia and Dagestan developed during the flourishing of Kievan Rus from the IX to early XIII centuries. "As archaeological data shows, the ancient farmers of Dagestan developed their agronomy from the coastal plain below sea level, to the highland altitudes of 1,800m to 2,100 m" [3] with widespread cultivation of local cereals, legumes, melons and other crops (chapter 21) [4]. Locally bred cattle, horses, sheep and goats were widespread. In addition to viticulture and horticulture, "Derbent madder was known far beyond the borders of the Caucasus" [5], successfully selling in India [6], as well as coloured yarn and fabrics in local markets. In the V century BCE, Herodotus noted "the manufacture of woollen fabrics in the Western Caspian was coloured with vegetable dyes" [7].

It follows that at the time of the first trade contacts of Kievan Rus, Dagestan was part of a "lively international commerce, both importing and exporting" [8]. "From the VII to VIII centuries important trade routes connecting the countries of the Middle East with Southeast Europe, the Lower Volga Region and the North Caucasus extended to the Caspian Sea basin" [5]. The Arab Caliphate, Byzantium, the Great

DOI: 10.4324/9781003388579-4

Khazaria, Volga Bulgaria and other states actively traded in this region. The main craft and trade centres were Derbent, Semender, Ardabil and Barda (east of Ganje). Lowland Dagestan was absorbed into Great Khazaria in the north and the Arab Caliphate in the south. Borders between the warring Khazars and Arabs often shifted.

From time to time, one local mountain state dominated the others, for example Sarir, Kaitag, Gumik, Lakz, or Zerekhgeran were both enemies and then allies.

From the VII to early XIII century Derbent, at the junction of land, river and sea trade routes, was the largest market of the region with an active seaport [9]. Master handcrafts and raw materials were traded in Derbent with its links to the known world, where regional rulers accommodated the policies of neighbouring states. Dagestan trade over the mountains with Barda and Semender declined.

After the steady disappearance of Great Khazaria during the IX century as the main player in the profitable Asia-Europe transit trade, the Kievan Rus controlled the northern Black Sea, the Azov Sea and most of the eastern Baltic through the unique system of river routes. The Baltic was the source of "furs, leathers, amber, walrus bone, wax, linen, and silver products" [8] and gave access to the markets of Europe. As early as the VIII and IX centuries, Kievan Rus integrated the East Slavic tribes of the Vyatichi, Radimichi, Northerners, Krivichi and Ilmen Slovenes [10]. "Foreign coins, both eastern i.e. Sasanian and later Arab, and western i.e. Roman, and later Byzantine, circulated in large numbers there" [1]. Furthermore, "In the area of the Dnieper were found many treasuries with VIII to X century Arab coins, including silver dirhams" [11]. The Baltic trade [7] was accessible both via land routes and more safely through the more convenient network of rivers interlinked by porterage.

"Foreign trade was traditionally considered the main pillar of the Kiev economy" [1, 11]. The Old Russian state traded with Byzantium, the Baltic states, Scandinavia, Bohemia, Hungary, Poland, Bulgaria (during its struggle for independence from Constantinople), Volga Bulgaria, the Caucasus, and with Central Asia and the Middle East. Russian merchants were seen in Persia and Baghdad. "In the East, Russia sold furs, wax, walrus fangs and, in certain periods, woollen cloth and linen, and bought there spices, precious stones, silk and satin fabrics, as well as weapons of Damascus steel and horses" [1]. Goods purchased by Kievan Rus merchants from eastern merchants, "such as precious stones, spices, carpets, etc., passed through Novgorod to Western Europe" [1]. Russian cities of Kiev and Smolensk, at the intersection of important land and river routes linked both Slavic and non-Slavic merchants with Poland, Bohemia, Hungary, Byzantium, the Baltic states, and hence the Scandinavian and other Western European countries. Greeks, Armenians, Germans, Scandinavians, Bukharans, Persians, Caucasians and others had permanent trade delegations in Kievan Rus. In turn, the Rus also had warehouses and trading offices in Itil, Semender and Derbent. Goods were sold-on to agents to send them further east where they accessed Chinese, Indian, Central Asian, Middle Eastern and Persian wares. Rus merchants bought a limited supply of copper, tin, silver, gold and other non-ferrous metals from within Kievan Rus. Horses, cattle and camels were

20 *Dagestan – History, Culture, Identity*

also purchased in the West Caspian region from "Turkic nomads – Pechenegs and, later, Polovtsians" [1] who almost surrounded Russia from the south-east.

Dagestan during the VIII to XIII centuries traded agricultural and manufactured products with the East, which was a richer market than Europe. Russian and foreign merchants after local high-quality fabrics and other master-handicrafts met in Derbent with the local merchants of Zerekhgeran [Kubachi and Amuzgi], Sarir [Avaria], Kaitag and Kumukh.

Imported technical and cultural innovations rapidly appeared in the plains and high mountains of Dagestan [2, 7], balanced by the renowned exports of steel mail and bulat blades of the Amuzgi armourers and the jewellery and niello-work of nearby Kubachi [5]. With regard to the origin of the 'Avar helmets' mentioned in Vernadsky's *Words about Igor's Regiment*, they were not products of the 'modern' Avars "that passed through the southern part of Russia and settled in Hungary", but forged by "a tribe with the same name, whose place of residence was Dagestan" [1]. It is likely that the 'Avar helmets' were made in Kubachi or Amuzgi, as they were the only armourers in Dagestan. The Russian merchants likely came across these Avars inhabiting Sarir (another name of Avaria), which is how these helmets got their name. Kubachis also arguably produced the famous helmet 'of eastern work' of Grand Prince Alexander Nevsky, presented to him by Sartaq Khan of the Golden Horde at their meeting in 1252.

Through the VIII, IX and X centuries [11] the Grand Princes of Kiev, Oleg (d. 912), Igor (878 to 945), and especially Svyatoslav (r. c.942 to 972) became dominant in eastern trade. However, the adoption of Orthodoxy in 988 and gravitation westwards meant that "the Black Sea began to play a more important role in Russian trade than the Caspian" [1]. Moreover Grand Prince of Kiev Vladimir I (c.960– 1015) was married to the Princess Anna of Constantinople in the first of a century of dynastic marriages. The so-called route 'from the Varangians to the Greeks' became preferred, and Byzantium became the main trading partner of the Kievan state.

The nomadic world was also changing. From east to west, the powerful Polovtsy pressed the Pechenegs and occupied their vast steppes of the northern Black Sea region, the Caspian region and Ciscaucasia. Now they controlled one continuous arc from the Urals to the Danube, cutting the south-eastern routes, which had previously connected Kievan Rus with the West Caspian region. "Nevertheless, the Russians continued to desperately defend their route to the Caspian" [1], though, by the end of the XI century, it was completely blocked. "The growing ties of Dagestan with Russia were dealt a severe blow" [8], though insignificant compared to the Mongol-Tatar invasion.

"The Mongol expansion from the early XIII century until the XIV century changed the face of the world, comparable with the barbarian invasions of the V century, which overthrew the Roman Empire and the Ancient World, or with the triumphal march of Islam in the VII century. Despite all its effects on Europe, the Crusaders' counterattack against Islam achieved more limited goals and brought less territorial changes than the Arabs or the Mongols" [12]. Flowering cities and civilizations

Trade with the Kievan Russ and the Golden Horde 21

were torched and devastated. Borders were redrawn as the old trade ties were violated. China, Central Asia, Persia, the Middle East, the Caucasus, Siberia and Eastern Europe became part of Genghis Khan's united Empire. Feudal-fragmented Kievan Rus fell in an unequal war with the Mongols, finally at the siege of Kiev in 1240. The Old Russian state disappeared into oblivion. The centre of power of the Russian lands, which had smoothly moved to the northeast in the middle of the XII century, was finally settled in the Vladimir-Suzdal principality, the Russian homelands, containing most of the Great Russian population under the Mongols. Moscow rose to replace Kiev and became the political centre of the ancient Russian lands. (Great Russia or Great Rus' – *Velikaya Rus'*, *Velikaya Rossiya* – was formerly applied to the territories of 'Russia proper,' the core of Muscovy and later Russia where the Great Russian ethnogenesis took place. Probably from the Byzantine Greek Μεγάλη Ῥωσ(σ)ία, Megálē Rhōs(s)ía was used for the northern part of the lands of Rus and later from 1654–1721 adopted by the Tsars.)

The Mongol invasion also cut off Russia from the Caspian region. The area later called Great Russia just survived under the Genghisid state, and thought only about escape from the heavy Mongol yoke. Vladimir-Suzdal was far from the Caucasus. Great Russia was clearly not up to the restoration of contacts with distant regions. The Caucasus itself at that time was also ravaged by repeated Mongol invasions, although "in fact those who lived in the high valleys were never completely conquered by the Mongols" [12, 13]. However, the steppes of Ciscaucasia, Transcaucasia, the Northern, Southern and Western Caspian were in the hands of the Mongol army. Pyatigorye and the mouth of the river Terek accommodated the famous nomad khans of the Golden Horde. On the plains of northern Azerbaijan and southern Dagestan, the Ilkhanids periodically staged their royal hunts [9]. The roads connecting the lowlands to the mountains were cut off by the Mongols.

The resumption of trade followed the unification of Russian lands under Moscow and their release from the Mongol-Tatar yoke. It was unlikely that in the late XIII century Russia, recently razed to the ground (except for Veliky Novgorod and Pskov which depended first on Karakorum, and then on the Sarai) and whose spirit was broken, could make any trade initiatives, any more than the remaining regions lost from the influence of Kievan Rus. The above areas mainly traded with Northern and Western Europe, Pomerania, the Kama River basin, Perm lands and the Urals [11, 14, 15]. Through the late XIII century Russia was bled to stagnation by the Horde tribute.

The GSR passing through Derbent suffered damage during the Mongol invasions, and more harm was done by the collapse of the unified empire of Genghis Khan into four: two parts of which the Golden Horde and the state of the Ilkhanids fought to control the Caspian part of the GSR. "Military operations, punitive expeditions, troop transfers of both Chingizid powers depopulated the plain" [9]. The once great port of Derbent was almost deserted. The Golden Horde controlled the route from "Central and Central Asia to the lower reaches of the Volga and on to the Northern Black Sea Region" [2]. The Ilkhanids controlled trade from Persia and the South

22 Dagestan – History, Culture, Identity

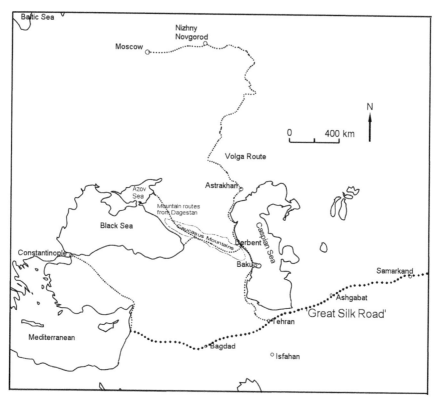

Map 4.1 The Great Silk Roads from China to Constantinople – Dagestan connections

Caspian to the Middle East. Dagestan's Caspian coastal area, earlier united during the XIII to XV centuries, lost its significance by fragmenting [9]. In *Nagorny* (Mountain) Dagestan locals created their own "strategic and commercial route along the Samur river from Kurakh through Kumukh, Chokh Gidatl, along the Andi Koisu river to Chechnya" [7] joining the North Caucasus and Azerbaijan, "aptly called the great route of peoples, essential for the economic life of Dagestan." However, in reality these routes were no longer of international significance.

The Italian maritime trading republics Venice and Genoa attempted to restore the trade route along the West Caspian lowlands of Dagestan. While fighting among themselves, from the XIII century they opened manufactories and warehouses in the Crimea and along the western coast of the Black Sea, promising impressive dividends. The northern highway of the GSR came out on the western and northern coasts of the Black Sea. Taman and Kerch guarded the entry to the sea of Azov and the Crimean peninsula. Initially, while the Latin Crusader Empire existed (1204–1261), almost "all Black Sea trade was monopolized by the Venetians" [12]. "However, after the restoration of the Byzantine Empire by Michael VIII Palaiologos, the

Genoese not only returned to the Black Sea, but also found themselves in a more privileged position than the Venetians." By the 1260s "they reached Dagestan and, having opened a route with cargoes along the Caspian Sea", established favourable economic relations with the indigenous population [2]. "Around 1267, Mengu-Timur granted them special privileges for trading in Cafes (modern Theodosius) and in 1274 they established themselves in Soldaiya (now Sudak) in Crimea" [12]. Genoese trading posts were also established in Constantinople along the Bosphorus. The Venetians were blocked and eventually driven out of the region. However, "the Genoese did not limit themselves to asserting their influence only in the Black Sea zone, but took measures to extend their trade activities in the more eastern regions of the Caucasus, including its mountainous region." At the end of the XIII century, "taking advantage of political stabilization in the Eastern Caucasus" [9], they finally extended their trade throughout the North Caucasus and part of Transcaucasia. The Genoese cunningly – the sleight *Genovese e dunque mercato* 'Genovese and therefore a merchant' became a compliment – tacked between the powerful interests of the Golden Horde and the Ilkhanids. For Genoa, the Black Sea was a door to the West, and the Caspian Sea, to the East.

In order to further develop trade between Europe and Asia, the Genoese attempted to emulate their Black Sea mercantile empire in the West Caspian by gaining a foothold in Derbent and other cities of Transcaucasia. They established trade offices and probably built ships on the Caspian – the Vatican heard an appeal against these Genoese activities by a Dagestani Catholic bishop representing the Kaitag rulers [9] – to open the sea route East.

Catholicism (as opposed to Orthodoxy) was considered the main self-justification through which the Genoese and Venetians hoped to establish themselves in the West Caspian. Thus two bishoprics of Tarki and Nuka (Sheki) were founded in the Transcaucasus and the Caspian region, where missions were repeatedly sent. The calculated interests of the Genoese in the plains of Dagestan and the Black Sea coast, coupled with their diplomacy with the Golden Horde and Ilkhanids, allowed them to revive the western Caspian lowland trade route, at least during times of Genghisid peace. But instability harmed Genoese interests there and Tokhtamysh in his confrontation with the Khan of the Golden Horde in 1395–1396 rode with 'fire and sword' in the Dagestan and throughout the North Caucasus [16] ending their competitive competition for Dagestan.

Saray-Berke the new capital of the Golden Horde on the Aktuba, 300 km northwest of Astrakhan, was described by contemporary travellers as a large city "with wide streets and beautiful markets." Mongols shared it with Russians, Greeks, Kipchaks, Alans and Circassians [12] as well as some immigrants from Dagestan. Ibn Batuta wrote that a Dagestan Shafiite theologian, named Sadreddin Suleiman al-Lekzi (the Lak), lived there [5, 17], to illustrate how well the Caspian region was integrated into the Genghis state, where Kipchaks lived on the northern plains. Archaeological excavations of 'typical Kubachi bronze lamps' confirmed the Dagestani presence in Saray-Berke [18]. The Golden Horde khans gathered the best artisans from all the conquered lands to their capital, and strongly supported trade, which likely included Dagestan ordnance and jewellery. The Russian export merchants also had a permanent presence in the local markets and it seems reasonable that they bargained there with merchants from Dagestan.

Having destroyed Saray-Berke, Timur did not spare the Genoese colonies located on the Black Sea coast and in Taman. In the XV century they recovered in a diminished state. The Genoese and Venetian Black Sea-Caspian ventures ended when "The capture of Constantinople by the Turks in 1453 closed the Black Sea to Western Europeans . . ." [9], and the Ottomans secured both the northern and southern routes of the GSR. Thus the road through lowland Dagestan lost its international importance.

In 1404, Russian merchants were recorded in Derbent [8]. They likely had travelled down the Volga and along the Caspian. By this time Derbent, "heavily destroyed as a result of the Tatar-Mongol invasions, had lost its former significance as the main seaport of the Caucasus" [8]. "The decline of Derbent went together with the flourishing of Baku, where merchant ships preferred the safe haven of Baku to the open waves of Derbent" [19]. However, in Derbent, it was still possible to purchase oriental goods, as in Astrakhan, then called Hadji Tarkhan. They were bought by Italian merchants, who exported to the West, or were resold on the Black Sea coast, in Taman or Crimea. Although almost nothing is known of the quantities or value of Dagestani weaponry, handicrafts and raw materials bought by Russian merchants in the Italian trading posts, in Astrakhan, or in Derbent, it is known that the Caspian's winter storms curtailed the trading period. Also in 1466 it is recorded that Afanasy Nikitin of Tver was trading in Derbent.

Moscow exploited its position at the crossroads of river and land routes connecting the southeast of Great Russian lands with its northwest. Goods from the markets of Nizhny Novgorod and Ryazan could not pass to Veliky Novgorod and Pskov without the protection of the Mother See (periphrasis for 'Moscow'). Russia tried to gain influence in the great markets/ *yamarki* of its main partners, Kazan, Bakhchisaray and the Hanseatic League.

Diplomats representing the Russian State appeared regularly in Poland, Italy or Lithuania and periodically visited Istanbul, the Holy Roman Empire, Persia and the Caucasus, with reciprocal visits to Moscow. Moscow was strong enough to openly challenge paying tribute to the Golden Horde by the end of the XIV century, having eliminated its other competitors, but the weakened Horde was only overthrown in 1480, a century after their first defeat of the Horde at the battle of Kulikovo.

References

[1] Vernadsky G.V. Kievan Rus. LEAN, Argraf. 2000. pp66, 69, 70, 201, 203.

[2] Ed. Narochnitsky A.L. The history of the peoples of the North Caucasus from ancient times to the end of the XVIII century. ed. A.L. Narochnitsky and M. Nauka.1988. pp102, 202–3.

[3] Daniyalov G.D. The historical path of development of the peoples of Dagestan before it became part of Russia. Daguchpedgiz. 1996. p7.

[4] Vavilov N.I. World resources of varieties of cereals, legumes, flax and their use in breeding. Agroecological Review of the Most Important Field Crops. Publishing House of the Academy of Sciences of the USSR. 1957. pp87–8.

[5] Shikhsaidov A.R. Islam in medieval Dagestan VII-XV centuries. 1969. pp34, 49, 51–2, 163.

[6] Kozubsky E.I. History of the city of Derbent. Bk. 1. Nagy Evi. 2012. p83.

[7] History of Dagestan. Vol. I. Nauka. 1967. pp97, 173, 180–1.

[8] Gadzhiev V.G. The role of Russia in the history of Dagestan. Nauka. 1965. pp47, 52, 60–1.

[9] Krishtopa A.E. Dagestan in the XIII- early XV centuries. Mamont. 2007. pp7, 111, 125, 185.

[10] Vernadsky G.V. Ancient Russia. LEAN, Argraf. 2000. p185.

[11] Klyuchevsky V.O. The course of Russian history. Vols. I. & II. Thought, 1987. pp58, 68.

[12] Vernadsky G.V. Mongols and Russia. LEAN, Argraf. 2000. p4, 96, 97, 111, 193.

[13] Carpini Giovani. Travels. Rubruk Guillaume. History of the Mongols. Travel to the Eastern countries. Tr. Malein A.I. Ed. Shastina N.P. State Publishing House of Geographical Literature. 1957.

[14] Grekov B.D. Kievan Rus. Publishing House of the Academy of Sciences of the USSR. 1944.

[15] Mavrodin V.V. Ancient and medieval Russia. Nauka. 2009.

[16] Jean-Paul Roux. Tamerlan. Young Guard. 2007.

[17] Islam in the territory of the former Russian Empire. Encyclopedic Dictionary. Vol. I. Oriental Literature. 2006.

[18] Grekov B.D. Yakubovsky A.Y. The Golden Horde and its fall. 1950. p91.

[19] Bartold V.V. Works on historical geography. Eastern Literature. 2002. p427.

5 Trade with the Moscow Tsardom XV–XVI centuries

The XV and XVI centuries, from a European perspective, were driven by merchant adventurers, often state-sponsored, seeking the wealth of the East. Russia sought to establish trading links for the same purpose through control of the lower Volga and the west coast of the Caspian, whence it could access the main Great Silk Road (GSR) as it came through Persia. At the same time the English pioneered a northern trading route through the White Sea, initially hoping to reach the East directly but then learning to utilise Russia's Volga route. The area to the north of Dagestan was fiercely fought over, not least by the Ottomans, both to secure the trade routes and for other power-political reasons. However, when the north-east conduit to the GSR via Russia, Volga and Caspian was working, Dagestan, in the middle, could import European goods and export its own.

Despite the gradual development of sea routes through European expansion, the GSR remained the safer and often quicker route – stormy sea routes risked shipwreck – and so continued to dominate east-west trade. In the late XV century the Ottoman empire, known after the palace gate in conquered Constantinople as 'the Sublime Porte', dominated both the southern and northern routes of the GSR near the Caucasus. The year-round accessibility of Dagestan, with its less-stormy coastal sea route never far from its ports, was attractive to the surrounding rival states. After the collapse of Timur's empire, the Caucasus found itself squeezed between the Ottoman Empire, Safavid Persia and a powerful and ambitious Russian State. The colossal potential of the GSR meant great interest in the Caucasus, where it arrived from the East, by Constantinople, Moscow, Tabriz and then Isfahan.

The Ottomans controlled the northern branch, of reducing importance compared to the past, through its Black Sea possessions, as well as Taman, Priazovye, and Crimea. The Safavid state was blocked in the centre of the southern route, so the Persian Gulf, which was open to European merchant fleets, could not reliably be connected through the Caspian with the Old World. At the same time, Russia remained practically isolated both from the Black Sea and the GSR without her main exit to the East, along the lowlands of Dagestan, where "lay the southern

DOI: 10.4324/9781003388579-5

(land) segment of the ancient Volga-Astrakhan-Shirvan route . . ." which connected "Eastern Europe and, first of all, Russian lands with Persia and some other countries of the Near and Middle East."

Russia's claim to the Volga-Caspian trade artery, her link to the East, began in 1392 when the Grand Duchy of Moscow annexed Nizhny Novgorod. As the nearest city to Moscow on the Volga route, Nizhny Novgorod guarded their access to the rich eastern trade route. In the XV to first half of the XVI century, Russian trade was concentrated in the markets of the Black Sea, Kazan and Astrakhan. From the accession of Ivan the Terrible in 1547, Great Russia began to operate on the principle of 'one trade route – one master.'

The conquest of the Kazan Khanate and adjacent lands in 1552 completed the ambitions of Ivan III [1] in sweet revenge for 200 years under the Mongol yoke, enabling the Russians to exploit the Middle Volga [2]. "Who was sovereign there controlled Russia's main market with the East, and must assert his authority in the Lower Volga – that is Kazan's trade with the East" [3]. In 1556 the tsardom of Moscow subordinated the Astrakhan Khanate so "the entire Volga basin was now in the hands of the Russians" [2]. Russia was now able to transport goods safely through the entire Volga region. In Astrakhan "Russian furs were traded for raw silk and silk products brought from the Caucasus and Persia" [3].

"In December 1556 the Astrakhan governors Cheremisinov and Kolupaev informed the Tsar that they had been sent peace proposals from the rulers from Shemakha, Shevkal and Tyumen. Two months later they were informed that merchants from Shemakha, Derbent, and Shevkal, had come to Astrakhan, Tyumen in present-day Kizlyar district of Dagestan, and Urgench in western Uzbekistan, laden with all kinds of goods" [4].

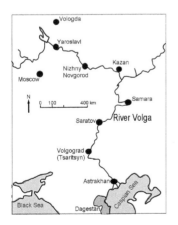

Map 5.1 The Volga route from the Caspian to and from Moscow

Russia exported "leathers, skins, wooden utensils, bridles, saddles, knives and other trifles, as well as bread" [5], in exchange for spices, products of Chinese, Indian, Persian, Central Asian, Middle Eastern, North Caucasian, and Transcaucasian craft industries, natural dyes, agricultural and livestock products, and coveted silk, likely from modern Azerbaijan and Dagestan.

All the peoples of the Caspian region, one way or another, "were engaged in the processing of wood, stone, clay, leather, wool." Dagestanis produced first-class hairy felt burka cloaks and other felts and fabrics. In addition, they wove ornamental carpets and also "engaged in artistic embroidery," and metalworkers made cutlery,

28 Dagestan – History, Culture, Identity

axes, sickles, scythes, iron vats, pans, chains, utensils and other household items and agricultural equipment, all from local ores – iron, copper, zinc, nickel, tin, lead, mercury, gold and silver. They continued to make weapons and military equipment from iron and steel [5], as well as ornamented jewellery.

Later examples of these unfamiliar and beautiful objects have been collected in the museums of Dagestan in Makhachkala and Derbent, which I understand were encouraged by my visits in the 1980s when I drew attention to the spoonboxes and other chip- or relief-carved wood wares, Davaghin and *dum* tapestry-woven carpets, magic bright-coloured Kaitag embroideries, *kinjal* silver-mounted daggers and *shashki* sabres and golden and silver filigree and niello jewellery with mounted stones. Outside Dagestan the main collection is in the Russian Ethnographic Museum in St Petersburg, founded in 1902. Dr Ramazan Khappoulaev the Museum's director helped me collect several duplicate examples and books because he feared that Dagestan might suffer the same destruction as Chechnya in the 1990s [7–9].

The city of Derbent became "one of the largest centres in the North Caucasus for the production of silk and silk fabrics, as well as satin, which were exported in large quantities even to Western Europe" [10]. During the XI to XV centuries in the Caspian region "paper and ink were produced" [11]. Other industrial centres throughout Dagestan were large villages known as *auls*. Many were in the mountains such as Kubachi, Amuzgi, Gotsatl, Sogratl, Archi, Tindi, Tsudakhar, Mekegi, Kumukh, Tsovkra, Andi, Karata, Ansalta, Akusha, Usisha, Untsukul Ruguja, Balkhar, Kharbuk and Khunzakh; Sulevkent and Endirey in the northern inland plain near present-day Khasavyurt; some further south on the coastal plain V. Kazanishche, Tarki; Kurakh, Ikra and Ispik on the Kurakh river, and to the south Akhty and Rutul along the Samur river. Both plains and mountain agriculture was well developed [12] and the use of land resources in mountain Dagestan was foremost in the world [13] (chapter 21).

Also along the Caspian coast the equally important "military trade route connected the Caspian coast of the Caucasus with the Black Sea-Azov highway." It joined Kaffa, Bakhchisaray, Temryuk, Pyatigorye, Tarki, and Derbent to Tabriz and Isfahan. The busiest mountain route was the Northern Azerbaijan road from r. Samur, Kurakh, Chokh, Gidatl, r. Andi Koisu to Chechnya [11] associated with other lesser trade routes, such as the North Caucasus transit via Tarki, Kafir-Kumukh, Kazanishche, Kazikumukh with Iverskaya Gore in Abkhazia [6]. Parts of the surviving northern Azerbaijan mountain-pass roads in Tlyarata, Tsumada and Tsuntinsky districts were also routes to Georgia and Armenia.

A united Dagestan [14] maintained economic ties with Great Russia, Central Asia and Asia Minor, Transcaucasia, the Near and Middle East, and Eastern Europe, and even such a "remote country as China" [15]. By these routes Dagestan merchants "travelled to the large trade, craft and cultural centres of Persia and the Caucasus – to the cities of Tabriz, Isfahan, Nuka, Shemakha, Ganja, Baku, Tiflis,

Erivan . . ." [15]. Alpine herders drove cattle and calves to market, "bringing wool, leather, butter, meat, cheese, as well as household products: carpets, cloth, felt, cloaks, weapons, pottery and wooden utensils, cotton, paper, and madder (for red dyes) and much more" [6]. They exported similar goods in smaller quantities to the north-western Black Sea region, to Kaffa, the fortress-port of Sunzhuk-Kale, Temryuk and Bakhchisaray (Crimean khanate). The Kubachi gunsmiths, and Avar and Lak jewellers worked successfully in the large markets of "Persia, Iraq, Syria, Anatolia, Egypt" [15]. Indeed "sabres, shields and other weapons, jewellery made of silver and gold, burka cloaks, and carpets made by the inhabitants of the Land of Mountains" were in steady demand [6], as was the high-quality Dagestan madder. In return Caspian traders kept their gold or silver money or purchased grain, spices, silk and cotton fabrics from the markets of Transcaucasia, Persia and the north-western Black Sea, products of the Transcaucasus, North Caucasus, China, Central Asia, Persia, Middle East, India and Asia Minor. They also bought raw materials: iron, copper, tin, oil, lead and salt. The great markets were mainly controlled by the Safavid state or the Sublime Porte, though European goods were also traded. The north-east Caucasus acted as both an offensive and defensive bridgehead for any dominant power. Russia's attention and powers were stretched, however, distracted by the lengthy Livonian war from 1558–83.

Russia strengthened its hold along the west coast of the Caspian to protect its interests, developing in particular fortifications along the Terek river that ran east-west across Dagestan.

The Sublime Port at first protested: "bring back the Cossacks from Terek, demolish the city set on Kabardia's land, and unblock the Astrakhan road to allow passage to all visitors from everywhere" [3], which Russia duly ignored. Moscow erected Tersky [16], "a new Russian town" on the lower Terek river "contrary to previous agreements" with the Ottomans, in 1588 (see map 5). Tensions rose and to defend this new claim to control the trading links in the area, Russia entered negotiations with the Shah of Persia [2]. In response, the Ottomans, together with the Crimean khan and other allies, took arms to within 75 km of Moscow, and forced Russia to demolish its Terek fortifications.

The confrontation was resolved by tacit recognition by the Ottomans of Russia's rights to the north-western part of the Caspian region. However, Russia's local allies were shifting allegiance, and Russia's attempt to keep them in line by force failed. "Premature interference in the Transcaucasus had cost Moscow dear under Fedor (1586–1598), but it cost even more in the reign of Boris [Godunov]" [5]. During the campaign the mountaineers slaughtered 3,000 Russian troops. To secure the city of Terki, Moscow next attempted to conquer northern Dagestan. At the decisive battle of Karaman 1605 [5], the Kumyk Sultan-Mahmud killed 7,000 Russian soldiers routed in retreat. Tarki/Terki maintained independence for 118 years. Russia could not hold on to more in the north-east Caucasus than the

30   Dagestan – History, Culture, Identity

Settlement of Tersky throughout the XVII century, although they more than once passed through northern Dagestan 'by fire and sword' [17, 18].

Tersky Settlement, Derbent and Shemakha were the main markets for Russian merchants and traders from Persia and Central Asia, the Caucasus, China and India [19]. From the XVI and XVII centuries, Shemakha was "the leading centre for silk production and trade" in the entire Caspian region. Derbent was nevertheless still a regional centre despite no longer being a functioning seaport and despite Shemakha's rise in importance [20]. There were Russian caravanserais in Derbent and Shemakha and Dagestani caravanserais in Shemakha [6]. Brisk trade also made profits in Baku and Nizabad. Russian merchants offered tin, copper, *yuft* Russian tough birch-oiled leather, cold steel for knives and swords, as well as gold or silver money, to purchase products from both plains and mountainous Dagestan.

Neither the Nogais (the destroyers of Sergei Posad) nor the Kumyks (the victors of Karaman) went to Tersky [21]. Instead, from 1580 to 1605, they were welcomed by Russia's enemy the Turks. During this period its relations with the northern Caucasus regressed. In 1556 traders of the Tyumen possession, Tarkovsky Shamkhal and Derbent had received permission from the tsar's governors to settle in the markets of Astrakhan. In 1569 Astrakhan was sacked by the Ottomans, who by the 1580s ousted the Safavids from Transcaucasia. Russia was distracted by defeat in 1583 ending the draining Livonian war. By 1586 the new Tsar Fedor ordered the Astrakhan governors to "exclude Schevkad and Kizylbashi, Turkish for 'red-head' some of the first supporters of the Safavids, from Georgia." Such a decision was made because there was instability in the markets of Astrakhan where Russian trading activity had lasted for at most 25 years. The revival of Great Russian trade in Transcaucasia took advantage of Persia's domination of the southwestern Caspian region.

Russia's trade with the East both as middlemen for European goods and exporters of raw materials was also hindered by the lack of reliable ports in the Baltic. At the time when "the conquest of Kazan and Astrakhan opened the way for Russia to the southeast, its window to Europe was Livonia" [2]. Russian trade with the Baltic states, Novgorod the Great and Pskov was blocked. European national trading companies took advantage of being the only buyers present by cheaply buying up Great Russian raw materials and Russian-supplied oriental raw materials, diminishing Russia's income. Russia started the Livonian War intending to rapidly resolve this issue with access to rich European markets, connecting the Baltic to the Caspian through the Volga. However, Moscow unconditionally lost the war and the English unilaterally connected the Caspian region with the White Sea and not the Baltic.

Moscow, trying to control the Baltic, forced Europe to attempt routes elsewhere [5]. The Netherlands, France, Portugal, Spain, and England competed fiercely to reach the East and its goods, initially by the hazardous route around Africa. Hope of an easier 'north-east passage' led English merchant-adventurers to attempt the route north of Norway and into the unknown Arctic Ocean. The sea routes of the Atlantic and Indian oceans were busy with England's rivals Portugal, Spain, the Netherlands and France, so in 1552, with a royal blessing Richard Chancellor's English flotilla set sail from Scotland to northern waters, supposedly towards the East. The English were baulked of a direct route to the East but found instead a conduit through the White Sea to a Russia eager to trade. The risks were high but so were the profits.

The English also keenly sought "to find a trade route from Muscovy to the East" [2]. London focused on the Volga-Caspian trade artery associated with Dagestan. The English learned from Russian merchants that land routes to India and China could be reached through the Volga and the Caspian. In 1558, Anthony Jenkinson (1529- c.1610), of the Muscovy Company, with permission from Moscow, visited

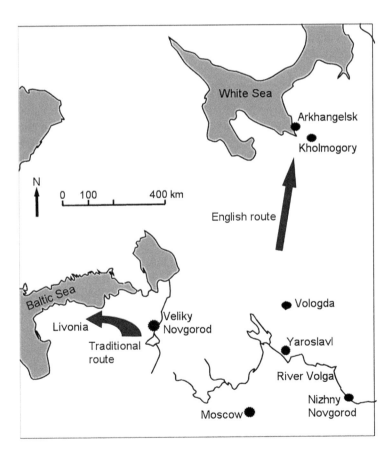

Map 5.2 Trading routes between Moscow and Europe

32 *Dagestan – History, Culture, Identity*

Bukhara and, in 1562, Safavid Persia. The discovery of this route to Persia seemed to present vast potential to the English, who hoped to capitalise on their monopoly of this access to Eastern trade [2, 21].

England opened depots and offices along this route, in Dagestan, Transcaucasia and Persia. The English sold English and European fabrics, as well as iron, copper, tin, and lead and bought Oriental and Caucasian: silk, spices, cotton, paper, carpets, jewellery and other handicrafts, as well as natural dyes. They were interested in "how Russians dye woollen and linen fabrics, leathers, etc.", as well as what dyes Great Russian merchants bought from the Turks and Tatars [5]. In Baku, Shemakha and Derbent, the English likely bought high-quality madder roots grown in Dagestan and Northern Azerbaijan, which gave the strongest reds in the world. English purchases from Persia and Transcaucasia journeyed across the Caspian and along the Volga to Astrakhan and Kazan and on to Yaroslavl, Moscow and Vologda. The goods continued by land to Arkhangelsk and Kholmogorsk ports on the White Sea, in summer by carts and in winter by sleighs. From there they were shipped to England and Western Europe. Although the ships' cargoes were usually carefully listed, little is known of the Volga and the Caspian traffic to Persia and the Transcaucasus. Thus, although cargoes from Moscow to and from the Caucasus are not listed as carefully as those from Moscow to England, a Londoner of Queen Elizabeth's time could see and use (and profit from) products of mountainous Dagestan.

The journey from England to the White Sea coast, and further to the southwest Caspian Sea and back took two or three years. The Russian evidence is that during the 25 years of their presence in the western Caspian, the English were able to make six return journeys from Arkhangelsk to Baku and Gilyan [22]. Noting that Jenkinson in the 1560s sent at one time "five transports with English goods to the Caspian Sea" [19], it appears that only about 30 English ship-loads visited Transcaucasia, but there is no conclusive evidence. Bronevsky estimated the value of one such English transport ship, fully loaded, at £30–40,000 pounds sterling at 1560 values [23], so it appears that London made great profits.

The English enterprise exploited a brief window of opportunity that lasted for 25 years until. the Ottomans took control of the Transcaucasus. The last Londoner who brought laden vessels to the Caspian was Christopher Barrow the cartographer and traveller, in 1581 [19].

The establishment of the Ottomans in Transcaucasia, resulting from their confident victory over the Safavids in the wars of 1578 to 1590 ended the English adventurers' hopes. The English were seen by Constantinople as hostile allies and commercial partners of the Russians and in 1581 were duly expelled by the Sublime Porte from the West Caspian [19]. Next the Muscovy Company tried to gain a foothold in the markets of Astrakhan and Kazan. However, the presence of the English in these cities went against Moscow's plans to protect its own merchants by imposing tariffs. Moscow also opened the White Sea ports in 1584 to European traders other than the English, diluting the latter's hopes there too.

Constantinople controlled the rich western Caspian trade until the two defeats by Safavid Persia in the wars of 1604–16 and 1616–8. As a result Isfahan recovered north and south Azerbaijan, Eastern Georgia and Armenia, the cities of Tiflis, Nakhichevan, Tabriz, Ganja, Erivan, Derbent, Baku and Shemakha, which had been taken in the late 1500s. Now Russia overcame the set-backs of the Time of Troubles (1584–1613) and rapidly increased its trade in the rest of the Caspian.

References

[1] Borisov N.S. Ivan III. Young Guard. 2003.

[2] Vernadsky G.V. Moscow Tsardom. Leon-Agraf. 2000. pp7, 37, 39–40, 50, 66, 101, 109.

[3] Lyubavsky M.K. A review of the history of Russian colonization from ancient times to the XX century. Moscow University. 1996. pp266, 268–9, 271, 394, 395ff.

[4] Tsagarelli A.A. Relations of Russia with the Caucasus in the XVI-XVIII centuries. V. Kirshbaum. 1891. p10.

[5] Soloviev S.M. History of Russia since ancient times. Bk IV. Vols. 6–7. Thought. 1989. pp132, 268, 363.

[6] The history of the peoples of the North Caucasus from ancient times to the end of the XVIII century. Ed. A.L. Narochnitsky. Science, 1988. pp281, 306–7, 316, 357.

[7] Chenciner R. Dagestan Today. Catalogue Zamana exhibition. 1989.

[8] Chenciner R. Carved and coloured village art from tsarist lands. Catalogue. Pushkin House exhibition. 2009.

[9] Chenciner R., Ismailov G. and Magomedkhan M. Tattooed mountain women and spoon boxes of Daghestan. 2006.

[10] Kudryavtsev A.A. Feudal Derbent. Science, 1993. p167.

[11] History of Dagestan. Vol. I. Science, 1967. pp180–3.

[12] Osmanov M.O. Economic and cultural examples of Dagestan from ancient times to the beginning of XX century. Makhachkala, IIAE DSC RAS. 1996.

[13] Vavilov N.I. Mountain agriculture of the North Caucasus and the prospects for its development. USSR Academy of Sciences, biological series. No. 5. 1957. pp78–86.

[14] Ancient crafts, craft and trade in Dagestan. Ed. M.M. Mammaev. Makhachkala, DF AN SSSR IIAE. 1984. pp149, 152.

[15] Mammaev M.M. Zirichgeran – Kubachi essays on history and culture. Makhachkala, IIAE DSC RAS. 2005. pp171–4.

[16] Magomedkhanov M.M., Bakanov A.V. and Garunova S.M. To the background of the Russian governance of the North-East Caucasus. Klio No. 12. 2018. pp80–6.

[17] Potto V.A. Two centuries of Terek Cossacks. Electrotype Printing House of the Terek Regional Board. 1912. p21.

[18] Klyuchevsky V.O. Course of Russian History. Vol. III. Thought. 1987.

[19] Kozubsky E.I. History of the city of Derbent. Bk. I. Baku, Headed Evi. 2012. pp122–3.

[20] Bartold V.V. Works on historical geography. Oriental Literature RAS. 2002. pp427, 571.

[21] Belorukov S.A. Relations of Russia with the Caucasus. University type. 1889. pp94, 208.

[22] English travellers in the Moscow state in the XVI century. Ed. N.L. Rubinstein. Tr. V.Y. Gauthier. Sotsekgiz. 1938.

[23] Bronevsky S. News of the Caucasus. S. Selivanovsky. 1823. p191.

6 Trade with Muscovy XVII–XVIII centuries

After the accession of Tsar Mikhail Fedorovich Romanov in 1613 and the ending of the Time of Troubles in 1618, the Russian administration needed to restore its ruined finances, and so re-established trade with Safavid Persia and softened its Caspian policy from aggression to diplomacy. "The Volga, Astrakhan, Tersky city, Tarki, Derbent, Shemakha, Shirvan trade route ran via Dagestan, to Persia and Mughal India" [1]. However Derbent's harbour was dilapidated, which ruled out the possible sea route.

Russian-Dagestan trade had stagnated (chapter 5), while "the Khans' merchants traded at Tersky, Astrakhan, and even Moscow" [2].

In the chess game between Moscow, Constantinople, the Safavids and the Crimean Khanate, Dagestan's 'Khans' – the Zasulak (near r. Sulak) Kumyk possessions, Shamkhal Tarkovsky and the nearby Kaitag Utsmi – found their niche, guided by their history of dealing with larger powers such as Byzantium and Timur [3].

Excluding the Cossack villages, Tersky *gorod* (city) on the Terek river delta was the only large Russian settlement on the margins of the Caspian, so its history is pivotal to this period.

About 1600, Constantinople banned Great Russian merchants from the markets of Shemakha, Derbent and Baku [4], which was reversed in the Safavid-Ottoman war from 1603 to 1618, when "having crossed the Transcaucasus with fire and sword, the Shah's troops drove the Ottomans out of Azerbaijan, Derbent and Eastern Georgia" [5] taking the south-eastern Caucasus.

The sole reliable coastal sea route for Russia (or other powers) to access the Great Silk Road (GSR) coming in via Persia was from Astrakhan via Nizabad in Dagestan, to Baku. Derbent could not accept heavy vessels, and the Khans could not guarantee a safe mooring. The stormy Caspian was unsafe for both the Russian and Persian lightweight merchant ship caravans [6]. In emergencies they were forced to land along the coast from Derbent to Tarki (near present-day Makhachkala), controlled by the variously titled local Dagestani rulers (called 'feudal elites' by Soviet historians to fit their communist theology). The valuable 114 km long strip ran from Tarki to the Safavid city of Derbent. Thus the safety of the trade-route depended

DOI: 10.4324/9781003388579-6

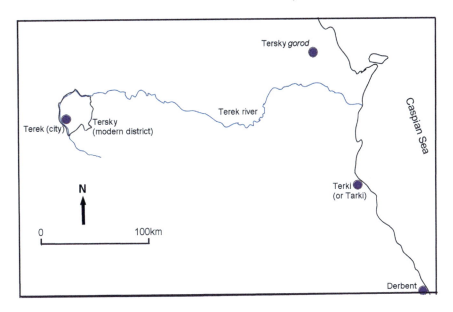

Map 6.1 Locating Tersky

This city, abandoned in early XVIII century, is not to be confused with Tersky *district* in the present day Kabardino-Balkarian Republic, also on the Terek river and with the Terek city in it, nor with the also-similarly named Tarki (or 'Terki'), on the edge of Makhachkala some 120km to the south.

on the loyalty of the Khans. Nevertheless "Derbent merchants who owned light vessels, periodically visited Astrakhan" [5]. Their ships could not take large loads or sail on open waters away from the coast, and their cargo was similar to Russian market wares, as described below.

These independent small states were unstable so to protect the Russia-Persia route the tsar's governors in Tersky had to negotiate with an increasing number of local rulers and please everyone. Soviet historians called it "classical vassal feudalism", but it was actually based on mutual benefits and oaths recognizing local sovereignty. "In the early XVII century some nine Kumyk rulers . . . and many other Avar leaders concluded a military-political alliance with the Russian State." At peace with the Shah, the Russian government turned a blind eye to the Caspian leaders simultaneously having friendly relations with them (the Russians) and Shiite Safavid Isfahan [5] and its antagonist the predominantly Sunni Ottoman empire.

The next war of 1623–1639 turned the Caucasus "into an arena of violent clashes where the Sultan waged war with Persia, as before . . . to ensure the free passage of Turkish-Crimean troops along the 'Ottoman road'" [2] to once more crush Isfahan from the rear. In reply, the Ottomans had "to seize strategic positions in the North Caucasus" and take control of the plains of Dagestan. The Persian shahs tried to win over local rulers [5], so that Dagestan, as a buffer, would protect their rear. Thus Isfahan and Moscow were equally interested in distancing the Khans from the Ottomans.

36   Dagestan – History, Culture, Identity

While eastern Transcaucasia was under Constantinople, Isfahan flourished under the reforms of Shah Abbas I the Great (d.1629), who, as with his successors, Shah Sefi I (d.1642) and Shah Abbas II (d.1667), invested in the 'Ottoman road', which was partly controlled by the canny Tabasaran Maysum and Kadis, and the Khans. Thinking on their recent military failures Persia bribed "the rulers of Dagestan who willingly accepted letters and all kinds of gifts of the Shah" [5].

Tsar Mikhail (d.1645) watched on as his Persian allies clashed with the Ottomans in the Caspian, saving Russia the expense. His policy was justified by the defeats of the Ottomans who were forced to withdraw from Dagestan, creating the opportunity for "the capture of Azov by the Don Cossacks in June 1637. However this created a crisis between Moscow and the Ottomans and the Crimean Tatars: "in response to the Cossacks, the Crimean Khan Safat-Girey raided the southern regions of Muscovy . . ." as "Tatars once more raided the southern regions of Muscovy, war with the Ottomans was only avoided by withdrawing the Don Cossacks from Azov in 1642" [1].

The Crimean khans supported by the Ottomans continued to oppress Kabardia, but they no longer threatened Tersky city [1]. Bakhchisaray was harried by the Don Cossacks, who were on 'bread and weapons' rations from the Tsar or acting independently [1, 7, 8]. The local Russian colonizers consisted of a relatively disciplined complex of Cossack settlements, located in the lower river Terek, the southern boundary of the tsardom of Moscow, the so-called 'serif line'. Tersky city "depended on the good relations established under Mikhail Fedorovich between Moscow and Persia and the Moscow's conciliatory policy towards the Ottomans" [9]. This balance contributed to better relations with the Dagestani khans who from 1614 to 1650 made unilateral peace arrangements with Russia [10].

The agreed obligations to Russia were to carry out so-called 'sovereign service', guard roads, provide guides, monitor the safety of Russian merchants, and punish local transgressors [2]. In his letter of autumn 1614 Shamkhal Tarkovsky, the leading Dagestani khan, swore that "there will be no disorder on the cities of his union of khans and no herds will be rustled, and no one will capture or beat or kill the khans" [10]. In response Moscow guaranteed similar terms. The union of khans were additionally allowed to conduct 'non-clipping' tariff-free trade in the internal Russian markets. Rewards for the Dagestanis were established for observance of fidelity and service to the feudal lords. They were paid regularly in bread and in cash, according to rank. The tsar's governors on their own initiative also took hostages of the khans' sons and relatives [2] to guarantee protection of the road from Tersky to Derbent. Tersky Kremlin ('small town'), containing 150 houses, was fortified with canon, several hundred archers [1], Cossack regiments [11, 12] and newly baptized highlanders, to maintain control of the lower Terek.

On the outskirts numerous Cossack encampments were "occupied by North Caucasians – Circassians, Okotsks, Novokreschenskayas and Tatars" [5]. This stability, helped by constant negotiations that balanced interested powers, ensured that the trade route was often open, protected by the Dagestani Khans whose loyalty was bought by regular bribes of gold and silver.

Tersky city "contained caravanserais, shopping malls, bazaars, luxurious gardens, public baths, customs offices and public places . . ." [9]. Russian, Armenian, Azerbaijani, Persian, Central Asian, Karaite and other merchants lived there, as well as north Caucasians and Transcaucasians and artisans from other lands [1]. Trade flourished between Russians and Caucasians and Russians and Persians, but slightly less between Russians and Central Asians, and periodically between Russians and Mughals from India. "The most important goods were manufactured in Russia, or were Western European rarities that passed through Russia." Volumes of cloth, canvas, leather, furs, expensive and cheap fur coats, sable hats, shoes and boots were traded [5]. Wooden utensils and Russian painted boxes, caskets, sieves, dishes and chests were in demand. Metal water vats, needles, pins, thimbles, wire, mirrors, scissors and basins, manufactured both in the West and Russia, were sold in bulk. Russian merchants also supplied salt, flour, and other agricultural products to Tersky city. "Twice a week, on market days, local north Caucasians called "*savdagars*" (?Afghans), arrived" [13], selling cattle and horses, all kinds of fruit, cheese, butter, honey, *sorochene* (alpine) millet, first-class ordinance, steel mail, cold steel, quality saddles, harnesses, fur coats, formed leather products, rough canvas, jewellery, other handicrafts, silk, cotton, paper, earthenware adobe dishes, madder and magnificent carpets [5]. North Caucasian caravans arrived loaded with oriental goods and their own products [2]. Tersky city was a bubbling place to live.

Moscow merchants bought saddles, harnesses, bridles, whips, silverware, and rough canvas. The Grebensky and Terek Cossacks acquired *arba* carts and accessories from the Kumyks and Kabardins, and from the Circassians: cloaks, fancy leather boots, *cherkess* jackets, and sheepskins [12]. Merchants of the Khans brought cotton, paper, natural dyes and silk, some of local cultivation, some re-exported from Transcaucasia and Persia, also expensive oriental fabrics and porcelain and Kaitag and Derbent earthenware dishes. They also brought suede, Morocco leather, felts and pile carpets, hazelnuts, walnuts and dried fruits.

For the Volga route the Caucasians used *strugs* – Volga long barges – lent by the tsar's agents from Astrakhan to Tsaritsyn, Samara, Saratov, Kazan, and by freight cart from Nizhny Novgorod and Yaroslavl to Moscow. Winter journeys north from Astrakhan used sleighs along the ice-bound Volga. Laden carts journeyed up the Volga to Nizhny Novgorod and Yaroslavl in caravans made of light river craft, from the north Caspian. Merchants also traded *en route*, due to storms, vehicle repairs, replenishment of supplies and changes of towing horses.

In addition, Shamkhal merchants Ildar Tarkovsky (1623–1635), and Surkhai (1641–1668), and Kaitag Utsmi Rustam Khan made the Dagestan to Volga r. and Moscow journey five times. "Ildar sold goods in Moscow in 1621 for 1,980 roubles; and in 1623, for 1,463 roubles; and a similar amount in 1627. He also brought 707 pieces of silk and cotton fabric, about 450 kgs of raw silk, 200 yufts of Safiyan or Morocco leather. At the beginning of the 1640s, Surkhai brought 8,910 roubles worth of goods."

In 1635, the ambassador Badarkhan and the merchant Kaitag Utsmi Vardanas brought to Moscow Zlatoglava 'the Golden-domed city', 333 pieces of silk and

38   Dagestan – History, Culture, Identity

cotton fabric, and about 60 kgs of raw silk and delivered to the tsar's warehouses 8 (bundles/bales) of red and yellow Morocco leather [2]. These were impressive quantities for those times.

The purchasing power of the XVII century rouble "equalled about seventeen" times that at the beginning of the XX century [1]. For example at the beginning of the XX century, one bull in the markets of Dagestan and Terek region cost about 16 roubles [14, 15]. Exporting food to Russia showed that the mountaineers had more than enough to feed themselves, contrary to later Soviet propaganda.

Upon arrival in Tersky city or Astrakhan or Moscow, and the intermediate cities on the Volga, Dagestan Khans' merchants received permission from the tsar's officials to store their goods in state-owned warehouses. They also periodically received 'sovereign feasts' of cash and concession benefits [10], although usually only diplomatic representatives could apply. They were subject to the same rules as merchants from eastern countries. The provincial governors and their officials vigilantly prevented the merchants of the East from trading on the Russian domestic markets, so bypassing the 'domestic guests' trading with each other or with Western merchants, with severe fines for transgressors, including seizure of goods sold directly to foreigners stored in 'sovereign bins' or all their goods [1, 7]. Any attempted partnerships between eastern and western merchants in the domestic retail markets was also forbidden. The prerogative of retail trade belonged to 'domestic guests'. For example Dagestanis, like the Persians, Indians and Bukharans, could not visit the markets of the White Sea region, Novgorod the Great and Pskov, which prospered through wholesale trade with the Western powers. Also, having sold all their goods, without official permission they could not purchase from the (non-Dagestani) 'domestic guests' so-called 'patterned goods' of Russian or European manufacture such as furs, guns, military ordinance, gunpowder, iron and lead [10], cheap goods such as cloth, dishes, agricultural implements, and household utensils. In spite of all these restrictive measures, the first half of the XVII century was a time of increase of Russian-Dagestan trade.

"When ambassadors of the Khans reached Moscow their goods were first shown to the court or even to the Tsar, who took his pick" [5]. After this 'gift' they were given permission to conduct wholesale trading exclusively with Russian merchants at the Moscow markets. If the Dagestani merchants stayed in Astrakhan or in Tersky, the local sovereign governors or agents representing hundreds of small merchants [16, 17] assessed their wares and took a selection of the best. Most of the silk and sulphur for gunpowder were reserved goods purchased at special rates that on arrival went directly to government warehouses [1, 7, 18]. Unclaimed surpluses could be sold in bulk to domestic merchants. In spite of these constraints "the resale of silk brought huge profits" to all merchants. "In Tersky and Astrakhan, a *pood* (over 16 kg) of raw silk cost 45–50 roubles, in Yaroslavl 50–60 roubles, and about 70 roubles in far-off Arkhangelsk" [5]. Silk traded in Moscow came from the Persian province of Gilan and the Transcaucasian Shirvan [19], partly from Dagestani merchants as local exports and re-exports.

Despite frequent trading visits the Khans' merchants were not allowed to open sales offices in Tersky city or Astrakhan or any of the cities on the Volga route.

Only the boldest merchants made the long and difficult Volga journey. Smaller merchants "often merged into small corporations to share navigation or land road expenses" [5], and only aspired to Astrakhan or Tersky city, though sometimes they paid a fee and joined the more adventurous caravans.

To avoid misunderstandings and theft the Russian governors urged the Khans to send documentation with their caravans so that the local militias could verify their identities and lists of goods. In return the governor would provide them with passports to show to potential violent robbers, especially in the remoter parts of the Caucasus mountains. The most expensive goods went to Moscow but greater bulk went to Terek city and Astrakhan. Russian-Dagestan transactions were by barter or cash – Persian fogs and Great Russian roubles [10].

Trading costs were high for foreigners; transport itself was expensive, but so were customs fees, typically ten per cent, *en route* – and they were subject to gruelling negotiation. The Khans had reciprocal rights to enforce and collect the tenth duty which was levied at each border crossing [20], sometimes five or six times on the same goods [2, 5, 20]. It is recorded that officials overvalued Fartag Ildar's goods, estimated at 1,430, by 33 roubles, seemingly because they were after extra transit duty. After a long debate they agreed on 144 roubles 24 altyns and 2 dengi/ kopeks transit duty. In 1631 Moscow granted the Khans and their merchants a duty-free incentive for the transit of goods, for theoretical duties of up to 150 roubles a year. The tenth duty continued for excess goods. To try to avoid misunderstandings [10], Moscow dispatched fast riders to inform the Khans and the Russian governors in Astrakhan and in Tersky city. Dagestani merchants were subject to Russian law and legal proceedings. In turn, Russian 'guest' merchants in the Caspian were subject to local laws. The fragmentary micro-states, each wanting their cut, drove up costs partly by making the area unstable. Moscow regularly dispatched patrols of newly baptized and co-opted foreigners "for reconnaissance in the Shamkhal, Kabardian and Nogai lands, on Kuma r., Quban, and even in Crimea" [9].

Such were the difficulties and risks that about 1635, only private caravans made up of Persian, North Caucasian, Azerbaijani, Georgian, Jewish and Armenian merchant venturers dared to travel to Safavid Persia via the Caspian by the Volga to Astrakhan to Shirvan route. For the Tarki to Derbent passage they needed the advance agreement of each Dagestani khan or Free Society. The polyglot Armenians, like the Kyzylbashs, were specialists in connecting Moscow with Persia. Armenian merchants had mastered commerce with the Ottomans and Safavid Persia [21], and as such were hired as agents by the Khans, the Russians and the Safavids. They operated from the Black Sea and the Mediterranean to Isfahan south of the Caspian, including the Persian markets of Isfahan, Tabriz, Ardabil and Gilyan; Baku, Shemakha, Quba in Azerbaijan; Derbent in Dagestan; the Crimean Bakhchisaray and Kaffa, and the Ottoman Trabzon, Samsun, Constantinople, Smyrna, Konya, Beirut, and Aleppo. From the 1600s they permanently settled in Astrakhan

40 *Dagestan – History, Culture, Identity*

and in Tersky City [22], where an Armenian named Vardanas was the agent of Kaitag Utsmi [10]. The Utsmi was the title of both the ruler elected by a Dagestani Free Society a democratic city-state and the area of his authority. Frustratingly there are no details from Russian sources about the Armenian merchants.

Despite the opportunities apparent as the Khans wavered through exposure to Russian comforts and bribes, Moscow abstained from taking advantage by picking sides, recalling their failures of 1593 and 1604–1605 against the northern Dagestanis. Any encroachment of the Russian State on the territory of modern Dagestan could be regarded by Isfahan as an encroachment on Safavid interests breaking their tacit mutually beneficial agreement. Any encroachment by Persia on Dagestan would displease the Russians. The Khans balanced the greater powers against each other to maintain their own independence. The Tsar's modest principle 'it is better to have a song-bird in the hand than a crane in the sky' meant that Moscow had to acquiesce to the smaller trade to Tersky.

As an attempt to get more out of the region because of not trading beyond Tersky, "in 1628, the German mineralogists Fritsch and Herold were sent by the Tsar to find silver and copper ore in the Caucasus Mountains and Ciscaucasia" [9], but nothing came of it.

The XVII century inhabitants of modern Dagestan were wholesalers of agricultural and craft products in their local markets of Shemakha, Baku and Derbent where Transcaucasian, Persian, Indian and Central Asian traders took them on to Safavid markets in Isfahan, Tabriz, Ardebil and Gilan. These markets to their south-west and south-east were more important than Moscow to the north [4].

As a rule, all exports arriving in Astrakhan were classified by the Russian authorities as Persian goods. The customs ledgers recorded where goods were bought and where the goods were taken from, but never by whom they were made. Some entries of "Gilan and Taurian" manufacture could actually be from Dagestan [13, 23]. The famous Shemakha bronze cauldron is now identified with the Quban south Dagestan and not the Persian or Azerbaijani types [24]. Travelling forward to XIX century, according to Robert Chenciner, similar misnaming of origin by Azerbaijan state-sponsored scholars and European rug dealers is found in Lezgin 'Sumak' rugs from Derbent and Avar and Kumyk dum and Davaghin rugs and perhaps so-called 'Shirvan' rugs as well [25]. Even today their identity is inaccurately given in auction catalogues, western and Azerbaijan books and museum labels in a failure to recognise their ethnic origin.

References

[1] Vernadsky G.V. Moscow Kingdom. Vol. II. Leon - Agraf. 2000. pp198–9, 351, 355, 359–60, 362.

[2] Gadzhiev V.G. The role of Russia in the history of Dagestan. Science. 1965. pp80, 86–7.

[3] Magomedkhanov M.M., Bakanov A.V. and Garunova S.M. Russian-Dagestan trade and economic relations during the existence of Kievan Rus and the Golden Horde. Clio No. 12. 2019. pp122–32.

[4] Magomedkhanov M.M., Bakanov A.V., Garunova S.M. and Emirova M.N. Russian-Dagestan trade and economic relations during the Kingdom of Moscow Pt. 1. Clio No. 1. 2020. pp74–87.

[5] Ed. Narochnitsky A.L. History of the peoples of the North Caucasus from ancient times to the end of XVIII century. Science. 1988. pp208–11, 307, 311, 320, 324–5ff, 330–4, 355–8.

[6] Tushin Y.P. Russian navigation in the Caspian, Azov and Black seas: XVII century. Science. 1978.

[7] Soloviev S.M. History of Russia since ancient times. Bk. V. Vols. 9–10. Mysl. 1990.

[8] Andreev I. Alexey Mikhailovich. Young Guard. 2004.

[9] Lyubavsky M.K. Review of the history of Russian colonization from ancient times to the XX century. Moscow University Press. 1996. pp395–8.

[10] Russian-Dagestan relations of the XVII – first quarter of the XVIII century. Documents and materials. Makhachkala, DF AN IYAL. 1958. pp35, 72–5, 77, 91–2, 113–14.

[11] Esadze B.S. Memo to Grebenets. Petrograd, P. Usov. 1916.

[12] Potto V.A. Two centuries of the Terek Cossacks. Electroprinting Printing House of Tersk Regional Board. 1912.

[13] Gadzhiev V.G. Works by I. Gerber "Description of the countries and peoples between Astrakhan and the Kura River". Science. 1979. pp108–9.

[14] Dagestan collection. Bk. I. Compiled by E.I. Kozubsky. Temir-Khan-Shura. 1902.

[15] Dagestan collection. Bk. II. Compiled by E.I. Kozubsky. Temir-Khan-Shura. 1904.

[16] Klyuchevsky V.O. Russian history course. Vol. II. Myal. 1988.

[17] Klyuchevsky V.O. Russian history course. Vol. III. Thought. 1988.

[18] Soloviev S.M. History of Russia since ancient times. Bk. IV. Vols. 7–8. Mysl. 1989.

[19] Bronevsky S. News of the Caucasus. Pt. 1. S. Selivanovsky. 1823. p196.

[20] History of Dagestan. Vol. I. Science. 1967. p289.

[21] Ter-Sarkisyan A.E. History and culture of the Armenian people from ancient times to the beginning of the XIX century. Eastern Literature, RAS. 2005.

[22] Shidlovsky Y. Notes on Kizlyar. Journal of the Ministry of Internal Affairs, Pt. 4. St. Petersburg, 1843. pp161–208.

[23] Bartold V.V. Works on historical geography. Moscow: Eastern Literature. 2002.

[24] Mammaev M.M. Zirikhgeran. Kubachi essays on history and culture. Makhachkala, IIAE DSC RAS. 2005.

[25] Chenciner R., Garunova S. and Magomedkhanov M. A survey of rugs and textiles with dragons from Azerbaijan and Dagestan. Azerbaijani carpets. Vol. 7. No. 24. Baku. 2018. pp62–71.

7 Under Russian governance 1801–1859

The XIX century saw the growth of Russian power and the expansion of its territories in the Caucasus causing radical changes between Russia and Dagestan. The annexation of Orthodox Georgia (Kartli-Kakheti kingdom) to the Russian Empire in 1801 anticipated the inclusion of the north Caucasus. Published by the printing house of the HQ of the Caucasian Army, in 1860: the highlanders, "once foreign to us, were absorbed, so Russia needed to subordinate them" [1]. Imperial officers noted: "One of the most 'interesting' parts of the Transcaucasus is without doubt Dagestan" [2].

At that time in Dagestan there were some 10 'feudal' estates and 60 unions of rural communities called *jamaat*, like Ancient Greek *polis*, which did not recognize external control and were fundamentally different from settlements in the Great Russian outback. "Most of the 'free societies' (*vol'nye obshchestva*) did not have feudal khans but consisted of free and equal members known as *uzdens*" [3]. In 1833 Baron Rosen pondered on the ruler of the Avars: "the property belonging to the khan himself consisting of several villages paying him a small tax is but a small part of Avaria. The rest of the Avars, although they consider the khan to be their ruler and sometimes pay tribute, only obeyed him if he had *auctoritas*" [4].

The Zulak Kumyk possessions including Endri, Aksai, and Kostek were the first to become absorbed into the Russian Empire. From the 1800s in each administrative unit, under the senior Khan was a Russian police bailiff or *pristav* of the Caucasian corps. Control was entrusted to the main Kumyk pristav, subordinate to officers from the Left Flank of the Caucasian defensive line.

The Tarkovsky Shamkhalstvo also submitted. Its khan received an annual pension of 6,000 silver roubles with the imperial ranks of Major-General and Privy Councillor. Under him was a Russian officer. Internal management both in the Zasulak Kumyk possessions and the Tarkovsky Shamkhalstvo was not included in the agreement.

To strengthen its hold on Georgia and extend its influence in Dagestan, Russia accepted the Avar Khanate into its 'protection'. In 1803, in the Avar capital Khunzakh, Sultan-Ahmed Khan swore allegiance to Russia before imperial officers, stipulating that he was acting for himself and his heirs. He was assigned cash gifts

DOI: 10.4324/9781003388579-7

Under Russian governance 1801–1859 43

and an annual pension of 5,000 silver roubles. As Governor Count Paskevich-Erivansky hoped, acquiring this territory "adjacent to the Georgian provinces, would prevent the Dagestanis and the Adjarians from engaging in predation and eventually serve to tame them into submission" [4].

Sultan-Ahmed gave the other side's point of view: "The warlike Avars in my neighbourhood consider themselves free and serve neither me nor others, except for mercy and money" [5]. The Kaitag Utsmi, Tabasaran Maysum (leader) and Kadis, and the Kazikumukh Khan, also only spoke for a small number of their nominal subjects. "In 1806, rural jamaats (communities) of western Dagestan entered piecemeal into Russian citizenship followed in 1809–10 by several free societies of Mountain and southern Dagestan. In July 1810 the commander in chief of the Caucasus general A. Tormasov accepted a number of Dagestanis into the Russian army" [5, 6]. Russia needed to augment the Caucasian corps, depleted by the full-scale war against Napoleon. Many free societies volunteered to serve in the Russian-Persian (1804–13) and the Russian-Turkish (1806–13) wars. "In 1812, representatives of the Akusha Confederation of free societies arrived at the imperial headquarters and took the oath of allegiance to His Imperial Majesty" [6].

Sheikh Ali Khan of Quba and Derbent, as well as Surkhay-khan of Kazikumukh, wanted to regain their former independence and sovereignty. They "repeatedly changed their position" [7], more than once swearing allegiance to St. Petersburg and then reneging. They repeatedly resisted the Russian troops, whose commanders, with St Petersburg's support, decided to remove them from power. In 1806, general S.A. Bulgakov captured Quba without a fight. He ousted Sheikh Ali Khan and in his place installed the loyal Khadzhi-bek with the rank of Naib, to govern the khanate traditionally, but under Russian supervision. In 1809 the administration of the Quban possession was transferred to a council of four Beks, reporting to the Russian military commander of Quba.

In 1806 the Tsar pronounced, "Regarding Derbent, We, guided by the constant care of the benefits of the residents of the city of Derbent, Our loyal subjects, have recognized the need both for themselves and this city to be taken into our administration, and you as a reward of zeal for service and loyalty to Our imperial throne, welcome the dignity (title) of the khan of Derbent . . . We allow you to use all the income of the Khanate of Derbent according to your previous rights and customs, with the exception of the city of Derbent and the income thereof, which shall pass to Our imperial treasury" [2]. The suburbs were transferred to Shamkhalstvo Tarkovsky. This continued until 1812, when "the head administration of the Derbent and Kuban provinces was established in Derbent" [7].

The removal of Sheikh Ali Khan, coupled with the Russian victories over Persian forces, had a decisive effect on Surkhay-khan of Kazikumukh who in 1806, and again in 1810, swore allegiance to the Tsar who still doubted his loyalty. In 1812 Surkhay-khan once again broke his word, so the Russians decided to annex the Kurakh Khanate, which included Kurakh, Koshan, Richa and a number of other Agul free societies. Aslan-khan, nephew of Surkhay-khan was appointed the ruler

44   *Dagestan – History, Culture, Identity*

of this new khanate, swearing that he "forever refused on his own behalf and on behalf of his heirs and successors" [8] to be vassal to any power except Russia and pledged personal loyalty to the Tsar. General A.P. Ermolov who took over the Russian Caucasus in 1812 commented: "the people of Kazikumukh cannot do without the bread of the Kurakh khanate and so Kazikumukh can be kept subservient" [9]. The Kura Khanate became a buffer between unreliable Kazikumukh and recently annexed Quba.

Through the XVII and XVIII centuries the Russians pursued a consistent strategy to attract Dagestani rulers and free societies to their side, with direct and indirect bribery and salaries for the rulers and their families, elders of the free societies, religious leaders and other influential people. The Dagestanis were further awarded high military and civilian ranks and granted commercial and social privileges. As part of the continued strategy used to conclude any agreement the Russians took hostages (*amanat*) both from Khans' possessions and from free societies [10], who were detained at the state's expense. Many became pupils of military academies and later served in the tsar's army.

Their agreements recognized their internal self-government and status of other groups that they brought into Russian citizenship. "Voluntary entry of the North Caucasians into Russia . . . did not mean that they were included in the military-administrative establishment or the laws of Russia" [7]. They were understandably forbidden to have contacts with states hostile to Russia. Mountaineers lost the right to declare war on their own, and to collect taxes including transit fees and tolls on goods from other peoples of the Russian Empire.

In the Gulistan Peace Treaty of 1813, concluded between the Russian Empire and Persia, Persia "universally recognized" and transferred to Russia political rights to Georgia, and the khanates of Azerbaijan and Dagestan. Moreover, "the highlanders living near the Caspian Sea ceased to depend on decisions from Tehran" [11].

Ignoring all previous agreements with Dagestan's Khans, Russia asserted its authority, replacing vassal relations by direct subordination. Having defeated Napoleon, Russia had become the 'gendarme' of Europe and disregarded the defeated Ottomans and Persians as serious opponents. The time had passed when every small ally counted. In the Winter Palace, the highlanders of Dagestan were considered merely as another group of natives. "The North Caucasus is increasingly becoming part of the sphere of Russia's domestic policy" [7].

St. Petersburg used military encirclement in an attempt to take control of the northeast Caucasus. They expected to "conquer Dagestan and Chechnya step by step, blockading on all sides with fortresses, roads and forest clearings" [10]. As early as 1816–7 a plan was developed to move the defensive line from r. Terek to r. Sunzha and the adjacent Caucasus Mountain Range. "Russian fortifications controlled the plain and its exits to the mountain gorges" [7]. In 1818 fortress Grozny (Terrible) was erected "threatening Chechnya and the Khankal gorge leading to it." In 1819, Vnezapnaia (Sudden) fortress was built near the Kumyk village of Endery, and in

Under Russian governance 1801–1859   45

1820 the new Burnaya (Stormy) fortress threatened Tarki, the capital of Shamkhalstvo Tarkovsky. A new fortified line cut the Kumyk plain, to "tear off the Kumyks from the Chechens, and make them subordinate to Russian troops" [12].

In the 1830s the Lezgin line was completed in the south. In 1832 the Temir-Khan-Shura fortress was built at the intersection of the roads to the Dagestan uplands and was later made the administrative centre of Dagestan. "Temir-Khan-Shura dominated a fertile plain, the breadbasket for the highlanders, with pastures for their cattle, down to the Caspian. A network of roads and postal tracks interconnected the forts, under the command of Russian officers who organized the police and decided taxes. At their command an investigation could be started and litigation be decided." Their judgements demonstrate that their universal power knew no bounds. The commandants "based all their actions on arbitrary personal considerations." By 1837 "the locals became troublesome, protesting as victims of the authority's whims" [2] but the abuses continued. In 1842 Petrovsk a fortress-harbour was built near Tarki. A few years earlier, the Kizilyurt fortification was completed, to control "the Shamkhalstvo possessions" [8].

The imperial administration's next form of repression was to transplant a Russian-speaking population equal to or greater than the indigenous Dagestanis. About 1800 there were no more than 3,000 Russian serfs and eight regiments of about 30,000 Cossacks stationed near the Left Flank Caucasian defensive line [13], too few for the planned repopulation. Resettlement of Don, Khoper and Volga Cossacks significantly increased numbers by the 1830s, when more than 25 new Cossack villages were established. "In 1840, in the Caucasus region, there were already 41 settlements in thirteen _volosts_ (Russian administrations) with 112,413 (at the census) Russian peasants" [7]. The transported Cossack population there was approximately 165,000, increasing to 240,000 over the decade [13]. In addition Armenian migrants "lived in almost all the cities, headquarters and settlements" and large numbers of Georgians were resettled there [7].

After Gulistan "the political choice to resist or submit to the Tsar faced all the Khans, free societies and rural jamaats" [14]. In Dagestan, the Avars, Mehtuli and Kazikumukh khans, Utsmi of Kaitag, Maysum and Kadis of Tabasaran, the Akusha Confederation and several other free societies had opposed the advancement of the defensive line. But the imperial troops defeated every opponent in short order. All who were discredited in the eyes of the tsarist administration were replaced by pro-Russian locals.

Many possessions were abolished or redrawn. In 1818, the Mehtuli Khanate was abolished but was restored in February 1820 under the rule of Ahmed-khan the former khan's son. After his death in 1844, he was succeeded by his wife Nukh-bika and "a Russian officer was appointed who rapidly took charge of her affairs" [7]. In 1819 Sultan-Ahmed the resisting Avar Khan was replaced by Surkhay-khan, who was originally a _chanka_ (arrivistes) of mixed descent. As Paskevich-Erivansky commented: "They have absolutely no devotion to Surkhay-khan, not for his limited ability, but though he is descended from the ancient Avar Khans through his

46 Dagestan – History, Culture, Identity

father, his mother is of much lower birth . . ." and according to tradition, he did not have the right to be a khan. He would not have been appointed "if all the other members of this clan were not our obvious enemies" [4]. To raise Surkhay-khan's prestige in the eyes of his 'subjects', in 1821 the imperial administrators tried to arrange his marriage to the daughter of Shamkhal, who found the proposal "indecent to Shamkhal's dignity" – adding that even uzdens did not marry off their daughters to chankas! General Ermolov pleaded without success "What matters his origin, when he is recognized by the government as the Avar ruler, and so equal to all the other Dagestan rulers?" [9] Nevertheless Surkhay-khan's nominal rule over Avaria continued until 1828, when it was divided in two. In 1830 power was transferred to Abu Sultan-Nutsal Khan, then in 1836 to Aslan-khan Kazikumukh, and after his death to Akhmed Khan Mehtulinsky. From 1843, the Khanate was seized by Imam Shamil and restored to the Russian authorities only after the end of the Caucasian war.

For participating in armed protests against the Russian presence in the Caucasus in 1820 Surkhay-khan was deprived of his possessions, which were transferred to his nephew Aslan-khan, the Kurakh Khan. Ermolov described Aslan as a drunkard and the weakest of his nephews. "Hounded by his vengeful uncle and exiled from Kazikumukh, he had been given refuge and an allowance by the Russians. In his unexpected transition to happiness, he was overwhelmed and did not bother to study the situation of the provinces entrusted to him, their economies or the condition of the inhabitants, but willingly signed the agreement" [9]. With these two possessions combined under his authority, the Russians counted on his total submission. For peace of mind they ordered him to put a *naib* in charge of Kurakh, with the warning "but do not unite these khanates" [2]. After Aslan-khan's death, the Kurakh-Kazikumukh Khanate was divided as before. Garun-bek ruled in Kurakh, soon succeeded by Yusuf-khan. The ruler of Kazikumukh until 1838 was Muhammad Mirza-khan, and then Aslan-khan's widow Umukusum-bike, with a Russian officer to oversee her affairs. From 1842, to assist him "an advisory body was established consisting of the Kazikumukh Kadi and two elders of noble origin" [7].

In 1815 St. Petersburg abolished the Tabasaran Maysumate and Kadiyate because of their support of out-of-favour Surkhab-bek Bek, Rustam-kadi and Sheikh Ali Khan the ruler of Quba and Derbent. The governance of these territories was initially entrusted to Russian commandants, handed over from 1823 to the loyal Beks of Tabasaran.

In 1820 the Kaitag Utsmi was also stripped of his title for resisting Russia. "All his revenues from his family estates and tithes from the villages were passed to the state treasury. The management of his territory was transferred to the Kaitag Beks, loyal to Russia, under a Russian officer who reported to Derbent." "Elected *kevkhs* and their *chaushes* (assistants)" were charged with the day-to-day management, as the administration recommended. Chaushes had to be approved by the Russian governor of Dagestan. "Kevkhs were to litigate in the villages that were not subject to sharia," for which the Russian commandant personally appointed a *kadi*. A kevkh's decisions could be appealed. Surviving documents show that the Governor had the sole right to pronounce sentence [9].

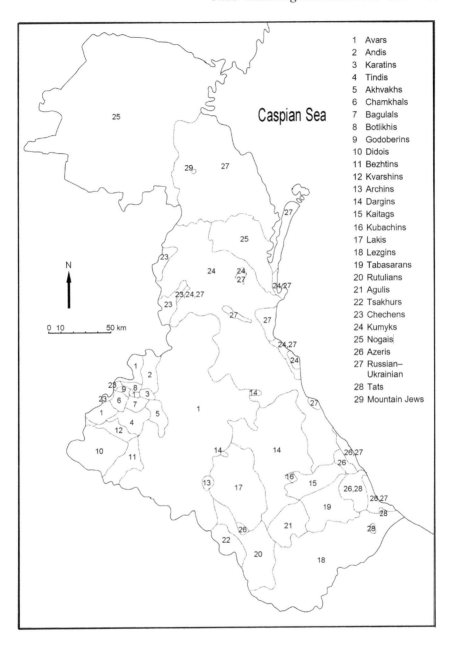

Map 7.1 Ethnic lands of Dagestan c. 1900

Preservation of the traditional customary laws was also discussed in General Ermolov's letter to Zukhum-kadi, a Russian appointee who was granted authority over the Akusha Confederation after their defeat by Russia in 1820. He was told to "refer to the commander in chief on all primary issues . . . for there is no other power over you" [9]. He received an annual pension of 500 silver roubles and

48   Dagestan – History, Culture, Identity

implemented all his orders unquestioningly, but after some years, he was removed from power after the Akushins complained about his ignorance and drunkenness. The position of kadi was abolished. The new district formed on the territory of the Akusha Confederation was short-lived after the appointed Russian chief was killed within a year. Russia was forced to restore the former Confederation, which lasted until 1854.

St. Petersburg aimed to consolidate its local "alliance with the Khans on the basis of transforming them into obedient vassals of the emperor." Russian politicians recommended swift transfer to a system of governorship, transforming the region it into a fully-fledged part of the Russian state and transferring power to direct control from the 'centre', but the local Russian authorities in Dagestan did not dare to proceed which meant that Russia "still strictly pursued its policy of controlling subordinate peoples through local khans" [12]. Behind every Khan, even if loyal to Russia, there was a pristav charged with "informing about all rebellious intentions, protecting public peace, to conduct a census of auls, *saklya* and residents, to hand out tasks according to auls' capacities, to collect fines for minor infringements of customary law and to arrest and process criminal suspects" [2]. These police-bailiffs were often previously Russian civil servants chosen because their ethnicity or clan was different and hostile to the locals. "Bailiffs were put in charge of migrants" [15]. Up to 1850 nine bailiffs were appointed, who reported to the command of the Left Flank of the Caucasian defensive line.

To nourish the loyalty of the Dagestan Khans the government increased their privileges and prerequisites. They were established as Great Russian landowners, supposedly with absolute power over their (non-existent) serfs. Local khans, beks, chankas and such were granted land, land rights and "all help and support" in return for their vanishing political freedoms [7]. Thus the Russians tried to become accepted, and at the same time subordinate the region – as it was customary to say in the Winter Palace – 'once and for all!'

To facilitate the transformation the Russians tried to suppress rural self-sufficiency to force acceptance of centralized authority. It was in Russia's interests to "destroy democratic forms of government not only among the non-peaceful, but also among the peaceful" which should stimulate "an aristocratic direction of governance" [11].

An eloquent example was the attempt to control a number of Chechen free societies by putting them under the authority of Shamkhalstvo Tarkovsky. In their swift complaint to the Governor Count Paskevich-Erivansky in April 1829, the outraged Chechens wrote: "Against our expectations, we learned that Shamkhal Tarkovsky, who invited us to join him, arranged our own vile people whom he had bribed to swear that since ancient times he was our ruler. In return the Shamkhal reassures them with promises of salary and mercy. He deceives them, and they deceive him . . . We inform the High Court that we disagree and cannot accept the Shamkhal for our lord. We will remove him with our *kinjals* (daggers) if he doesn't leave us alone" [4].

The unwillingness of free societies to be ruled by a Russian-backed khan was fear of new or increased taxes, unlawful legal proceedings, and arrogant behaviour of the khan or his patronage. It "especially" annoyed the "mountaineers" and drove the jamaats to armed insurrection [4]. In their attempts to crush them, the quislings relied on the "bayonets of the Russian autocracy" [12], threatening that "each rebel should be punished to the level of his guilt," and that pacification was possible only "with the presence of the victorious Russian army".

Some Russian officials and military were sceptical, believing that "to expect a perfect rapprochement" between the highlanders and Russia is possible "only when a cross is raised on every mountain and plain and when churches replace mosques" [2]. However cynical this may sound and no matter how many advocates it had, Russia never tried to Christianize the northeast Caucasus. Nevertheless, in political circles Orthodox subjects were thought to be more reliable compared to Russians of other faiths, particularly the Islamic.

Many civilian officials and the military did not see "the difference between the submissive and the enemy; between communication of complaints and criminality." They "arrested, abducted, hanged and exiled to Siberia many of those who, having submitted, had served the great Tsar." However, local residents "did not trust or talk to their Russian bosses," of whom they "were extremely afraid" [4]. Although they were assured that after submission "religion, the old internal order, previous relations between estates, courts and blood-feuds would be respected according to *adat* (customary law)" [16]. Violation of the last three assurances was the main reason for the decades-long Caucasian War.

"On paper [tsarist officials] saw almost all of Dagestan as conquered" [11]. State propaganda news reports claimed the complete extermination of the rebels and the pacification of the region. Reforms were long overdue, which was the reason Tsar Nicholas I sponsored the grand plan of Senator P.V. Ghan on the reorganization of the entire Caucasus. The creation of the Caucasus Committee was considered a positive achievement by the Russian Empire, but Ghan's model of civil society did not work.

Ghan proposed that Dagestan should consist of two parts: Derbent province and the lands of Northern and Mountain Dagestan. Derbent province included: Derbent city, Derbent and Quba counties, Samur and Dargin districts, Kurakh and Kazikumukh khanates, and lands south of r. Avar Koisu. Northern and Mountain Dagestan was to include the Khanate of Mehtuli, Shamkhalstvo Tarkovsky and the auls Ishkarty, Karanay, Erpeli, Chirkey, Chiri-Yurt, Miatly, Sultan-Yangiyurt and Otar-Aukh [16]. Repopulation of the province was to be according to current imperial civil law, as had been previously adopted in internal Russian provinces.

Shamkhalstvo Tarkovsky and the Khanate of Mehtuli were to remain under the jurisdiction of natural rulers but Ghan recommended that imperial institutions supervise their possessions. The auls of Ishkarta, Karanai, Erpeli, Chirkey,

50   Dagestan – History, Culture, Identity

Chiri-Yurt, Miatly, Sultan-Yangiyurt and Otar-Aukh were to be under military command, under an elected pristav.

Ghan's program, implemented in 1840, soon met many obstacles in Dagestan where the conservative population was unfamiliar with the procedures of the Russian Empire; it was "accustomed to customs inherited from their mountaineer ancestors, strictly abided by them and hated innovations" [11]. The new program was launched in three districts of Derbent province – Derbent, Ulus Magal, and Quba Uyezd (a secondary-level Russian administrative division). For the remainder "it turned out to be premature . . ." and locals demanded "a special kind of management based on adat" [16]. Military rule was imposed. On a Machiavellian note: "maintaining the khans is the best way, because if they are smart, they will be indispensable opponents of Shamil" but "everything bad that happens from the people will be attributed to them, and not ours" [11]. "In the 1850s very few representatives of the tsarist administration had doubts about imposing quisling khans onto democratic societies" [12].

In 1845, to improve communication and coordinate the activities of the centre and the periphery, an extraordinary governing body – the Caucasus Committee – was created. Other such Committees had appeared to be effective in Siberia, the Kingdom of Poland and the Western provinces. The Caucasus Committee replicated the Cabinet of Ministers in St. Petersburg, and was in charge of the North Caucasus and Transcaucasia, where it "oversaw the issues of trade, industry and agriculture, land tenure, resettlement, public education and health care in the Caucasus" [15]. Its members were selected by the Tsar himself. They were highly educated professionals and higher state officials; for Dagestanis they were simply another level of duplicit bureaucracy.

Thus, due to local resistance and conservatism, the Russian government failed to create a unified administrative system in Dagestan until after the end of the Caucasian War in the 1860.

After 1800 Russia became "the largest trading partner of Dagestan" [6]. In 1811 six exchange yards and four salt shops were opened locally. By the 1840s there were seventeen exchange yards, in addition to 41 markets where the mountaineers had the opportunity to sell their agricultural and livestock products, handicrafts, and other goods, exchanged for Russian and European manufactured goods.

The famous Dagestan knotted pile carpets which are mainly found in Europe and USA were woven in the XIX century after the pacification of Derbent and the south. By 1900 there were 40,000 women quasi-industrial carpet-weavers. The small number of Derbent dye works were called *kuchasi* and dye merchants were given Persian titles *ranginfarush, nilfarush* and *hnafarush*. In 1913 A.S. Piralov noted "that Dagestan *sumakhs* [weft-float brocades] are in great demand abroad for their original designs, colour selection, large sizes (from 10 sq.m/ *arshin* to 25 and up to 50) and fetched good prices from 60 to 150 roubles, and rare in size, quality of wool and design, or especially old . . . 200 to 350 roubles." In 1914, the average [monthly] wage of a worker was 22 roubles 53 kopeks [17]. Large motif Avar

Davaghins and Kumyk dums long tapestry-weave blue-ground rugs were for home use and unknown in the west until 1980s.

Military purchases authorized by Russia included weapons, military equipment, sheet steel, cast iron, tin, lead, iron and gunpowder. Export of gold and silver bullion was not allowed, neither the local sale of gold coins, partly to discourage clipping. The salt trade was a state monopoly. Russian vodka was first mentioned by the XVII c German envoy Olearius as drunk from long cow horns in Tarki in 1638, and in greater amounts with the Russian invading army and after Russian subjugation of north Caucasus.

Selective blockades, quotas or bans were usually determined by current wars. Rebellious highlanders were forbidden to trade in the Transcaucasus, in Russian exchange yards and fairs, or with peoples subordinate to the Russian Empire. "In case of violations, it was permitted to arrest traders on arrival and confiscate their goods" [8]. It was admitted that by 1850 the prohibitions significantly increased smuggling [7], which was blamed on Jews and Armenians, who were periodically expelled [9]. From the 1840s the benefits of the Russian markets and deterrent of being banned increasingly coerced Dagestanis to be included "in the all-Russian system" [12].

References

[1] Fadeev R. Sixty years of the Caucasian war. Marching Printing House of the Main Headquarters of the Caucasian Army. 1860. p4.

[2] Eds. Bushuyev S. and Magomedov R. Materials on the history of Dagestan and Chechnya first half of the XIX century. Dagestan State Publishing House. 1940. pp91–2, 329, 375, 385, 400, 423.

[3] Gammer M. Elements of democracy in Dagestan on the eve of accession to Russia. Bulletin of the IAE Institute. 2007. pp48–54.

[4] Ed. Berger A. AKAK. Vol. VII. Printing House of the Head Office of the Viceroy of the Caucasus. 1878. pp524–5, 532, 537, 567, 912–13.

[5] Ed. Berger A. AKAK. Vol. IV. Printing House of the Head Office of the Viceroy of the Caucasus. 1870. pp614, 628.

[6] Gadzhiev V.G. Russian-Dagestan relations in the XVIII- early XIX century. Science. 1988. pp13, 18, 20.

[7] Ed Narochnitsky A.L. The history of the peoples of the North Caucasus: The end of the XVIII century- 1917. Science. 1988. pp10, 11, 30, 36, 57, 59, 83, 94, 112–13, 136.

[8] Gadzhiev V.G. The role of Russia in the history of Dagestan. Science. 1965. pp201, 233–4, 263–4.

[9] Ed. Berger A. AKAK. Vol. VI. Pt. II. Printing House of the Head Office of the Viceroy of the Caucasus. 1875. pp8, 41, 69–70, 85, 102.

[10] Degoev V. The big game in the Caucasus: History and modernity. Russian Panorama. 2001.

[11] Mochulsky V.I. The war in the Caucasus and Dagestan. Makhachkala. 2012. pp8, 41, 70.

[12] Pokrovsky N.I. Caucasian wars and Imamate Shamil. ROSSPEN. 2000. pp112–13, 134, 137–8, 140, 367.

52 *Dagestan – History, Culture, Identity*

[13] Lyubavsky M.K. A review of the history of Russian colonization from ancient times to the 20th century. Moscow University. 1996.

[14] Magomedkhanov M.M. Dagestanis: Milestones of Ethnosocial History of the XIX-XX Centuries. Makhachkala. 2008.

[15] Eds. Bobrovnikova V.O. and Babich I.L. The North Caucasus as part of the Russian Empire. 2007. New Literary Review. p68.

[16] Fadeev R.A. Notes on Caucasian affairs. St Petersburg, V.V. Komarova. 1890.

[17] Piralov A.S. *Kustar* production in Russia. Vol. II. St Petersburg. 1913. p84.

8 XIX Century historical consciousness

Lenin had declared that the Caucasus was "populated by mountaineers who stood aloof from the world economy and even aloof from history," but Marxist historians, lost in the 51 volumes of his *Complete Works*, came up with 'Highland feudalism' anyway in their efforts to apply theory to the area. Much work was spent demonstrating the patrimonial nature and patriarchy of the social structure of the Dagestan peoples during the XIX century [1].

The creation of Soviet ethnography in Dagestan took place in the shadow of the unconditional acceptance of ideas of class inequalities, exploitation of the working masses, and the inevitable progress of feudalism [2].

In contrast to this imposed dialectical materialism, materials collected by estate-land commissions that worked throughout Dagestan until 1917 cast some light on the actual development of social relations and on the forms of feudal power.

The members of the commissions scrupulously analysed textual evidence of estate-land relations. They also recorded oral evidence about the estates, legal (adat and Sharia) land tenure, land use, and so on. Their reliable materials are distinguished by an abundance of information on a wide range of issues about the history of public life in Dagestan.

For example, the estate-land commission of 1873 recorded 12 families calling themselves Rutulian Beks in southern Dagestan, who all traced their family tree to Kazibek three centuries earlier. They could be confidently assigned to the privileged class. Representatives of these families had *firmans* (decrees) from Ottoman and Persian rulers, indicating that members of the surname Kazibek were considered Beks and recognized as the rulers of Rutul. The commission concluded that from the moment the Rutul Society became part of the Russian Empire, the Beks of Rutul were recognized by the St. Petersburg government as a privileged estate, like the other Beks of Dagestan, who did not pay any taxes or duties. Due to its democratic structure and liberty, Rutul society had never been dependent on the Beks who lived among this society and "apart from the honour were not distinct from the 'simple' class and did not benefit from the other inhabitants" [3].

DOI: 10.4324/9781003388579-8

54   *Dagestan – History, Culture, Identity*

Another study of the community governance of the r. Samur Lezgins in southern Dagestan concluded that the buttermilk custom (according to which the male representatives of the village of the free society once a year visited and dined at the villages belonging to the Akhtynians, Kurushis and Rutuls) could not be categorized as feudal relations [4, 5]. Also, that the Samur Lezgins' social structure, based on *Uzden* (free people) was similar to the free societies of northern-mountain Dagestan.

Original sources were allowed to speak for themselves. Sultan-Ahmed the Avar Khan wrote to General A.P. Tormasov in 1809, that "the number of Dagestan villages exceeds ants and grains: the number of Avar *Magals* (rural communities) is more than can be counted." One part of them was under his authority, another part under the authority of Shamkhal Tarkovsky, the third part under the Kaitag Utsmi and the Kazikumukh rulers. The rest were not subordinate to anyone and considered as free and belligerent.

In Kumyk society, which Soviet scholars usually endow with hierarchical power and strict regulation of both legal and domestic relations [6], jamaats enjoyed the same self-government as the Avar and Dargin free societies.

Among the Dido (Tsez) by the early XIX century there was property inequality, which, however, did not lead to the formation of a class of feudal lords [7]. For a long time the rural communities of western Dagestan were able to function autonomously, resisting both internal and external enslavement [8].

Among the Kumyks, in the old days the relationship between the Kumyk princes and the Uzden was as in one large family. They were held together by mutual trust, affection and devotion. "Now (1846), this class of princely Uzden has almost disappeared . . . The princes' yards were empty and, in the sunset of a valiant service, their proud cavalry dispersed."

This occurred because the princely uzdens built up fortunes and acquired land in the first half of the XIX century in Russian service. Becoming wealthy and independent of the princes, the uzden stopped serving them. With this Russian support they joined "the class of *sala-uzden* . . . and began to interfere with minor princely uzdens."

The deliberate removal by the imperial administration of princely uzdens from the rule of the Kumyk princes led to the destruction of their independent government. It caused a decline in moral social relations. Kumyk princes changed from 'fathers of the people' into imperial puppets.

Prior to this change, every Kumyk village or jamaat rural community "had as many senior princes as there were auls in the village." They met to resolve current issues and jointly made a decision acceptable to everyone, after which each of them communicated it to the inhabitants of each aul. For important matters, a popular gathering was organized, usually at the main mosque of the village. After explaining the essence of the problem, the princes made a decision based on the opinion of the people. The villagers could also have a general gathering without the princes, usually when they wanted to "discuss their needs by submitting a request to the princes" or when they were oppressed by them and agreed "to resist them."

In contrast, the remote administration of Russia dealt with only one senior prince, who was supposed to force residents to fulfil the duties required of them through a structure of administrators in each Kumyk 'village' (a rural community consisting of several villages) [9]. After the end of hostilities in the north-cast Caucasus in August 1859, the Dagestan Region was established by Russia. This preserved the old divisions of Dagestan which were in use during the Imamate, and promised retention of existing systems; however, "after the Caucasian war, in the most critical points, power and law were concentrated in the hands of the tsarist administration" [10]. In practice, this simplification was a continuation of the earlier repression, and often brutal.

"The new relations of the Russia state developed with the semi-wild tribes of the Caucasus. Previously they were seen as foreigners, alien to us. But when they became internal, Russia had to subordinate them to its power" [11]. The new colonial redivision of the world was based on the 'right of the strong', the idea of historical inevitability and the 'state necessity' of conquering the weak. As with other empires, Russia claimed a civilizing mission with respect to the peoples of the East. The new world order determined the causes of the Caucasian war, and not its mythical social roots developed by Russian writers or the political claims about the *abreks*' 'raiding system'.

"Mountains of literature comparable in height to the Main Caucasus Range" [12] were written about the Caucasian War, the "predations of the Highlanders," and about the 'fact' that the Highlanders were politically naive, unaware of the self-interest of Turkey, Persia, England, and puppets in their anti-Russian politics.

Many Dagestanis doubted the feasibility of armed opposition to Russian power. With the tightening of Russia's grip on the North-east Caucasus, Dagestanis, in their own interests, took a central role in numerous projects to support Russia, related to the strategy of war and the conquest of the highlanders. In Russia "there was no doubt about the legitimacy and inevitability of the conquest of the Caucasus, [fulfilling a 'state need']" [13]. The weighty arguments for Russia's dominant presence and 'arrangement' of the Caucasus were further acknowledged by Turkey and Persia [14].

In Dagestan the jamaats and khanates were split. Some tried to take advantage of the Russian incursion, others endured patiently, and others desperately resisted. The first were considered subjects or pacified; the second duplicit and prone to treason; the third were 'hostile'. In St. Petersburg the oath of Russian citizenship was understood as submission and promise of service to the Tsar; but "they only dreamed of an equal alliance with us, and by no means entertained thoughts of submission" [15]. They just wanted to stop the ruin of war and would say anything and even adopt Russian citizenship. At first, "the Russian government, wanting

56 Dagestan – History, Culture, Identity

to have, in the rulers of Dagestan, if not direct subjects, then at least not enemies, condescendingly over-looked all their tricks, paid them salaries and granted them ranks" [16].

General Ermolov, distinguished in the battles of Austerlitz (1805) and Borodino (1814) was appointed commander in chief of the Russian forces in 1816. He brought a more sophisticated and a more cynical approach to the Caucasus struggle. Dreaming of Bonaparte's laurels, his 'innovative' strategy consisted chiefly of destroying villages, setting fire to fields, stealing cattle, and looting provisions. His creed was "everyone is subject to hunger, and hunger will lead to obedience." His name became a byword for brutality. In a reply to the outraged Alexander I, he wrote, "I desire that the terror of my name shall guard our frontiers more potently than chains or fortresses" [17].

"Far from subduing the population, as his admirers up to the present have asserted, his activities rather intensified hatred to Russia, stiffened resistance to it and helped to enhance the role of Islam, in the form of the spread of the Naqshbandi Sufi *tariqat* brotherhood" [18]. This subtle remark of the prominent historian Moshe Gammer is of particular note to those historians who view the Imamate as a theocratic state, and the Imam's very status only in the religious-hierarchical sense, contrary to what Shamil called himself, *amirul'mu'minin*, the ruler (emir) of Muslims. In fact power and religion were separated in the Imamate [19].

"Initially, I [Ermolov] set them against each other so that they would not want to be together, against us, and some already promised the extermination, and others the execution of the *amanats* (hostages). If necessary, some need to be honoured with an excellent elevation, that is, the gallows" [20]. Ermolov also offered bribes and intimidation, even interfering in the family affairs of local rulers. Not a single serious military event of the Caucasian War was without the participation of the khans and their 'native police' [21].

The brutalizing war dictated its own rules of survival, for both social relations and political self-organization. In the hope of peace and patronage, entire societies and peoples of the Caucasus swore obedience to the Tsar. "Some went with the infidels even in the war against Muslims. Others mixed with infidels, day and night, whole families: children, brothers and grandchildren. Still others gave their children as hostages to the unfaithful, in return for their handouts. Other appointed as the rulers over their houses some devil-seducer from the infidels, [or became quislings themselves]" [22].

The feudal lords who accepted the citizenship of Russia pledged to pay taxes and form the 'native militia' in return for keeping their power, military ranks, pensions and privileges.

"The idea that the only true, historically necessary way was the war with Russia, and that the Avars, especially, were dominated by anti-Russian sentiments is wrong" [23]. Notably, the only bloodless accession to Russia, Merv, was under the Avar general A.M. Alikhanov-Avarsky.

Shamil led the unification of Dagestan and the North Caucasus into a single state – the Imamate. With hindsight, he "sought to be more a Muslim than a Dagestani, through which he lost his enormous charisma in Dagestan" [24]. As well as his personality, there were other nuanced pressures for unity, now called 'national liberation struggles' or *muridism*. (For Shamil and his *murids*, the meaning of the term muridism was incomprehensible. As he said, "I've only been a simple uzden, who has been fighting for freedom for thirty years.")

Most studies of the Caucasian War use an 'ethnological subtext' to explain the 'mountain mentality' that was so resistant. One may ask "to what extent is it legitimate to project conceptual, ideological, or semiotic theories, or Europeanist complexes onto [the Caucasian warriors] that arise from outside other existential grounds?" [25] An irony was that Russian historians of the war were forced into self-analysis.

Figure 8.1 Shamil by Denier

Some more sophisticated historians thought that the courage of the warring parties lengthened the war. In 1851, Adjutant-General Argutinsky perspicuously commented on the extraordinary losses of the highlanders: "the gradual breakdown of the enemy's households will cause discontent and bitterness among our former supporters" [26]. The hardships of wartime tested the patience of the already stretched Imamate's population. The worse the Dagestani military situation, the more stringent and strict were Shamil's requirements for the population. Naibs had to follow military commands without question, even if unpopular with the locals.

The population gained little from any of their oppressors – 'their' khans, Shamil's naibs or the tsarist administration. Many Dagestanis "saw that the life of peaceful villages under the auspices of the Russians was much calmer and abundant" [27], while others remained indifferent to the Russians and even hostile to the Imamate. According to Shamil's ground-rules, the naibs, his commanders (chapter 9) found "it's all the same . . . whether it will be in accordance with the thoughts of the person who received the order, or he disagrees, or even if he considered himself smarter, more restrained and religious than the imam." The naibs had to "leave the decision on cases under sharia to the Muftis and Kadis and not argue, even if they were *alims* (Islamic scholars). They are only allowed to conduct military business" [19]. This distinction shows that some military decisions might (of necessity) go against sharia.

The latter part of the XIX century saw the new generation of Russian-European educated bourgeoisie gradually rallying to the Russian cry, "unity of the Tsar and the people," although ironically the same period saw the revival of Caucasian [or

58   Dagestan – History, Culture, Identity

mountaineer – a synonym for Dagestanis] spirituality and national culture under Shamil [28] in the Arab-Muslim tradition, see also the next chapter.

By 1912 it seemed that all was forgotten. A Dagestani wrote "We love and are always faithful to Russia. We proved this both in the Sevastopol campaign, and in the Polish uprising of 1863, and in Skobelev's Akhal-Tekinsky campaign, and in the Russian-Turkish War of 1877–78, and in the last Manchurian War [1904]. We always responded to the call of the Tsar and went to die as volunteer combatants. We did this loving Russia, which became our motherland. And of course, for all this, we expected maternal care for ourselves from the Russian government" [29].

References

[1] Kovalevsky M.M. Law and custom in the Caucasus. A.I. Mamontova and Co. 1890.

[2] Kosven M.O. Family community and patrimonia. Academy of Sciences of the USSR. 1963.

[3] Khashaev M.O. Feudal Relations in Dagestan XIX – beginning of XX century. Archival materials. Science. 1969. Pp121–2.

[4] Ragimova B.R. Forms of community governance of the Samur Lezgis late XVIII- first half of the XIX century. Questions of public life of the peoples of Dagestan in the XIX – early XX century. Makhachkala. 1987. P107.

[5] Karpov Y.Y. Dzhigit and the wolf. Men's unions in the sociocultural tradition of the highlanders of the Caucasus. St Petersburg, Ros. Acad. Sciences.1996. P108.

[6] Gadzhieva S.S. On the estate relations of the Kumyks in the first half of the XIX century IYAL. Vol. IX. Makhachkala. 1961. Pp191–216.

[7] Luguev S.A. and Magomedov D.M. Didoians (Cesus). Historical and ethnographic research XIX – beginning of XX century. Makhachkala. 2000. P59.

[8] Daniyalov G.D. The class struggle in Dagestan in the second half of the XIX – early XX centuries. Makhachkala. 1970. P16.

[9] The Tiflis newspaper "Caucasus". No. 37. Tiflis. 1848. P152.

[10] Aglarov M.A. Andeans: Historical and ethnographic research. Makhachkala. 2002. Pp65–6.

[11] Fadeev R.A. Sixty years of the Caucasian war. Tiflis. 1860. P2.

[12] Karpeev I.V. Documents RGVIA about the XIX century Caucasian war. Russia and the Caucasus through two centuries. St. Petersburg. 2001. P239.

[13] Gordin Y.A. Caucasus: Earth and blood. Russia in the Caucasian war of the XIX century. St. Petersburg. 2000. P11.

[14] Gadzhiev B.T. and Ramazanov X.X. The movement of the highlanders of the North-East Caucasus in the 20–50s. XIX century: Coll. Docs. Ramazanov Makhachkala. 1959.

[15] Yurov A. Three years in the Caucasus (1837–1839). Caucasian calendar. Vol. IX. Tiflis. 1885. Pp1–2.

[16] History of the Apsheron Regiment. 1700–1892. Vol. 1. St. Petersburg. 1892. P346.

[17] Blanch L. The Sabres of Paradise. 1960. P24.

[18] Gammer Moshe. Empire and mountains: The case of Russia and the Caucasus. Uchitel. 2013.

[19] Codex of Shamil. Makhachkala. 1992. Pp9–10.

[20] Letter of Ermolov to Zakrevsky 18 November 1816. Rus. State libr. Ms. F. 325. Ed. Chrn. 33. L. 66.

[21] Lapin V.V. National formations in the Caucasian war. Russia and the Caucasus through two centuries. St. Petersburg. 2001. Pp108–25.

[22] Chronicle of Muhammad Tahir al-Karahi "On the Dagestan wars during the period of Shamil." Makhachkala. 1998. Pp34–5.

[23] Islammagomedov A. Avars. Historical and ethnographic study XVIII to early XX centuries. Makhachkala. 2002. Pp66–7.

[24] Voronov N.I. From a trip to Dagestan. SSKG. Vol. III. 1870. P25.

[25] Sukhachev V.Y. Ethical and national component in the Caucasian conflict: The advent of the "alien". St Petersburg. 2001. P178.

[26] History of the Apsheron Regiment. Vol. II. 1700–1892. P208.

[27] Dobrolyubova N.A. First complete collection. Ed. L.T.K. Lemke. Vol. 4. St. Petersburg. 1911. P157.

[28] Gamzatov G.G. Dagestan phenomenon of rebirth, XVIII – XIX centuries. Makhachkala. 2000. P324.

[29] Dawn of Dagestan. NQ 1, 28 February 1912.

9 Shamil's Ethno-religious Imamate

The Laki Abdurakhman from Gazikumukhi (abbr. AG) pioneered Dagestani ethnography in his Book of Memoirs [1] much quoted in this chapter with "unprecedented material in the historical literature of Dagestan" (Shikhsaidov), capturing the internal workings of society from 1820–50, instead of the usual military-political studies. He gave uniquely detailed descriptions of customs and adat norms of individual villages and their various industries, clothes, food and climates, as in the following selections.

1. Shamil's name

"Initially, Shamil was called Ali. He was a sickly child, and as was the custom [to avert the evil eye], they changed his name to Shamil-Ali, abbreviated to Shamil. This name was nowhere to be found in his family, in their village Gimry or in its surroundings. When he discovered that Shamil was not his original name, he was pleased to discover that it was taken from the Hebrew prophet Shamuel/ Samuel."

2. Shamil's naibs

Shamil's *naibs* (companions and commanders) confounded their Russian opponents with legendary bravery and ultra-human abilities and endurance, combined with theology and mysticism, redolent of Caucasian Nart giants and Arthurian knights. In war courage was as desirable as theology but there was no direct connection between courage and scholarship, though mostly alims were appointed naibs, because "they had God's grace and were lucky".

"[Naibs] should not," said *nizam* (the organizer) Shamil, "listen to their people's opinions which threaten to disrupt decisions to build defensive walls, protect borders, or destroy the enemy's pathways. If a naib showed weakness, he was demoted to the rank of chief of hundreds."

Many of Shamil's 58 listed naibs were described as brave alims (theologians) [1]. Others were praised for *amanat* (loyalty) or were noticeable as thin or well-built or spoke eloquently, wittily or as windbags.

DOI: 10.4324/9781003388579-9

Some appointments seemed nepotic (the Arabic *min nasl* means 'birth', as in 'descent'): Gazimuhammed, "since he was the son of Shamil, people respected him and often turned to him" and his close friend Gitinav Gidatli; Nurmuhammad Karakhi, ". . . an alim descended from alim Musalav Khushtadi, al-Hajj al-Asam the deaf Haji from Chokh . . . authoritative among us" was popular for his courage and marrying his daughter to Shamil's son. He was one of the best naibs and "did not spare Shamil his fortune or even his life, like the caliph Abu Bakr's sacrifices for the Prophet Muhammad." Talhik – "a famous daredevil for his attacks and campaigns was father of the wife of Jamaluddin, son of Shamil. He kept his restless people on Shamil's side by curbing the spies and others who wove intrigues in his province. Other descendants of famous *ulama* (Islamic scholars) included Aydemir "son of the venerated Sheikh Jamal Chirkeyi" and Zakariyahadzhiyav Khushtadi. A rare outsider was Naib Giada Charbili who "was bold in battle . . . he was not an alim but no less intelligent."

"The naibs who are listed here, I saw with my own eyes several times and knew about them personally, excepting Akhberdilmuhammed, Sukhaib and Shuayb, who lived before me, but I heard about them from Shamil, my father and other trustworthy people" [1]. The following descriptions of 24 naibs are illuminating.

During the long wars, cruelty at home was evidently excusable:

a) Labazan Andreusi – "He was brave, intelligent, eloquent, fair and authoritative. He had 100 people executed in Andi his *vilayet* and not one was innocent. Some had spied for the Russians, others were thieves or adulterers. If he was not bold and hard-hearted, there would have been more lawlessness, since the Andis are bad-natured, liars and debauched, afraid only of firm rule. However, they are always brave and each time they encountered the Russians, they returned with many 'scalps'." "He, Muhammadamin Harahi [b below] and Musa Balakhani [c] were 'naked sabres', similar to predatory animals, devoted to revenge and robbing their subjects, that caused many to defect. Humiliated, others preferred death. They deceived Shamil with fine words and false information, but ignored his orders. God save us from the devils of the human race!"

b) Muhammadamin Harahi – "He was a long-serving alim and not a coward, though he tortured and killed many throwing them into the river, for which when Shamil moved to Dagestan, he was expelled to Ichichal village."

c) Musa Balakhani – ". . . known for his uncouthness and ruthlessness especially in matters of faith."

d) Musahadzhiyav Chokhi – "a notorious bastard who was subsequently removed."

e) Bukmammad Gazikumukhi – ". . . one of the best naibs, a famously brave *muhajir* always friendly to his troops. He was a sincere worshiper, skilled in battle, and a devoted favourite of the Imam. His name thundered as he repeatedly raided his fearful subjects and burnt down their villages."

62 Dagestan – History, Culture, Identity

f) Miklik Murtazali Chirkeyi – "He was an arrogant despot who took bribes. After too many complaints he was demoted, his illegally acquired property confiscated, and he was sent to Baytulmal for active service."

g) Khursh Sogratli – ". . . warlike . . . who ruled his people fairly, faithfully and bravely. He tried to eradicate viciousness among his people and follow Shamil's orders."

Hurtful nicknames were less usual:

h) MaxIahIajiyav Kudutli – "the famous stuttering alim, nicknamed 'shorty' was Shamil's favourite."

i) Kurbanalimuhammed Batsadi – ". . . an eloquent and educated alim. He was not a warrior, but managed the affairs of his people. He was ridiculed by his nickname *Genibikh* (Pear-cutter-in-half). A lot of pears grew in the aul, and before becoming a naib, he had been a pear merchant."

j) Kurbanilali son of Muhammad Batsadi, *Muhajir* Umar Salti and Idris (Effendi) Andyreusi – may have spoken eloquently with the imam, but aside from their courage and orderly management, they really became famous for their meanness.

Shamil was plagued by infighting and slander:

k) Hadji Murat Avari – ". . . the well-known leader, feared by all near the borders of Dagestan . . . big-hearted, and a famed administrator . . . Shamil regretted 'truly they lied to me denouncing Hadji Murat, and now I see only his honesty and reliability.'"

l) Galbatsdiber Karati – ". . . a respected alim, and a sane, decisive, zealous and thorough defender of sharia. He was deposed by [the] Andis because their slanders separated him from Shamil. However, he never deserted Shamil, even on the final battle of Mount Gunib. He died later a *gIabid* (pilgrim) on *hajj*."

m) Kebdmuhammed Teletli – ". . . eventually became a *mudir* mystic. Shamil said that although neither brave, nor wise, nor respected, he prayed earnestly. 'I honoured him as naib, introduced him to my retinue, and thanks to my respect, people also respected him. In return he began to resist me.'"

n) Daniyalbek Ilisui – "He joined Shamil as a major general having served Emperor Nicholas . . . When he became a mudir, he equipped his troops and muhajirs, built a mosque in Iriba, and donned a turban with a long dangling end and became a hajj . . . His detractors spread rumours that he wanted to run away, or surrender Iriba fortress to the Russians. His bitterest enemies were Khadzhimurad, Kebdmuhammed Teletli and Aglarkhan who accused him of killing the son of his sister married to an uzden of Ilisu . . ."

Valour in battle clearly extended the resistance, and vice-versa:

o) Sukhayb – ". . . a close assistant to Shamil who fell for his faith in battle with Prince Vorontsov's troops in Dargo."

Shamil's Ethno-religious Imamate 63

p) Rajab Tsubutli – "He ruled the people with complete justice, and tried mightily to improve their situation. Their hearts rejoiced and revived like grass in the rain after scorching heat, and they resisted the Russians more zealously than before."

q) Idris (Effendi) Andyreusi – "an eloquent alim and muhajir, but timid, clumsy and inconsistent in business. But since he was a theologian, Shamil did not want to lose his authority. In the end, he had to replace him with a more able battle commander, under Russian pressure from all sides."

r) Abakarhaji, the son of Qadi Muhammad Akushi – "Hero, alim and muhajir . . . a fair, God-fearing and brave man, but not successful in battles."

s) Zubair nicknamed Khusro – ". . . fought in the final battle *gazavat* on Mount Gunib. When we were under fire, surrounded by Russian troops, he and his followers bagged-up Shamil's sugar supplies, ignoring the gold and silver. You can see how wild the Dagestanis were!"

t) Akhberdilmuhammad Khunzakhi – "The [Ichkeri] people of Kekhi loved him greatly . . . for his justice and courage, so devoted that when he called them to battle, everyone flocked to him, like bees for honey."

u) Usman Zhalki – "The Imam loved him for his zeal in military service . . . he and his family accompanied Shamil when he left Chechnya for Dagestan, but when they retreated to Mount Gunib, Shamil ordered him to return to his homeland, ashamed to risk the lives of his numerous family and small children."

Others were less than valorous:

v) Saadullah – "did not know how to treat the people of Kekhi or respect their customs, he was considered the most courageous among the Chechens. The people's complaints increased but because he was a well-known daredevil Shamil delayed removing him and paid for it: 'Imam, you did not listen to our complaints, and forced us to join the Russians,' – leaving Shamil without an army. They mocked 'Now let Shamil keep him as naib in command of our trees.'"

w) Batak – "He was the naib commanding Shubut and made peace with the Russians without a fight."

And mitigating cases:

x) Ummah Zunsi – ". . . a true Muslim hero, still fighting the Russians more than a year after Chechnya was conquered. He hid in the woods and organized periodic attacks. Surrounded in his cave, he finally surrendered to Prince Mirsky's detachments. Exiled to Smolensk for four years, he returned to Dagestan early after appeals from his villagers. On his return, he stayed with Shamil for two weeks and explained that he had to surrender because his family almost died of starvation in the cave."

y) Umar Salti, Muhammadamin Harahi, and Hajiyav Shodrodi – were also not brave, but not cowards.

64   Dagestan – History, Culture, Identity

Even less than valorous were:

z)   Muhammad Baktlukhi, Kebdmuhammed Teletli, Shahmandaril Hajiyav Chirkeyi and Idris (Effendi) Andyreusi – not brave.

3.   The alim 'Islamic scholar'

The righteous alim devoted his energies and exhortations to God, against all indecency in society (*glavam*), but above all in himself. To keep young people upright, Abusufyan Akayev wrote '*Qilik kitap*' (book of table etiquette) in Kumyk: "I translated the Arabic into Lak for the ignorant and the young." Kurban Giali Gumchukatli selected from the Arabic "what was profitable or useful . . . and needed because the alims were gone and there was no one to ask and no one to tell, so people remained in ignorance and darkness" [2].

Many of the naibs were learned alims, who calculated the times of prayer, resolved personal quandaries, or discussed the philosophy of the universe, though a few had unworthy, weak and even vicious characters.

When consulted an alim usually wrote down both the question and his careful response to avoid less learned distortions. The best were unafraid to consult their seniors, as it avoided making a mistake that could damage their life-long reputation. It was disloyal for a villager to consult an outside alim. However an alim could visit a mutually respected colleague in another village to deepen his knowledge, without diminishing his status.

Only those already knowledgeable in Arabic grammar, jurisprudence, logic, and poetics were suited to be an alim.

An alim always acknowledged his sources, and followed Eastern tradition in giving enthusiastic reviews. However, falsely denying knowledgeable alims was considered a great sin: "*Gielmu lalel glalimal glodoreglanlun gari.*" Authors always thanked Allah Almighty on completion of their work.

Naturally, alims were usually positive with "good news for Dagestan. In our country there are many meritorious deeds of hospitality and helping a neighbour. In Arab countries they do not encourage good deeds and prohibit the bad and are changeable in worldly affairs and religion. There is no leader against the enemies of religion [like Shamil] and they have more love for worldly goods than Dagestanis." Alims writing criticism never named individuals.

4.   Attitudes to alims

Sheikh Shuayb al-Bagini (1850–1920) in *Tabakat al-hwajakan* (Layers of important people) stated that neither he, nor all the sheikhs he listed, knew how many sheikhs were in Dagestan, "because, from the moment Islam appeared, the country became a fountain of knowledge, learned people, and sheikhs. The earth is mixed with their sacred ashes . . . then in knowledge of sharia, these ustaz can only be compared with sheikhs from Egypt and Hadividya in Kashmir."

Alims damned 'false sheikhs,' who, lacking even the smell of knowledge, "had ignored their mission to guide people on the path of truth, instead acquiring wealth," which inspired Hajimuhammad Husaini Gigatli's (1846–1945) poem:

> *Murshids* in the past/ stood like thorns against the khans/and those who are now tyrants./ Tea is drunk like *zamzam* healing water,/ Money from naibs is not hidden/in cracks in the wall, but in their marriage chests.
> . . .
> For the sheikhs in the past/ The gates of the khans were not closed/ But they didn't enter their courts,/ fearing that the gates of Paradise would be shut.
> . . .
> An aspiring murshida answered:/ "You found the worst in yourself,/ I'd be looking for someone better, now the one who distributes places in the *wird*/ claims that he is one of the best."

5. Shamil governing Chechnya during the Imamate

"The Chechens were less committed to Islam than the Dagestanis. Shamil carefully studied both regions and decided that it was necessary to explain and fulfil all the laws of sharia. Shamil appointed Chechen *Muftis*, *Mukhtasibs*, *Mudirs*, *Kadis*, from whom he appointed commanders of a thousand and five-hundreders. As far as possible he avoided reprobates, instead revealing to them the gates of humility and worship, mosques and madrasahs, *saadak*, *waqfs* and other charitable works. He condemned indecent intoxicating drinks, smoking tobacco, pagan verses, chants (*zikr*) and all kinds of gatherings. He also ignored their adats that disagreed with the Koran and the *hadiths* on robbery and assault and murder (i.e. blood feuds) excluding retaliation."

6. The fall of the Imamate

As explanation for the fall of the Imamate [3]: "Shamil's naibs oppressed the people hard . . . Their injustice and greed finally reached the limit . . . It was impossible to appeal to Shamil, who only listened to complaints with written authorization from the naibs, who would hardly incriminate themselves. The highlanders, already tired of fighting, grew weaker and poorer every day, despaired: 'For us it does not matter what happens in this world.' First the villagers began negotiations with Russian border officers, who received them kindly with generous gifts. Their naibs followed, though Shamil was ignorant of his treacherous naibs on whom he relied. They undermined his power, opening the door to the Russians, lubricated with Russian gold."

7. Good Character as promoted by Shamil

The following are characteristic of the Imamate, though some concepts were also valued throughout Islam. In Dagestani languages, the concept of 'character' is conveyed by *'amal* ('habit' or 'behaviour') *hasiyat* ('character'), of Arabic origin is closer to the latter meaning, in Russian *kharakter* means temperament. Although the Arabic root *'amal* means 'work', 'action' or 'method', it has not replaced the Kumyk/ Turkic *ish*, the general Dagestan word for 'writing', Avar *hlaltli* and *gyavudi*, Lak *Dava* or Archin *Ari*. The meaning of *'amal* varies depending on the context, as the Avar: '*Matzal, Kveral, Cherkhal Gyarulel Giamalalal'* – actions performed by language, hands, body, '*Giamal kvesh'* – a person of bad character, '*Hiamal klodoli'* – arrogance, '*tslugyaduleb glamal'* and '*qiadrab glamal'* – habit of stealing and vile disposition.

Alongside knowledge (*glilmu*), deeds (*glamal*) and purity of intentions (*ihlyas*) form an integral part of sharia. Knowing and mastering what is permitted and forbidden is only possible with religious upbringing. In Islam, these concepts of *hlalal-hlaram* permeate Islamic life – from satisfying food and clothing needs to economic activity and trade, ethics of behaviour, momentary obsessions and deeper existential thoughts.

8.   Social economics of '*maglishatl*' in the time of Shamil

The Avar *maglishatl* approximates to today's 'life support' not only in a narrow economic sense, but including the beneficiary's business dealings and social and family status. *Maglishatl* meaning 'create and collect worldly goods' is partly equivalent to *dunyal gabi* (Avar), *dynyal dava* (Lak), *dunyal mas* (Dargin), in contrast to spiritual capital (*ahirat gabi, ahitar bavu*). The concepts of *maglishatl*, *dunyal*, and *qadar* described human destinies, predetermined by the Most High and considered by the alims in terms of eternal or transitory values. Aligaji Inholi an Avar recommended: "In worldly affairs, be God-fearing/ compassionate and generous, my friend./ Enrich your behaviour with theology to increase your kindness,/ be open-faced./ The Creator always values goodness, my friend."

Interdependence of the economy and ethnic culture are well known. In Dagestan, with its long mercantile history, (chapters 3–6) the concept of 'economy' analysed and justified the accumulation of goods. The economy was divided into a) the economic activities of individual villages; b) the legal aspects of land tenure and land use (rent, joint management), land conflicts both inside rural communities and between them, precedents and disputes; c) inheritance and donation of land, movable and immovable property; d) monetary relations and debt obligations in trade. It shows what was considered important.

9.   The innovations of Imam Gazimuhammad, a staunch ally of Shamil, regarding leisure

"He began to forbid people to drink intoxicating drinks, smoke tobacco, play the tambourine and dance with women [although this is permitted in *Sharh al-Muhazzaba*], and as for dance, in general it is not forbidden for men [in sharia]) but for women."

10. About clothes

For the Dagestani alim, what today is called traditional material culture and economy were so familiar that they were unworthy of description. They were interested in a proper inclusion of the material world within the framework of the sharia, Sufi ethics, and ethnic moral values.

The naibs' regalia subtly became more modest. "[Shamil] established their distinctive yellow turban and two silver plated, gilded epaulettes inscribed 'This man proved himself in battle, rushing like a lion,' which was awarded as the seal of Shamil."

11. Fate, free will and the transience of worldly matters

For naibs, philosophy was of equal interest to practical matters, so the following proverbs translated via Russian may seem obscure and mystic.

One of the earliest of the alims' philosophical reflections belongs to Khadzhimuhammad-Musalav, the son of Musa Kudutli (1651–1715):

"You may be the lord of the Maghreb-Mashrik/ but Azrael will take your poor soul/ . . . Allah gave dear life,/ a fickle guest, – she disappears in vain./ Allah granted your house in which you are a guest/ but only as decoration,/ for you will not stay in it."

Abubakar Aimaki (1711–1797) and Aligaji Inholi (1845–1891) did not separate the predestination of fate from freewill as qualities with which the Lord endowed his slaves.

In Dagestan, ideas about the fragility of the world and the eternity of the afterlife existed since the adoption of Islam, and survived in epigraphic inscriptions from the XV century: "He moved from hell [on earth] to the afterlife, and he is Shams ad-Din b. Muhammad al-Hamahi" (Kamakh, 1432); "Death is truth, and life is deception. The owner of this grave Bagarchi son of Kurbach . . . – may Allah forgive them both" (Kadar, 1492–3). "The late Qadi Ali, the son of Muhammad al-Baghdadi, moved from the corrupt world to the everlasting world" (Tarki, XVI century). Although the perishability of worldly life preoccupied Hassan Kudali (1718–1795), he maintained that actions, not dreams, were the source of human well-being. His dictums, "Forgetting God, he amassed worldly shit" or "The abundance of gold and silver will no longer be useful as a simple white shroud for everyone in the end." But also: "The poor will not get rich from worthless dreams. But if you follow the Will, you don't lose the *sabab* (Means), and with the Mind, the words you say will not be false."

Two of Aligaji Inholi's epigrams became proverbs: "For he who wants peace without labour,/ a field without a sickle will not be ploughed," and "Destiny (*qadaru lagi*) is irreversible, even if avoided by cunning tricks. Everyone on

68   *Dagestan – History, Culture, Identity*

earth seeks salvation: When *takadiru* (fate) comes, *tabadiru* (safety measures) are cut away."

The famous Arabic proverb *'Ish al-yavma ka annaka tamutu gadan* ('live today as if you die tomorrow'), had different versions in Dagestan, as in the Avar: "Do worldly things so you live forever, but serve (Allah for the sake of) the afterlife (*akhirah*) as if you die tomorrow". Muhammad Gidatli (1850–1920) interpreted it thus: "Old hopes are meaningless. Do not postpone a good deed or worldly actions as if you're staying forever, or your heirs will take the credit demanded of you in the next world. Prepare for akhirah as if you were dying now, for tomorrow you will find only what you did today."

In the chapter "Making a living" of Sheikh Hassan Khilmi's book *Talhis al-maa'rif fi tahrib Muhammad 'Giarif* (scholars of *al-maa'rif* nourished on the hidden words of *Muhammad 'Giarif*), he quotes Sheikh Sayfullah Bashlarov: "A perfect mentor leads students on the true path without disturbing their daily work. The renunciation of worldly things by a perfected student in a cleansing of the world's heart by a *zuhd auliya* (disinterested protector), may not be completely, so he may earn money by trading or engaging in agriculture and crafts, in order to become 'closer to Allah.' For someone who is not working but dependent is no different from a pregnant woman!"

12.   Public life in suitable company

In *Gilmu-l-Basharia* (traditional socio-ethnology), to distribute *zakat* (alms) fairly, people were put into eight categories to decide their needs, depending on their situation, legal capacity and availability of appropriate work [4].

a) *Fakir* – one who does not have property, and who does not labour for subsistence; b) *Miskin* – one that has or produces a livelihood, but needs sustenance; c) *Giamil* – one who works; d) *Muallafat* – a convert to Islam; e) *Rikabal* (Arabic slaves); f) *Garimuna* – those in debt; g) *Gusatu-l-mutatlavvigati-Allagase glolo gazavat gabulel chagli rugo* (veteran fighters); h) Ibnu-sabil – a traveller on his journey, far from home.

If a villager became insolvent his community would never dehumanize him as a lumpen member of a dialectical class. In every village there was an unwritten method to share the expense of recognizing births, marriages and funerals. There was nothing to expect from someone who had nothing. As the Avars say, *Pankil kulgyu, kyolol bertin* ('for a funeral a cake, for a wedding a toast') *sto gram* (Russian for a hundred grams i.e. a measure of vodka). Although poverty never justified any sleight to personal dignity, the impecunious were tactfully reminded that they were still invited to celebrations and that they should not miss out on *sadaka* charity.

Sirazhudin found in his list of great sins: *Sordo-koyal kwanase kven rokob bougev chiyas, Chiyadasa jo gari, kurab jo badib chlvayi* (Avar: 'Having daily food at home, ingratitude and not welcoming a stranger').

For the better-off, it was reprehensible to be greedy or show too much enjoyment in front of a guest, through over-eating or drunkenness, and to forget *yah* (modesty) for worldly goods: "It's worth more to starve than being a louse/ The poor are more beautiful than living to excess/ Yah!"

13. Eating properly

"Whatever his blessings, a person who attains wisdom dreams without rest of the next world, seeing Allah who gave him life, earthly and heavenly blessings and Allah the omnipotent" [2]. "It is obligatory to gain knowledge by suitable behaviour and devotion to service of the Almighty. But he cannot serve Allah, if his body is not healthy and strong, for which he must take food correctly, being nourished by faith."

"A person who puts a piece of food in his mouth to serve Allah has his reward, keeping his body in order to better seek knowledge, pray and do what is permitted. It is sinful to eat or walk for *keyf* (enjoyment), not to do God-pleasing deeds to improve worldly life . . . and that *halal* food should be clean, not sinful or godless . . . The eldest and wisest says *Bismillah* before the others. Use three fingers of the right hand – the *sunna* – to eat a small amount, not to stuff your mouth, but chew well and swallow before putting more in. Do not eat from the middle of the dish, or the *barakat* (blessedness) will leave, but start from one end; or from another's dish . . . It is better to bite than cut your chosen fruit [i.e. to draw your kinjal] . . . salt the first three slices of meat before eating to increase the barakat and avoid food-poisoning. Salt can cure some 70 diseases and eating salt at the beginning and the end of the meal will protect you from 360 misfortunes, prevent *zhuzam baras* (sore throat), toothaches, heartaches and stomach pains . . . Eating too hot food risks seven ailments that can be treated by *karagat* (blackberries): weakened memory, dry mouth, decrease in hearing and vision, a darker face – all because there is too little barakat, further dissipated by blowing. You must wait for hot food to cool."

The best known book on food customs was Abusufyan Akaev's *Qilik Kitap* guide to table etiquette which was *nazmas* (praised) by Abdullah Chokhi in his *Ummul Bayan* (Old Lady) and Sirazhudin Obodi. In Sirazhudin's *Nazm Kvanil adab-Sunnatab* (Food Culture following Sunnah), he advised: "A khan asked his assembled sages/ 'What is the medicine without disease?' 'Do not eat, whether not hungry or not full.' On this they agreed – it is the best medicine," and on his verse: "Like a hungry dog, who dare not grab his master's food/ Like when a lover eats with his love,/ Eat nicely, with a prayer/ as if the Lord was watching." To which Aligaji Inholi added: "*Buza, alkohol* and tobacco, look, you gave them up/ otherwise in your dying hour you will lose the faith." As a treatment for *hirs* (gluttony), Sheikh Sayfullah-kadi Bashlarov proposed "the education of their *nafs* (egos) in worship of Almighty Allah by reducing food and drink along with an increase in *dhikr* and *murakaba* (remembrance of Allah); avoiding forbidden prayers and not looking at the beautiful faces of women, recognizing that this is the beginning of sin."

70   Dagestan – History, Culture, Identity

14.   Renunciation of worldly life

Fear of God does not require asceticism. Sharia does not deprive a person of permitted (halal) worldly pleasures, but obliges remembrance of Allah. Many alims and Sufis wrote about everyday concerns. They divided people observing mystic *wirds* into six categories:

First are those whose wird indulges in worship and prayers, day and night. The second wird is for those that are engaged in learning to benefit their community by study and teaching explaining decisions, which is more valued than routinely following farsh (religious obligations). Third wird are students following the path of Allah by studying the sharia in their search for knowledge which is also valuable. Fourth are those that cannot live without working, who must perform *farsh*, to commemorate the work of Allah and give alms if his earnings exceed his family's needs. He who needs his earnings must not leave his job to devote himself to worship. Fifth, the khan's worthy wird is to fulfil farsh and make decisions consistent with sharia law, establishing just order (*'hell*) to protect them from evil. Sixth wird are *zagyids* who only serve Allah and who have already completed another wird. They must perform farsh, remembrance of Allah, and eschew worldly riches.

Before joining a wird, the student should first decide which group he belongs to and follow the advice of his *ustaz* (mentor). Some spend time intoning 300, 500 or 1,000 indicated prayers, *sunnat* and at least 100 *raki'atov* daily prayers. Others read the Qur'an and others recite *astagfirullag* (seek forgiveness in God) or *subhI-anallag* (exclaiming God is perfect).

In addition to farsh, further obligations correspond to his position in society: Sheikh Kharda al-Rochi (sometimes 'Harda', 'Khadaa' and other variants; 'al-Rochi' or 'al-Ruchi' means 'of Archi') "divided into faith groups such as women, men, cattle breeders and traders, all are equal before Allah Almighty, excepting religious disciples who regularly study the Sunnah, as true Sunnis who do not talk about what they should be silent about, or delve into what they do not understand. However in the XIX-XX centuries others indulged in innovations, turning away from reading the Quran, the Sunnah of the Prophet and commentaries in Arabic."

15.   Social classes

Social classes are listed with indicated decent behaviour and obligations. The greatness or insignificance of deeds depends on their surroundings and participants. Since people have different *sipat* (qualities), *'amal* (characters), and abilities, each individual, whether a Sultan or a woman, needs to decide which *agl* (group of people) he/she belongs to, and accept their standards.

a)   Sultans, kings, khans, big bosses are obliged to act *insap* (fairly), establish a fair order in *gladlu* (society), impoverish any despot in restitution, fulfil the will of the people, and work for their people. Rulers are necessary, because

Shamil's Ethno-religious Imamate 71

wild, unruly people would tend towards cannibalism. Whatever the ruler's religion, Allah will be pleased with the faithful fulfilment of their duties.

b) Tribunes, *vezirs* (ministers), *Uman* (security services) AAG, are to appeal to the people, show mercy and *vahiza-nasihlat* (lead them on the path of truth), preventing deception or betrayal of their rights.

c) Seekers of wisdom should study and not seek worldly wealth and glory.

d) Pupils, students – their best behaviour is the mastery of knowledge.

e) The rich are to praise Allah for his grace, and be generous and compassionate.

f) Merchants – should buy and sell correctly and honestly and not lie or cheat.

g) Artisans – should complete their work in good faith, without fraud, and on time.

h) Beggars (*fukara*) have no valuable property and cannot subsist by their labour.

i) The disadvantaged (*zuglafa*).

j) The poor (*miskin*) have insignificant property but are paid too little to live. They should accept their poverty and diligently earn a righteous livelihood.

k) Saints (*Glubad, Zugiad, Mukhlis*) glorify the people and love for Allah.

l) The unhappy, or sick should be patient (*sabra*).

m) The ignorant do not know the difference between good and evil. They should recognize what they don't know.

n) Unrestrained youth should subjugate their body, avoiding bodily lusts.

o) Old men should pray more.

p) Women – Their most charitable actions are to satisfy the well-being of their husband, to fulfil his will and please him, to curb his mouth and curtail gossip.

If the many categories above are reminiscent of mystic incantations, they are put in perspective by Sheikh Kharda al-Rochi's [5] "To know the taste of sea water, it is not necessary to drink the whole sea," an appropriate introduction to his own list of vices and how to overcome them, to combat the *nafs* (ego):

"Hypocrisy – with sincerity;

Envy – by a desire for good to another person;

Malevolence – by prayers that he is not overwhelmed by troubles;

Hostility – by understanding the benefits of suppressing anger and the cost of unfriendliness;

Lust for power and pride – by understanding that this is not needed by anyone except to flatter a narcissist, manifesting modesty in word and deed, with dignity, but without ingratiation;

Cowardice – through repeated facing up to what the ego fears, focusing on the benefits of courage and the flaws in cowardice until it is replaced by righteous anger;

Waste – by purification of greed replaced by greater generosity;

Laziness – through fellowship in the company of the diligent, fear of friendship with the wicked and avoidance of idle meetings;

72 *Dagestan – History, Culture, Identity*

Light-headedness through seriousness – a sign of the power of knowledge, kindness and prudence, without ostentation and arrogance, signifying frankness, indignation at secrecy and disorder."

Well-read Dagestanis of the XIX century were brought up to recognize the role of Islam as the leading cultural resistance to Russian Christianity in the Caucasus. They knew of the extremist attitude of some Russian officials and military occupiers that "to expect a perfect rapprochement" between the highlanders and Russia is possible "only when a cross is raised on every mountain and plain and when churches replace mosques" (chapter 7) [6]. However the Russians faced up to reality and never attempted to convert the Dagestanis to Orthodox Christianity.

While Shamil's extreme form of Islam was rarely followed, his ethno-religious legacy reflected a stubbornness in the face of impossible odds that grew into a national-religious cult of Shamil. In 1871 Shamil died on hajj in Medina. His earliest heritage was the uprising against the Russians in 1877–8 [7] under the spiritual leadership of Sheikh Abdurahman-Haji al-Suguri, formerly in Shamil's circle. The uprising was brutally crushed. Their eventual recovery shows their strength of character that enabled Dagestanis to survive their subsequent existential suffering as part of Russia and USSR (chapter 11).

References

[1] Abdurakhman from Gazikumukh (abbr. AG). Book of Memoirs. Summary of a detailed description of the affairs of Imam Shamil.
[2] Kadi Kurbanali ibn Ibrahim al-Gumchukatli al-Gazikumuhi al Dagistani. Guidance to the people in gaining goodness. Temir-Khan-Shura. M.M. Mavraev. 1910.
[3] Hajj Ali from Chokh. An eyewitness account of Shamil.
[4] al-Karakhi Muhammad-Tahir. The Chronicle [of the wars of Shamil].
[5] Sheikh Kharda al-Rochi. Elixir of Torment. ms. pre-1824 (see also chapter 14).
[6] Eds. Bushuyev S. and Magomedov R. Materials on the history of Dagestan and Chechnya first half of the XIX century. 1940.
[7] Urminsky Ishaq and Saltinsky Ali. The history of the sharia uprising in Chechnya and Dagestan, and the Imamate of 1877.

10 Legal systems under the Russian government

The Russian Empire covered almost 22.5 million square km by the end of the XIX century, and of its 125.7 million population about 42% were actual Russians and the rest included some 200 different ethnicities. Followers of religions other than Christianity included Islam 11.1%, Judaism 4.2% and Buddhism 0.5%.

With the incorporation of Dagestan into Russia in 1868, the khanate was abolished. Its historical legal forms, partly adat, had been overlaid during the Imamate by Islamic sharia. The Russian overlordship subsumed – or attempted to subsume – these earlier structures. The institutions of civil self-government of rural societies were adapted to the imperial goals of subordination to the tsarist administration. In general, administrative and territorial delimitation at grassroots level corresponded to the traditional divisions of rural societies, for example the authority of *naibstva* from Arabic *nā'ib* (assistant, deputy head) was retained. The elected village administration was restored and rural and district courts were created, as well as a regional Dagestan people's court. The judges were elected, though the Russians had vetted the choices. Socially, Dagestanis vied to represent the royal power, to assimilate into the military and economic elites, to receive a Russian education and to absorb Russian culture. "When Dagestan was finally conquered, the khans' power became alien to the all-Russian state," a shadow of their earlier independence.

Like any administrative system, the new model as enshrined by the 'Regulation on the Administration of the Dagestan Region' *Dagestanskaya oblast'* of 1860 was far from ideal. Adat, sharia and Russian law were mixed under the *voenno-narodnoe upravleniye* (military-national government). Of course it could not satisfy everyone; but nothing else was on offer. Imperial rule was supposedly justified by the incorporation of Dagestani traditions in the new legal culture and caused little concern for the political stability to the tsar's administration.

The correlation of adat, sharia and Russian laws, and their correspondence to Dagestani ideals has been studied for some 150 years [1–9]. The recent discovery of a large number of judgements from the Temir-Khan-Shura higher court of 1864–1917 conclusively demonstrated the co-existence of Russian law with sharia and adat [10].

DOI: 10.4324/9781003388579-10

74   Dagestan – History, Culture, Identity

For adherents of sharia, the adat remained a relic of the times of ignorance (*jahili-yya*). Nevertheless, Dagestanis and Russians liberal attitude toward adat was maintained throughout the XIX century.

Even Imam Shamil's attempts to limit the scope of adat to conform to sharia norms failed. The conservative highlanders cherished their adats. Rural societies, where the Imams told villagers to accept sharia, were convinced that they had been following sharia for a long time and could not comprehend the admonitions.

Substituting blood with *diyat* (material compensation, from Arabic for 'ransom'), as well as in the custom of reconciliation of blood feuds, were ancient practices as evidenced in the adats. It also seems that the tukkhum could never be a claimant or defendant in the Imamate courts. Shamil strengthened this principle, imposing double individual responsibility for both the crime and any deviation from sharia.

Positively, the adoption of sharia law created alignment between degrees of guilt and severity of punishment; and introduced advanced methods of gathering evidence, based on Muslim *fiqh* (law).

A Russian general stated that "strong power [is essential] in stopping *krovomoscheniya* (blood feud)". In support he claimed that from 1860 to 1868, "In the former blood feuding districts of Avar and Andi, which were until 1859 under the close supervision of Shamil" there was not a single case of blood feud [5]. XIX century researchers found that murders in Dagestan happened, as a rule, for moral, not self-serving motives. The destruction of the house of the murderer and the spread of the blood feud to his relatives was prohibited.

Although at critical points power and law were concentrated in the hands of the tsarist administration, the adage that the "military-national government contained nothing national in itself" does not seem to be entirely correct [2].

Adat and sharia in 'divide and rule' policy

A Russian observed that "the Russian government in many cases took the side of adat in its struggle against sharia, first of all trying to weaken the action of sharia, and thus to paralyze the power of the Muslim clergy . . . seen as a main hindrance in pacifying the region" [7].

But hopes that by conflicting adat and sharia laws, the imperial law system would be more easily mastered and implemented were misplaced. In spite of Russian undermining those locals who had submitted (chapter 7), the Caucasian Committee established in 1845 in St. Petersburg was tediously and unsuccessfully continued until the October Revolution of 1917.

Trivial reasons for blood feud

The trivial reasons which led Dagestanis to bloody strife shocked the Russians.

For example in the Caucasus about 1900, carts continued to be used whose amazing construction echoed the Asian chariots and carts of the 2nd millennium BCE.

The *arba* (from Persian *arābe*) had four wheels without spokes, which rotated with the axle. When one *arbakesh (arba* 'driver') refused to give way to another, in a sort of road-rage, it led to injury and blood revenge, as in the following comment from the Russian director of the Tiflis Classical Gymnasium:

"No matter how respectful one is of everyone's self-esteem, no matter how great is the fear of public opinion, but the solution of all questions of honour only with the help of a dagger, and so the replacement of all religious and moral concepts with concepts of bloody violence . . . makes every insider or outsider involuntarily shudder" [11].

Robbery

In Dagestan, as elsewhere, there were many names for robbers. They were called *khachag'al* in Avar, *khachagatal* in Laki, *kachaglar* in Kumyk, and so on in the 28 other languages of Dagestan. "To the credit of Dagestanis, it should be mentioned that in the upland districts there are no robberies and robbers . . . Where the multi-battalion detachments with guns did not risk to pass before, now the batman was walking freely, even without a stick, and one can be sure that such security will prevail in the region until they will not lose the primitive purity of their morals . . . So, weapons in the hands of everyone, the inevitable revenge hanging like the sword of Damocles and, most importantly, the people's pride or public opinion that controls all the actions of their members – these are the reasons for the complete absence of looting and robbery of environments and those people who for some reason so readily are usually called brigands" [12].

Traditional commitment to order

The tsar's administration soon came to understand the motivation of the highlander's commitment to *a'dlu* – Arabic, which in all Dagestan languages means discipline. It was not his fear of the severity of his superiors and their punishments, but self-respect and the fear of being condemned by public opinion.

Alikhanov-Avarsky the Russian lieutenant-general wrote as an Avar: "Murders, injuries and other crimes in general never have a mercenary motive, at least in the mountainous part of Dagestan. Moreover the mountaineers of this region, if they are exceptionally sentenced to exile, it is usually for deeds that in their understanding are not something reprehensible, but – on the contrary – directly commendable. The weak understanding of legality and the habits of the traditional adats, which are more in keeping with their attitudes and temperament, lead to the fact that even street quarrels about the most empty excuses, which outside of Dagestan would peter out, here virtually all end with spilt blood. Even when given a sharp insult, the mountaineer responds with a dagger, and cannot do otherwise, else he will be ridiculed as a person who could not stand up for himself, and would not be able to continue to live in his village. If he immediately punished his offender, and escaped only with exile to Siberia, then he is sympathetically considered as a young man who has fulfilled his sacred duty, that a modern Dagestani folklorist called 'the motive of insulted honour.' A highlander was a man with a highly developed sense

76 Dagestan – History, Culture, Identity

of his own honour who demanded a proper attitude from another, equal to himself as adopted by his society. This feeling was exacerbated by the highlander's inherent awareness of his personal freedom and independence . . . deviations from these norms lead to conflicts that at first glance have only a moral cause, but they are socially determined . . . Moreover, such low, unworthy behaviour of a man can even affect his descendants position in society . . . his name will be a reproach to his children and even his grandchildren" [13].

The obligation of personal vengeance was so ingrained among the touchy highlanders, that it would never occur to one to complain to the authorities since, according to local opinion, it would lower him to the level of a woman.

"It's not the business of Qazi, the judges, the Naib, or the governor to wash off the insult inflicted on me, it is my duty: for that Allah supplied me with heart, and my father with a dagger" [12].

The fate of religion in the mainly Muslim Russian Empire was carefully recorded. In 1917 in tsarist Dagestan, with a population of just over 1 million, there were 2,060 mosques and about 1,000 *maktabs* (preliminary religious schools) and *madrasahs* (secondary religious schools). By 1924 education numbers had increased to 2,000 Muslim schools with 50,000 students and differing estimates of 151 secular schools with 10,721 students [14], or 211 secular schools with 16,783 students [15]. These numbers illustrate the falseness of widespread propaganda that the Soviet government only dealt with illiteracy in its cultural revolution.

The establishment of Soviet power in Dagestan, as elsewhere in the USSR, saw an irreconcilable struggle with religion. According to Soviet theorists, since the problems of interfaith relations were due to the very existence of religions, then the cardinal solution of these problems was their liquidation [16]. During the Soviet years in Dagestan, "about 12,000 people were repressed, of whom more than 5,000 were Muslim clergy . . . And how many Sheikhs and ulama were humiliated and offended! . . . In the eyes of atheists and communists, they were idealists, mystics, enemies of the people . . . thousands of holy buildings were destroyed, 670 mosque and private libraries were destroyed, mountains of spiritual literature and unique manuscripts were burned; about 165,000 mosque carpets, kilims, felt-carpets (*arbabashs*) were confiscated. In many places even gravestones were used in communist buildings" (chapter 11) [17].

By 1931 all the Muslim schools and almost all mosques were closed.

By 1980 less than 50 mosques functioned in the entire North Caucasus and the Volga region, and those were under the close supervision of the state and party structures.

Reluctant witnesses

The adaptation of the traditional civil self-government of rural societies in subordination to the tsarist administration emphasized the perception of the new law enforcement as a 'fatal reality'. Its representatives were hardly the best representatives of fairness and morality. The attitude of Dagestanis to justice and the criminal and civil courts, even when they corresponded to their own traditions, changed for the worse. Distrust of the court was the result of imposition of unclear imperial laws in 'administrative reprisals', that is, expulsion to Siberia without investigation or trial.

The adat courts were incompatible with the changed life and worldview of the highlanders. Seven years before the October Revolution of 1917, it was noted that "the adats of the Caucasian mountaineers . . . from their peculiar tribal origins even today serve them as a source of distinctive virtues, such as the layered customs of blood feud, family solidarity and an exaggerated concept of manliness." Thus, almost all civil cases are resolved in Dagestan on the basis of sharia, which in family, marriage and hereditary cases completely supplanted adat, even usurping its name . . . Instead of the former solid principles of specific morality, the highlanders have not received anything and are forced to roam in the dark labyrinth of the military administration, from which the only way out is to destroy it" [18].

Crackdown on crime

The authorities were serious about fighting crime, ensuring the political trustworthiness of their subjects, and keeping them in their place. To achieve this the intelligentsia expanded the network of educational and cultural institutions.

From 1860 rebels were either massacred or deported without trial to Siberia as a widespread administrative repression. Deportees came from Andi *okrug* (district) in 1862; Unkratl district in 1863 and 1871; Zakatala okrug in 1866; Gumbet district in 1866, and Kaitago-Tabasaran and Avar okrugs in 1871 [19]. In 1866, the village of Shilyagi of the Kaitago-Tabasaran District was burned down, and the inhabitants and their families were sent to Siberia. The fate of the rebels in 1877 was also tragic [20–22]: after the brutal suppression of the centres of the uprising that engulfed most of Dagestan, 300 people were executed in public, and 1,000 families, 4,875 people were exiled to Saratov, Novgorod and Pskov provinces [19].

Deep changes in public life due to the Russian revolution of 1905–1907, the First World War of 1914–1918, the October Revolution of 1917, and the Russian Civil War of 1918–1921, led to a crisis of law and order. During the first quarter of the XX century robbery and looting spread to Dagestan, as elsewhere in Russia.

The last Governor of the Mountain Republic, General Minkail Khalilov (d.1935) wrote in 1919 from exile in Turkey "Dagestan was always a country of order and long-established traditions and customs," a view seconded by his former political opponent imam Nazhmudin. A Dagestani wrote in 1925: "Not long ago, before the Revolution, which modernized petrified forms of family relationships, the highlander's family was a solid and coherent organization in which each member was given a certain place, role and responsibilities. These duties were carried out by

78 Dagestan – History, Culture, Identity

each of the family members with the highest conscientiousness, with clockwork precision, as the adats of their ancestors command" [23].

The Soviet response

The textbook Soviet propaganda portrayal of the ritual of blood feud reconciliation was an image of Party authorities in *stalinka* caps seated behind a table covered with a red cloth, against the background of portraits of the leaders of the proletariat; and in front two mountaineers in fur hats shaking hands. It mocked the symbolism of the traditional rite. Soviet justice also deprived the injured party of diyat for murder, which unintentionally encouraged blood feud. The traditional arbitration by Elders to agree reconciliation was either prohibited or replaced by the Soviet surrogate version, or aligned with Soviet law in the immediate arrest of the killer.

Unfortunately, the realities of bribery or falsification of evidence to avoid due punishment under the Soviet system meant that immoral conduct became commonplace.

The Party rotted people's souls. The following local story illustrates the constant undermining of human values in Dagestan. One of Gamzat the physician's *kunak* (traditional guests who always were obliged to stay with a single host) was called Javatkhan, with a beautiful white beard and magnificent boots. He worked as first secretary of the Tlyaratinsky district committee of the Communist Party of Soviet Union, (CPSU) as long ago as Leonid Brezhnev. In those days a person caused offence if he spent the night at the hotel and not with his kunak. So, when Javatkhan arrived in Makhachkala, he always stayed in Gamzat's house. Of course, as the first secretary of the party's district committee, de facto 'Soviet Naib' (chapter 16) he could reserve a room at any of the elite hotels – Hotel 'Dagestan', 'Kavkaz', 'Primorsky', or 'Kaspii'. But he was not *Parteigenosse* (Member of the Party) and he confidentially explained that he was always followed in hotels, and so could not pray in peace. Anyway, he could calmly drink 300 gram shots of cognac, from his experience at Party dinners where they suspected those who did not drink. Javatkhan recounted that he always gave a lot of vodka to the unwelcome atheistic lecturers from Makhachkala and sent them back with a hangover. One time the Dagestan CPSU sent a young party member (who later had a very noticeable career in Moscow and Dagestan and must remain anonymous) to Tlyarata to instruct the Agitation and Propaganda department. He was soon kicked out with the official reason *Za careerizm* (self-serving over ambitiousness) but it was actually because he was *Kveshav chi*, Avar for a "bad person."

References

[1] Abdulmazhidov R.S. On the introduction of civil (all-imperial) legislation in the Dagestan regions in the XIX century. 2017. Pp26–36.
[2] Aglarov M.A. and Magomedkhanov M.M. From the Imperial experience of managing the North Caucasus. 2015. P314.

Legal systems under the Russian government 79

[3] Bobrovnikov V.O. Muslims of the North Caucasus: Custom, law, violence: Essays on the history and ethnography of the law of Mountain-Dagestan. 2002.

[4] History of Dagestan. Bk. 4. Vol. 2. 1968. P122.

[5] Komarov A.V. Adats and legal proceedings from them (materials for statistics of the Dagestan region). 1868. P48.

[6] Kovalevskii M.M. Law and custom in the Caucasus. 1890.

[7] Leontovich F.I. Adats of Caucasian highlanders. Materials on the customary law of the Northern and Eastern Caucasus. 1882. P45.

[8] Matochkina A.I. Study of Islam and Arab-Muslim culture in works of Russian orientalist scholars about 1900. Study of Religion. No. 2. 2017. Pp107–19.

[9] Musaev M.A. The policy of the Russian Empire in relation to the Muslim clergy, sharia and adat in Dagestan after the fall of the Imamate. The World of Islam. hist. soc. culture. 2009. pp101–5.

[10] Magomedkhanov M.M. Adat, Sharia and Russian laws in Dagestan. Bulletin of the RDRN No. 16. 2004. pp75–83.

[11] Lilov A.I. Essays on the life of the Caucasian highlanders. 1892. p31.

[12] Alikhanov M. In the mountains of Dagestan. Travel impressions and stories. 2005. pp260–3.

[13] Akhalakov A.A. Historical songs of the peoples of Dagestan and the North Caucasus. 1981. p80.

[14] Magidov S.G. Implementation of the Leninist national-language policy in the North Caucasus. 1979. p92.

[15] Kaymarazov G.S. Enlightenment in pre-revolutionary Dagestan. 1989. p190.

[16] Khalidova O.B. Islam in religious structure of the soviet state in 1920s: Revisiting policies and regional practices in a national region for example Dagestan. Archivist's Herald. No. 4. 2017. pp223–35.

[17] Kurbanov M.R. and Kurbanov G.M. Religion in the culture of the peoples of Dagestan. 1996. pp20–1.

[18] Gabiev S. Customary Courts and Military-People's Government. 1910. pp18–25.

[19] Musaev M.A. Expulsion of Dagestanis for participating in an uprising led by Muhammad-Haji in 1877: Reconstruction of history. Modern Problems of Science and Education. No 4. 2012. p344.

[20] Gasanov M.M. The national liberation and class struggle of the peoples of Dagestan in the 60–70s of the XIX century. 1997. p20.

[21] Kovalevskii P.I. The uprising of Chechnya and Dagestan in 1877 and 1878. 1912.

[22] Magomedov R.M. Insurrection of the mountaineers of Dagestan in 1877. 1940.

[23] Samursky (Efendiev) N.P. Dagestan. 1925. p42.

[24] Musaev M.A. Muslim clergy in 60s-70s of the XIX century and the uprising of 1877 in Dagestan. 2005.

11 Repression and Sovietization

Dagestanis perceive historical events through a complex lens. They tend to identify themselves both with those who fought for or against the Soviet authorities, who were favoured by power, and with those who suffered from repressions [1]. Years of Soviet power has significantly changed their psychology, and left a lasting imprint on social life.

Obviously the Soviet system was not created by Dagestanis. Despite the non-existence in Dagestan of a so-called 'proletariat', the Soviet dictatorship was installed willy-nilly. The first rulers of Dagestan Autonomous Soviet Socialist Republic (ASSR) in 1922 assumed, without any evidence, the unacceptable existence of a 'class struggle' in the area, with its schemes of social gradation and class-hatred.

In fact the first secretary of Dagestan *obkom* (regional committee) N. Samursky noted in 1925 that, for Dagestanis, the concepts of class and political consciousness were insignificant, compared "with their strictest discipline," their "ancestral way of life" and "the will of the family-relative group (tukkhum)". The tukkhum had no basis of class stratification and the only class divisions related to vendetta. Thus the "class of workers and peasants" required for a proletarian revolution, and "the creation of the Communist Party" were hard to find [2].

M. Kovalevski and M. Kosven coined the phrase 'the tribal and patriarchal nature of the Dagestani social structure and way of life' to better impose Soviet thinking. Due to their recognition by Soviet ethnologists, their opinion became axiomatic. Even today's academics continue to refer to *perezhitki patriarkhalno-rodovogo stroya* ("remnants of the former patriarchal and tribal system"), misunderstanding (as M. Kosven) the differences between *rod* (clan), *plemya* (tribe), and *patronimiya* (patronymy). Unsurprisingly none of these words has an equivalent in any of the Dagestani languages. The XIX-XX centuries' tukkhum cannot be identified with *rod* or *patronimiya* in their 'pre-historical meaning', because of the fundamentally different structure of Dagestan society, based on independent, self-governed village communities, where the tukkhum was a united group of extended families [3].

In the time of Imam Shamil or Tsar Nicholas II uzdens (freemen) had no idea that they were "the poorest, most heavily exploited class of peasants" irrelevant

DOI: 10.4324/9781003388579-11

to Dagestani society. People who had been literate for centuries needed nobody to explain the concept that "society is divided."

Village communities needed to preserve their numbers, so even an insolvent villager was not excluded. For example, every village had evolved unwritten customs for rituals around birth, marriage or funerals, but always with a lower limit of expense. Poverty was no pretext for a humiliating insult, but public opinion delicately put pressure on the poor man. He was still invited to weddings, funerals, and public meals, where he was lent the amount for his contribution, and in return he had to pay for his family celebrations to which the village was invited.

"Vanity and pride, inherited from self-rule of equals explained the mountaineers' temperament," General M. Alikhanov wrote, "correlating their ritual hospitality with no need to beg, for even crippled or disadvantaged people. They would rather die of starvation than request alms. Stinginess resulting from extreme poverty, was set aside for a welcomed guest. A highlander would never work for his uzden" [4].

"The spiritual person," N. Samursky wrote "is not only a priest, but a judge, people's teacher, leader and freedom fighter, and steward of public funds and mutual assistance. Public life is in the hands of the clergy in Dagestan's Arab culture. The village sheikhs, imams, scholars and *muta'allims* are educated with deep study of old Arab culture, science and philosophy, understanding all religious subtleties." Moreover "in patriarchal family life, the clergy does not advocate any class interests" [2].

Despite Samursky's words the clergy were labelled obscurantists, exploiters of the working class, servants of the bourgeoisie and nationalists. Most of the clergy were 'disappeared' during the repressions of 1927–8, so that by 1937 only a few hundred were left.

General Khalilov wrote further: "as a consequence of the revolution, Bolshevism reached Dagestan, or rather invaded Dagestan with strong leadership and propaganda. However hateful its world-shattering anti-religious doctrine, it was not eternal. Mountaineers could not accept orders to destroy their traditional way of life from people who recognized only violence and the gratification of animal needs."

Before they seized power the Bolsheviks were moderate with their promises and their 'dialectical' fulfilment. At the Second Congress of the Russian Social Democratic Workers' Party in 1903, Bolsheviks set the task to overthrow the tsarist autocracy and replace it with a democratic Republic, providing civil liberties, including the "inviolability of the person and home," "unrestricted freedom of conscience, speech, press, meetings, strikes and unions," etc. All this was promised, as well as the "land to the peasants", and the abolition of *propiska* registration. Their "Declaration of the Rights of Peoples of Russia" at the peripheries, guaranteed "1. The equality and sovereignty of the Peoples of Russia. 2. The right of Nations to free self-determination excepting secession."

The imposition of Soviet power in Dagestan (March 1917–July 1918) followed by the creation of the United State of North Caucasus Mountain Peoples and of

82   Dagestan – History, Culture, Identity

the Cossack Mountain Republic (1918–1920), the fall of Bolshevism (July 1918–March 1920) and its restoration; and the dictatorship of the proletariat indicate the confusion of the times.

No one involved in these revolutions exploited sensitive ethno-national (such as Avar or Dargin) aims. The right-wing and left-wing, red and white, sheikhs and socialists, all proposed freedom and prosperity and claimed that they were acting for the long-suffering Dagestani peoples.

As described at the end of the previous chapter, in 1920 Stalin spoke in total support of sharia, adat and the Highlanders' way of life. In 1924 Samursky developed a similar doctrine for Dagestan called the 'Platform of 43', which in 1937–8 became the pretext to murder its 43 signatories as guilty of Trotskyism and 'bourgeois nationalism'.

To glorify the new Soviet power for the people, the past was called 'cursed', the national cultures of 'wrong heritage' and 'class defectiveness' were destroyed and religion was forbidden as harmful obscurantism.

The label *kulak* vilified middlingly prosperous farmers, leading to seizure of property, arrest and deportation to the frozen, barren North and Siberia. In 1925, 1926 and 1927, the Council of People's Commissars of Dagestan (CPCD) established several Commissions to evict former landowners, the first of which revealed 196 former *pomeshiki* (landlords). After ten meetings from 20 July to 2 August 1927 they resolved "the issue of eviction of 116 former landlords of which 65 were evicted and their assets seized – 34,000 Merino sheep, over 700 head of cattle, 50 horses and about a million roubles". Directives of the Central authorities to "liquidate the kulaks as a class" and to impose socialist forms on agriculture were executed with severity.

Religious servants did not constitute 'a separate class of clergy' but were the same uzdens who charitably discharged the duties of the imam, muezzin, or madrasah teacher. Soviet 'scientific atheists' could not pin a single case of illicit appropriation of *vakuf* (religious charitable foundation) property on them. The 23 June 1927 decree transferred all land and vakuf to *krestkom* (peasant committees), *bedkom* (poor peasants) or *batrakkom* (landless seasonal agricultural hired workers). By 1928 almost all of the mosques were closed, and the transfer was completed in 1930. The tradition of zakat for the poor (a pillar of Islam) continued, but to benefit the now-privileged bedkom.

In 1929–1930 a decree legitimized violent appropriation of grain, and prohibited the possession and distribution of bread. Anti-*kolkhoz* (state farm) uprisings took place in Don and northern Caucasus regions that had not known serfdom. The Manifesto of the Union of Farmers founded in April 1929 in Rostov-on-Don decried the move: "Taking advantage of the unorganized farmers and workers, the Stalinists, through the GPU, destroyed Lenin's worker-peasant Union and announced its dictatorship. Farmers were set against each other to ruin the economy. Beatings, torture, shooting, detention, and destruction of farms and persecution of bread producers are happening everywhere with impunity. After three years' suppression there is famine. Stalin's government exports our starving farmers' bread and cattle. So for our blood willingly shed in the revolutions, instead of freedom we received even greater enslavement and poverty" [5, 6].

Anti-kolkhoz mass-insurgencies spread in 1929–30. On 3 December 1929 in Temiraul village, Khasavyurt *raion* a meeting was convened on collectivization where Khasavyurt Communist Party and Komsomol members, members of *rai-krestkom* (regional citizens committee) and the Chairman of the village Council were beaten by villagers. Next day, in nearby Bata-Yurt, 300 women "armed with sticks, axes and daggers rallied under the slogan: "Down with collective farms, long live the Clergy!" During that night in nearby Bairam-aul village, the mother of a Komsomol collective farm organizer died from a shot through the window [5, 6].

These uprisings were decoded by the OGPU ('Joint State Political Directorate', i.e. secret police) on 15 January 1930: "1. 'A sharp increase of counter-revolutionary activity with the leadership inspirationally organizing the framework of the terror-ist counter-revolution, joined by ideologues and the Whites.' 2. '*Blok* (alliance) with bandit elements of kulaks.' 3. 'Erasure of ethnic and class distinctions'. 4. 'Liquidation of the White guard, Cossacks and bandit-Highlanders.' 5. 'Alliance of Cossacks with farmers'.'"

At the end of February, in Kandik village, Tabasaran *rayon* (Soviet administrative unit), women and children demonstrated against the *selkhozarteli* collective farm. One night in March in nearby Ashaga Yaril village "all the community surrounded the house of the Chairman of the village Council, where there was a brigade police-man, and demanded the restoration of rights of the kulaks and the dissolution of the *artel* (cooperative). Terrified of being lynched the policeman agreed to all requests. In the morning the women demonstrated again but were subdued by reinforce-ments from the district centre. On 11 March in Tabasaran the Ekendil commu-nity stormed the Executive Committee room and were granted the same demands. When the police tried to arrest their leader, the mob broke through into the police courtyard to free detainees. Frightened police and the Vice-Deputy of the Rayon Executive Committee fired into the air to attract help. The villagers were joined by 600 to 700 supporters led by kulaks from Tinit, Burgankent, Khurig, Genzir, Sirtich and Chulat villages. To avoid a serious confrontation, the officials accepted their illegal demands" [1, 5, 6].

"On 9 March in nearby Chulat village a demonstration protested against the gangs and all Soviet activities. They demanded that the lists kept by artel be destroyed in public, which was conceded and calmed the crowd." Next day in Tinit "women demonstrated under the slogan 'Soviets take away our faith!' but were subdued by compromises" [1, 5, 6].

At the end of March, anti-Soviet agitation started in the important Buynaksk rayon. Head of the Dagestan OGPU comrade Mamedbekov commented ominously that "mass protests and anti-kolkhoz uprisings have begun to take on a rebellious

84   *Dagestan – History, Culture, Identity*

nature." On 21 April in Nizhni Kazanishe near Buynaksk over 300 people, including 100 women, demanded the release of two arrested men, dissolution of the kolkhoz and restitution of its seized land. OGPU agents were "ordered to identify the active speakers and by 'group processing', calm the mood" [1, 5].

In spring-summer armed rebellion began in Dido region, Tsumada, Kurakh, Kasumkent and Tabasaran districts. In March 500 armed Didoi rebels led by Wali Daglarov of the new 'Shariah Council' neutralized Soviet power in Asakh, Khupro, Shaitl, Shauri, Mokok, Kidero, Ginukh and other villages. They offered the Communists and *Sovrabotniki* (Soviet Workers) safe passage to "depart from Dido auls and never return." On 30 and 31 March, Mamedbekov demanded the surrender of the Dido rebels and issued orders to liquidate the uprising. OGPU agents were to extend their 'disruptive work', reporting the leaders' identities and rebel numbers, ordnance, ethnicities and class. The Bezhta *udarnaya* shock group counterattacked with 250 red partisans and OGPU armed with light machine guns, part of the 48th and other divisions. The signal to attack was black smoke and air-attacks, bombing the villages Shauri, Mokok, Asakh and surrounding 'gang-centres'. The OGPU liquidated "politically unreliable auls who had failed us during the rebel uprising" [5].

The Chairman of Dagestan Central Executive Committee (CEC) comrade M. Dalgat and the Chairman of the CPCD comrade Dzh. Korkmasov appealed to the rebels in April 1930: "You Didoevtsi succumbed to the adventurism of your enemies! . . . [but] Soviet government has released the ancient chains of slavery of the people of Dagestan!" and the rebels responded "Let us live as we lived under Nicholas!" The government threatened "Daily we are delivering bread. throughout Dagestan. But in *Your* area delivery has stopped because, as armed enemies, *You* closed the road and *You* want to starve your people . . . The Soviet government wants to build a better life with *You*." Meanwhile, a few days earlier Soviets had seized 700 tons of grain from Shauri village, which was tantamount to death by starvation for the Didoi. They complained that the poorer peasant "women were forced to carry corn [instead of wheat], resulting in 60 miscarriages . . . , there was also evidence of rape, and foul language addressed to the clergy, etc.," carefully recorded by the OGPU. The rebels were invited to "promote the progress of the Red Army and the Red Partisans" or else "you adventurers are encircled and will starve."

On 29 April concerned Party members were instructed "to check mobilization readiness, weapons and ammunition." "During the night of 21/22 January 1930, in a planned operation, OGPU seized counter-revolutionary groups in seven districts: Khunzakh – 50 persons; Gunib – 67; Buynaksk – 45; Andi – 110; Khasavyurt – 52; Dargi – 9; and Kizlyar – 8, in total 482 persons including 141 already detained."

In accordance with the resolution of the All-Union Communist Party ('VKP' – bolsheviks), on 30 January 1930: "About measures on the elimination of kulak farms in areas of collectivization," six to eight thousand families from the North Caucasus and Dagestan were to be sent to gulags in the North, Siberia and Kazakhstan.

Another decree of 20 February condemned "2,950 kulak-activists of the 15 March events in the economically backward areas, including 350 Dagestanis

Repression and Sovietization 85

and 1,300 Transcaucasians to be imprisoned in 1st category 'anti-Soviet enemies of workers' gulags."

The repression was meticulously recorded in the OGPU review of 17 November, "on counteraction against the kulaks' policy against collectivization in 1929–1930 . . . from January to April 1930, 2,686 rebels and their leaders were killed and 7,310 voluntarily surrendered. From 1 January to 15 April 140,724 1st category persons were arrested. From 15 April to 1 October 142,993 1st category persons were arrested and 2nd category kulaks were deported from February to May. 10,595 families were evicted from the North Caucasus including 1st and 2nd category persons, and 32,253 families were resettled internally." Dagestan obkom of VKP approved the confiscation of property of 1,500 households to eliminate the kulaks as a class.

The situation of the deported families on arrival was desperate. From a Memorandum of the Northern periphery OGPU, "On March 26, of the planned 130 *echelons* ('military groups', as the euphemism described them), only 95 echelons arrived numbering 169,901–54,447 (32.0%) men, 51,967 (30.6%) women and 63,487 (37.4%) children. Able-bodied numbered 45,613 (26.8%), and disabled 124,288 (73.2%). How they found food remains unresolved: the elderly and disabled women with children were forbidden to bring belongings and left without food or money, as their descendants tell. In Dagestan they had been fed from collectivized reserves, but with the termination of kulak production, they had to pay for food, putting them in an impossible position. For kulak families the adequate diet was set at 1,300 calories. According to the *kraizdravotdel* (Regional health authority), "this diet is obviously insufficient, and will speed on total exhaustion" [6].

Only on 13 February did the Presidium of the Supreme Soviet of the USSR 'discover' that the OGPU "for a quick result of the counter-revolution, had activated the liquidation of the kulaks as a class."

'Troikas' were created of the VKP, OGPU, and a secretary of the regional Committee of Party, "with the participation of the Prosecutor". Three of them had the right to make final decisions on cases of counter-revolutionary crimes, "to ensure the highest measures of social protection." In 1930 179,620 persons were processed through Troikas, including 20,230 (11.3%) from the North Caucasus and 6,275 (3.5%) from Transcaucasia. 179,650 persons were condemned to "the highest measure of social protection": 18,996 (11%) were sentenced to death, 99,319 (55%) to forced-labour camps, 38,179 (21%) to internal resettlement, 8,869 (5%) to expulsion, and 14,287 (8%) were put on *uslovno* (probation).

The 7 August 1932 resolution of the CEC of the Council of People's Commissars was sadly-named "On the protection of property of state enterprises, collective farms and cooperatives, and the strengthening of public (socialist) property." People who encroached on public property were regarded as "enemies of the people," who, "without exemptions or amnesty," were punished commensurately by "shooting or up to 10 years imprisonment, with confiscation of property." In less than 11 months from 250,000 convictions at least 17,000 people were shot.

86 *Dagestan – History, Culture, Identity*

On 8 May 1933 VKP announced a Directive "About the termination of the mass evictions of farmers, streamlining of production arrests and decommissioning of places of detention. The last three years had . . . finally strengthened our socialist position in the village . . . , [so] that now the challenge is to meet the growing reception of individual peasants into collective farms, the only place where they can protect themselves from the risk of poverty and hunger." It was the bitter truth. A collective farmer, in contrast to a collective farm-horse, did not have a passport. Any possibility of migration to the city or rural resettlement was mired in administrative bureaucracy. The collective farm was really the only choice for locals, and exclusion was a real disadvantage often used by the chairmen of the collective farm to impose their power.

There were words about "our success in the village . . . and a moment when we don't need mass repressions, affecting, as it is well known, not only the kulaks, but also individual farmers and part of the collective farmers . . . we have evidence available, from which it is clear that the massive indiscriminate arrests in the village still continue to affect our employees . . . They arrest all who were not lazy and who, strictly speaking, have no right to be arrested. It is not surprising that . . . the mandated OGPU, and especially the police, are losing all sense of proportion. Arrest is often unfounded, acting according to the rule: first arrest, and then to investigate. VKP . . . agree to immediately cease mass evictions of farmers . . ." "Eviction is allowed only for 12,000 households . . . exceeding the North Caucasus quota of 1,000 . . . To cooperate . . . [they] immediately started emptying prisons and in two months reduced the number from 800,000 to 400,000." Within 18 months the 'limit' for resettlement from the North-Caucasus region was increased by five times. Samursky wrote to Stalin on 17 August 1937 boasting "In 1935 and 1936 we evicted a record 1,050 kulak households."

From Kh. Khashaev's speech at the Dagestan Regional Party Conference 12 March 1940: "During each of the years 1938 and 1939, 2.6% of the adult population was convicted, not to mention their families' suffering. This unjustified criminalization continues today."

Repression continued until the Great Patriotic War of 1941–1945, and then restarted, with varying intensity, until Stalin's death in 1953. Soviet Communism wanted to create 'new man' *homo sovieticus* and the National ethnic Republics were obliged to join the "irreconcilable offensive struggle to eliminate remnants of the past and bourgeois ideology in the people." To develop "new, progressive traditions and ceremonies," their propaganda focused on the "liberation of women" – Dagestan's *Goryanka* (Mountain women), with high-profile condemnations of polygamy, bride-kidnapping, and early marriages, which actually were not widespread.

On 31 May 1924 Commissar of Education and Prosecutor of Dagestan Alibek Takho-Godi, speaking at the 3rd Dagestan Congress of Goryankas, claimed: "A Goryanka is a slave from birth . . . abused by her husband. According to sharia a woman is equal to half a man, who may divorce her at any time or take a few more wives . . . But the Soviet government has created the people's court '*Narsud*' to protect women's rights. But Goryanka with her domestic and religious peculiarities isn't included in Narsud, and its sentences are not recognized by most the mountaineers . . . a woman who had divorced through Narsud had to return of her husband's house . . . But she often does not understand the evil damage of traditional customs, and does not want to be a free Soviet citizen" [7]. In practice her liberation was limited and she was never given the choice to work in the collective farm or a carpet factory. She was denied the Party's privileges, honorary diplomas and red pennants, and abused by the rude and mistrustful Soviet authorities.

The false achievements of the construction of socialism in Dagestan by the mediocre leaders of the party, puffed up by 70 year's propaganda regarding the liberation of the 'unfortunate' Goryanka from "centuries-old patriarchal religio-tribal oppression" were indefensible. How could the Soviets ever console the Goryankas who mourned their lost sons and brothers in the horrors of the 1877 uprising; the Russian-Japanese war; the First World war; the Civil War; and the Great Patriotic War? How could they forget their fathers and grandfathers exiled as 'spiritual Elders' in 1928, to die in Arkhangelsk and the Far North? How could they forget their relatives transported to Kyrgyzstan in 1930s as kulaks, and their menfolk lost in the repressions from 1937; or the victims of the tragic 1944 deportation to Kazakhstan?

According to the late academic researcher Magomed-Rasul Ibragimov [8], during the Great Patriotic War (1941–1945), Beria and Stalin bypassed the Dagestani Communist authorities by secret decrees and were responsible for the tragic deportations of 7,306 Volga Germans and 37,100 mainly rural Chechens from Dagestan, and 'unfoundedly' blamed the Dagestan government as motivated to seize Chechen lands. Inside Dagestan the forced migrations were suffered by the Avars and the Dargins, to Chechnya and back to Dagestan, and the Laks and the Kumyks resettled to former Chechen villages within Dagestan, with incalculable and continuing damage to interethnic society and individuals. Some were falsely condemned without trial as saboteurs or spies and others for treason and cooperation with the invading Germans. The most ambitious deportation was mobilization to the fronts of more than 180,000 (almost 19% of the population of Dagestan) and forced resettlement of more than 116,000 (or 12%). Despite the mobilisation and direct losses, the overall population of the republic actually increased by 90,000 due to the influx of refugees from the front-line regions.

The deportations were planned in meticulous detail, evidenced by Beria's letter to Stalin on the eve of the Chechen deportation, 17 February 1944, giving the total living in Chechnya and Dagestan at precisely 459,466. 20% to 33% perished.

The eviction of the Chechens was described by A. B. Baymurzaeva, an eyewitness and later a distinguished sociologist:

"On the night of February 22–23, at about one a.m., the 'responsible officers' (*ovetstvennie rabotniki*) of the Khasavyurt district party committee and the district executive committee were gathered. The Minister of the Interior of the DASSR Markaryan, the head of NKVD Kalininsky and the representative of the Regional

88 *Dagestan – History, Culture, Identity*

Committee Kh.M. Fataliev have already arrived in the city of Khasavyurt. We were read the resolution of the State Defence Committee (GKO) No. 5073ss dated January 31, 1944, 'On measures to accommodate special settlers within the Kazakh and Kyrgyz SSR', which stated that there were 'Cases of cooperation of the population of the Chechen-Ingush ASSR with the German fascist invaders.' Then it was announced that at 6am the Chechen population of the Aukhov and Khasavyurt districts and Khasavyurt city was being resettled outside the Caucasus. By this time, NKVD troops, NKGB secret police and SMERSH workers had cordoned off all the settlements, set up ambushes and patrols, and turned off radio broadcasting and telephone communications. We were not allowed to return home. Cars with district activists and 4–5 military drove up to the villages. They knew where and to whom to go. They drove up to the house and said: 'Open the gate, check passports.' Entering the house, the military stood at the door, and the activist announced the decision of the Soviet government to evict them outside the Caucasus; said that they can take with them up to 100 kg per person. He told me to take food, warm clothes and valuables. The family was gathered in a corner, searched for weapons and given about one hour to get ready. Many women began to cry, they were reassured as best they could, they said that their time together should be cherished. A card was drawn up for each Chechen family, indicating all the information about family members, property, including livestock, etc. An hour and a half later, the collection was completed and the Chechens were taken in an organized manner to the railway station in Khasavyurt, where echelons of freight trains equipped with potbelly stoves were waiting for them. As each echelon was completed, the trains were sent northward" [9].

Another Chechen victim Kh. Arapiev remembered that they were transported "in overcrowded cattle trucks without light and water, for almost a month to an unknown destination . . . Typhus was rampant. There was no treatment, there was a war . . . moving away more than five meters from the carriage meant execution on the spot" [9].

From the end of March to April 1944, some of the Avars, Dargins, Laks and Kumyks were forcibly resettled on former Chechen lands. District boundaries and all place names were sovietised. Although USSR had ordered relocation of 6,300 state farms, the zealous Dagestan Commissars resettled 16,100 farms from 21 mountain regions and one district of Georgia, 144 settlements and 109 collective farms and 110 villages, with about 62,000 souls, about a fifth of the population of mountain Dagestan. About 55,000 of them were transferred to four districts annexed to the Dagestan ASSR (DASSR) and some 15,000 to the foothills and lowlands within the former borders of Dagestan. Inside DASSR, about 7,000 Laks from the Kulinsky and Laksky districts were resettled in the former Aukhovsky region. In addition, about 3,000 Avars from Almak village were resettled to the Kazbekovsky district. About 3,000 Kumyks from three villages were resettled in the former Chechen villages in Khasavyurt region, as eyewitnesses later told ethnographers.

The collective farmers were promised prosperity and riches, with a year's tax holiday, but traditional life had been destroyed, many resettlements were ethnically mixed and climate conditions were different from their alpine villages. They could not adapt; some tried to return to their villages but were detained and sent back. To stop them, their villages were destroyed and neighbouring villagers were forced to dismantle the empty houses and take the stones to build new houses in their villages, especially in Tsuntinsky region. The psychological damage was immeasurable.

From materials in Central State Archive of Republic of Dagestan, "On the appointed day, a long line of carts loaded with simple belongings, with crying children, confused women and a few men, accompanied by the military and representatives of Soviet and party bodies, walked along mountain paths and roads to strictly prescribed settlements in the neighbouring former Chechen-Ingush ASSR, that was now annexed to DASSR. In the three districts (Vedensky, Andalal and Ritlyabsky) were settled more than 40,000 Avars, Andians, Godoberins, Chamalals, Tindals, Khvarshin, Tsez, Bezhtins, Ginukhs, Gunzibs, Akhvakhs, Karaumblyans, from Kakhibodsky Khunzakhsky, Gunibsky, Buinaksky, Untsukulsky, Botlikhsky, Tsumadinsky, Tsuntinsky, and Akhvakhsky districts. More than 3,000 Bezhtins, Ginukhs and Avars who until 1944 lived in the Kvareli region of Georgia SSR were also resettled to the annexed regions. And, finally, in the fourth Shuragat region, more than 10,000 Dargins were settled as well as Kaytags from Akushinsky, Sergokalinsky, Levashinsky, Dakhadayevsky and Kaitagsky districts." The resettlement of over half of the population of Ando-Tsez and Archi and part of the Kaitag and Kubachis resulted in assimilation into the larger Avar and Dargin communities, respectively. Similarly the sparse Aguls, Rutuls, Tsakhurs and Tabasarans were subsumed by the Lezgis.

It was reported to Beria that winter sowing was 61% of usual and inter alia 2,000 men and women had to manually plough 1,245 hectares. Epidemics of malaria, dysentery and other diseases, and hunger killed 20% to 25% in the first two years after resettlement. "In Novolak, Andalal, Ritlyab and Shuragat districts in August 1944 there were up to 7,500 cases of malaria."

On 9 January 1957 deportations were reversed but it was not clear what to do with the returning Chechens. Initially Moscow decided that the 60,000 resettled Dagestanis should be left in the Chechen-Ingush ASSR to strengthen the republic's multi-nationality. However, serious conflicts began between the Chechens who returned to their native villages and the Kumyks who had been resettled there after the Chechen expulsion in 1944. The remaining Dagestanis were then returned to their destroyed mountain villages or the unfamiliar plains of DASSR. The forcibly evicted Kumyks decided unilaterally to return to their villages. However the 2,020 hectares redistributed to Makhachkala city and other highlanders were not returned. The Laks and Avars remained in the formerly Chechen Novo-Lakski rayon. It is to their great credit that the Dagestanis avoided inter-ethnic conflicts in contrast with other parts of the Caucasus.

Another aspect of repression was the forced mass resettlement of residents of high-mountainous regions of Dagestan to the Caspian lowland since the 1920s which Rasul Gamzatov called turning 'shepherds into fishermen', and was justified as 'universal internationalization.' Since the 1950s this was connected to the increased

90 Dagestan – History, Culture, Identity

urban population, attracted by a better life. These phenomena had a desiccating impact on both physical and sociological mountain landscapes. The transported Highlanders were accused by some of violating the sharia by living in so-called occupied foreign ethnic territories displacing the previous inhabitants.

Institutionalized lying was another form of repression. Doubtless there was some mystical sense of modern progress but the agencies of modern communication were corrupted by the Soviet state to its own ends. In spite of irregular deficits, radios, telephone lines, roads, local airlines, educational institutions, creative groups of artists, writers' organizations, and theatre groups were part of Soviet moderniza-tion. Soviet achievements went unquestioned, such as the lightbulb, known as 'Lenin's Electric Lamp.'

Political and ideological anti-Semitism repressed the identity of the Mountain Jews of Dagestan from the late 1930s. From the end of the 1960s, they began to call themselves *Tats*, because in the past their language was officially referred to as Jewish-Tat. The official Soviet process of 'Tatization' was double-speak for 'de-Judaization' and led to an artificial formal division of their single ethnic group into Mountain Jews and Tats.

In addition, some were recorded as 'Jews' in passports and censuses, that is, as European Ashkenazi Jews instead of 'Mountain Jews' or 'Tats'.

Their logic was that as there was no place for religion in the country of *voinstvuy-ushii ateizm* (militant atheism), religious traditions were of negligible importance and therefore the existence of two peoples under one name *Tats* was meaning-less with regard to their unrecognized religions. The Mountain Jews self-named *Djuhurum* were classified as a *narodnosti* (nationality) a pejorative term as inferior to *natsionalnost* (ethnos). This awarded them less status and funding compared to the Tats who were officially recognized as a Soviet natsionalnost. In Dagestan the very concept of 'Mountain Jews' as a natsionalnost is still considered to be unofficial. On 28 March 2013 the head of the administration of the city of Derbent I.M. Yaraliev signed Decree No. 116 on the use of the name 'Mountain Jews' in the official terminology of Derbent city instead of the previously used 'Tats' [10].

Chernyi [11] c. 1870 unintentionally created an inaccurate image of Mountain Jews as both 'savage Asians' and 'primordial Jews' that played into anti-Semitism. The 1926 Census for Dagestan ASSR [1] counted 11,600 Mountain Jews and 200 Tats, while 9,500 Mountain Jews indicated their native language as Tat. In 1959 16,200 Mountain Jews and 3,000 Tats were counted. In the 1979 census, 77,400 were recorded as Tats, while the number of Mountain Jews was reduced to 4,700, to dis-enfranchise Mountain Jews for anti-Semitic political reasons. The 3,025 Ashkenazi Jews counted in 1926 increased to 14,000 about 1979 when emigration started. By 1989 there were only 9,400 remaining. The rest had gone to the capital cities of Russia and then abroad. Today, there are almost no Ashkenazi Jews in Dagestan.

Since 1990 almost half a million highlanders migrated from the mountains to the plains and the cities, double the number during all the Soviet years, while the

Repression and Sovietization 91

population of Makhachkala tripled and almost every third resident of Dagestan lives in this pluralistic city of a million. The mountain village's ability to preserve the ethno-cultural identity, image and native languages is a fantasy [10]. More common was the unfounded but never corrected prejudice that geopolitical instability ripened in the mountains of Dagestan.

The repression of migrant Dagestanis continues today. Typically the media accuses Dagestani (and other) ethnic city market traders of criminality, unaware that it is the only work open to migrants, as agents for Dagestani producers of sustainable traditional foods and handwork. 'Ethnic economics' refers to sectors of the urban economy of first-generation migrants, whom Robert Ezra Park the Chicago sociologist in 1914 first described as marginalized and isolated. Migrants who find themselves in the afflicted minority position can sometimes call on effective ethnic resources from their social capital, a trusted ready-made flexible ethnic network [12, 13] emulating the merchant Diasporas of the Jews, Chinese, Indians and Armenians. A successful ethnic business could grow into a great corporation leading to political influence that opened doors to assimilation and key positions in the host society [14], such as the Dagestani Diaspora in Turkey.

The host society ignored migrants' social status, level of education and traditional culture, and their industry was considered as a reaction to racist discrimination and exclusion from higher prestige careers [15]. It was slowly admitted that Dagestani (and other) migrants are permanently disadvantaged [12, 9, 16, 17, 18, 19] where second to fifth generation Highland migrants are still described as living in a 'foreign ethnic territory' when ethnic tensions arise, without allowing for the effects of wars, famine and epidemics.

The host society accuse ethnic entrepreneurs of criminal links to accumulate capital by any means, to capture and retain markets in the legal and shadow economies [20, 21]. Driven competitiveness is considered as aggressive expansionism in pseudo-communist behaviour, causing phobias which destabilize interethnic relations. In reality ethnic economic activity in developed countries is related to the integration of small ethnic groups.

References

[1] Butaev M.D., Kakagasanov G.I. and Dzhambulatova R.I. Repressions of the 30s in Dagestan. 1997. Pp165, 508–16.

[2] Samursky (Efendiev). Dagestan. Moscow-Leningrad. 1925. Pp5, 42.

[3] Aglarov M. Rural community in mountainous Dagestan, XVII to early XIX centuries. 1971.

[4] Alikhanov M. In the mountains of Dagestan. Travel impressions and stories of the highlanders. Epoch. 2005. Pp191–4, 225.

[5] Collectivization and anti-collective farm uprisings in Dagestan (1927–1940). Documents and Materials. Makhachkala. 2007. Pp3, 23–33.

[6] The tragedy of the Soviet village. Collectivization and dispossession. 1927–1939. Vol. 2. November 1929–December 1930. Moscow, 2000.

[7] Takho-Godi A. Revolution and counter-revolution in Dagestan. Makhachkala. 1927.

[8] Ibragimov M.-R.A. Deportation of the inhabitants of Dagestan during great patriotic war 1941–1945. Vestnik D.N.Ts. No. 43. 2011. Pp84–90.

[9] Waldinger R., Ward R. and Aldrich H. Ethnic business and occupational mobility in advanced societies. Sociology Vol. 19. No. 4. 1985. Pp586–97.

[10] Derbent Tats became Mountain Jews. 16 June 2017. http://flnka.ru/novosti/2081-derbentskie-taty-stali-gorskimi-evreyami.html.

[11] Chernyi I.Y. Mountain Jews. SSKG. Bk. III. Pt. 1. Tiflis. 1870. Pp4–6.

[12] Light I. and Karageorgis S. The ethnic economy, the handbook of economic sociology. Princeton. 1994. Pp646–71.

[13] Granovetter M.S. The strength of weak ties. American Journal of Sociology. Vol. 78. No. 6. Chicago. 1973. Pp1360–80.

[14] Eds. Peach C., Robinson V. and Smith S. Ethnic segregation in cities. London. 1981.

[15] Bonacich E.A. Theory of middleman minorities. American Sociological Review. Vol. 38. No. 5. 1973. Pp589–94.

[16] Waldinger R. Immigrant enterprise. A critique and reformulation. Theory and Society. Vol. 15. No. 1. 1986. Pp249–85.

[17] Radaev V.V. Ethnic entrepreneurship: Russian and international experience. Polis. No. 5. 1993. Pp79–87.

[18] Ryzhova N.P. Phenomenon of ethnic entrepreneurship: Western tradition and Russian reading. New Humanitarian Research. No. 3. 2008.

[19] Snisarenko A. Ethnic entrepreneurship in large cities in contemporary Russia informal economics. Russia and the World. 1999. Pp138–55.

[20] Grigoryeva K.S. and Mukomel V.I. Objectives and implementation of migration law reforms. Migration Law. No. 2. 2018. Pp3–8.

[21] Vendina O.I. Dagestan: Tradition as a condition for modernization. Science Innovation Technology. No. 3. 2016. P141. https://elibrary.ru/contents.asp?id=34266316.

12 Language policy of the USSR

Linguists and philologists have long wrestled with the 30 autochthonous languages of Dagestan. Ethno-linguists give general ethnographic information about native speakers, being primarily interested in linguistics. However, languages are also repositories for ethnographically-marked semantic meanings of words, and for ethnographic codes, as a kind of storehouse of the history of interethnic communications. Ethnographers bring out these nuances, beyond mere translation.

Many of the languages are closely-related and so easily confused, especially from the viewpoint of one used to the dominant lingua-franca, but to properly appreciate the differences between sub-cultures care must be taken to respect the (subtle) linguistic differences. For example in Russian, *umno sdelano* or *hitro sdelano* mean the same – 'cleverly done'. In Avar *t'sodorgo* and in Archi *t'sat'urshi* mean 'cleverly, thoughtfully, carefully'; *t'sodortli habe* in Avar and *t'saturkul a* in Archi mean 'do it cleverly, take care, do not let yourself to be deceived, work, walk in the mountains, ride a horse gently, intelligently' –! Ethno-linguists must consider all these meanings, and even more.

For example there is a wide range of similar words and phrases with the common root of *bakъ*, which means sheep gut sausage in Avar. In Avar there is no etymology for *bakъ'il zaman* ('adat time'). In Ingush, a truthful, just person is called *bakъdola* (*bakъ-* Sun) as well as in the Avar, Lak and other Dagestan languages *bakъ* and *barg*. In Archi *barxъ* means 'sun'. The Ingush noun *boklo* means 'norm, rule, permission, freedom, and prohibition' – the significance of these varies depending on the sub-culture, so care has to be taken to identify the linguistic context. By the way, the pronunciation of large numbers of aspirated consonants is virtually impossible for non-locals; *kъ* (a modulated kh or ch as in Scots 'loch') is pronounced as in *bakъ*.

Stalin and his ideologists believed that human development would make "the nation/ethnic group convinced in practice of the advantages of a common language over national languages." There will be a single, united, international world language, which "is neither German, nor Russian, nor English but a new language, which incorporates the best elements of national and zonal languages" [1].

DOI: 10.4324/9781003388579-12

94   Dagestan – History, Culture, Identity

Thus, the 'supreme values of humanity', a condition of human progress, were not derived from the peoples with their traditional cultures and writings, but from the class struggle for a new life. In Dagestan this meant the destruction of centuries-old manuscripts and everything else in Arabic script. A complementary policy was the elimination of traditional Arab-Muslim education and Muslim scholars; Arabic was declared a tool of the exploiters and a means of oppression and enslavement of the working masses. At the same time it must be admitted that from 1920 to 1960 unique conditions were created for the extension of social and cultural functions of local languages, for raising the prestige of these languages, and for raising the level of national artistic consciousness. This is the opposite of current thinking in Dagestan.

Since the 1960s the reducing trends of teaching literature, and use of spoken ethnic native languages, became more and more obvious. The role of the national languages in the transmission of ethnic cultures and in the appreciation of national-linguistic forms of folklore and traditional arts were similarly decreased.

According to the First General Census of the population of the Russian Empire in 1897, of the 16.5 million Muslims, some 14 million were Turkic peoples.

The tsarist authorities were less concerned by the religious, ritual practice of Muslims as by their political orientations, including 'revitalization' of religious and national identity, "alienation from Russia and all Russian culture" [2], political trustworthiness of the clergy, and manifestations of separatism. The authorities keenly and often repressively censored religious publications, monitoring the activities of clergy, and preventing the spread of feared pan-Islamism and pan-Turanism among Muslims of the Empire.

To ensure public peace, 'instilling citizenship' was encouraged through the integration of Muslims in Russian political and cultural life. It was a contradiction against the thoughtless widespread aim to make them "most Russian of all the subject peoples of the empire after the Russians" [2], to isolate them from the rest of the Muslim world [3].

An Azerbaijani Musavat reformer recognised that "the entire system of social ideology has already passed from the religious Islamism to the nationalistic Turkism" [4]. However, Ottoman influence on Russian Muslims remained significant. They respected the Sultan as the caliph of all Muslims, representing *Turkler* and *Turk*, that is, all Turkic peoples from Altai and Central Asia to the Danube and the Caucasus. The collapse of the Ottoman Empire meant that Arabs as well as pan-Islamist, and pan-Turkic ideas, became irrelevant.

Russian educated Tatar and Caucasian intellectuals influenced "the transition to the national system of Turkism . . . Sooner or later, Russian Islam, developed by Russia, will head the intellectual development of the rest of Islam" [3].

However the ideas of the All-Russian Congresses of Muslims, and the Muslim parliamentary factions in three State Dumas of 1905 to 1906 failed to unite an effective Muslim movement [5].

As a result of World War I, the socialist revolution in Russia radically broke old social structures and nation-states and replaced them with socialist constructions. The class struggle on the 'cultural front' was accompanied by the destruction of the old, and 'construction' of a new, socialist culture. As a result, many monuments of written culture in Arabic script were destroyed; religious institutions were razed or confiscated; religious schools were abolished, and thousands of clergy were repressed and exiled.

Against this background the Soviets developed a language policy, recognizing the importance of language as part of ethnic identity.

The Party and government bodies of the USSR decided to "help the labouring masses of non-Great Russian peoples catch up with central Russia that was more advanced:

a) to develop and strengthen Soviet statehood in forms that corresponded to the national living conditions of these peoples;
b) to develop and strengthen in their native language: the political structures, administration, economic authorities, and government bodies composed of local people who know the life and psychology of the local population;
c) to develop the press, schools, clubs, businesses and in general cultural and educational institutions in the native language;
d) to supply and develop a wide network of courses and schools of both a general educational and vocational character in their native language . . . for accelerated training of native cadres of skilled workers and Soviet-party workers in all areas of government and, above all, in the fields of education" [6].

This comprehensive program was to put in action the Soviet 'global' model for the modernization of national population centres.

In the 1920–1930s *Kultsansturm* (*kult* cultur(al); *san* sanitary; *sturm*, assault) was a key slogan of the cultural revolution, opening educational programs and 'huts' – reading rooms for peasant education and propaganda. The policy gained little traction, for example the founder of the Dagestan Soviet ethnographic institute, Professor Sakinat Gadzhieva, distinguished herself in the early 1930s as an active fighter against Kultsansturm.

Implementation of language rights remained unspecified, especially a key provision of the 1936 Constitution of the USSR "teaching in the mother tongue schools". The commitment was replaced by apparently non-binding formulae as in "the opportunity to use the native language and languages of other peoples of the USSR" or "the possibility of studying in a school in the native language; creating conditions for education."

New scripts were created for a number of non-written, as well as old-written languages of the peoples of the USSR. In the latter case it was simple switching from Arabic to Latin in 1928, and then in 1937 to Russian orthography. Experiments

Figure 12.1 Kultsansturm 1928 – compulsory Russian and Soviet indoctrination in Archi

created alphabets based on extended Cyrillic for Tsakhur (1932) and Akhwah (1936), and later for the Karatin and other languages. In practical terms, the compilation of the alphabet, primers, dictionaries or the publication of newspapers in any of the unwritten languages does not constitute any particular problem. Some languages considered to be unwritten by the Soviets were in fact not, for example Archi (chapter 14). However simplified tuition was not accessible to schools or ordinary people.

It was presented as the greatest gift of Soviet power to the oppressed and backward peoples: Azerbaijanis, Dagestanis, Chechens, Ingush, Kabardians, Karachais, Balkars, Volga Turkic peoples and Muslims of Central Asia. "Providing native languages with modern writing resources depended on the increasing functions they could fulfil, especially in the national republics. Schools in native languages were opened in the Russian provinces, as well as the republics. Teaching in the native language transformed the school into an instrument of ethnic self-identification of a person" [7]. New textbooks were created, and schools, technical schools, universities, national mass media, writers' unions, art groups and theatres.

The Agul language, as spoken by one of the smaller peoples of Dagestan covering 20 mountain villages in modern Agulsky and Kurakhsky districts, and not one of the languages protected by Soviet policy (Avar, Laki, Lezgi and Dargin), is an interesting example. The Agul language has five dialects, named after their respective gorges: Tpig (Agul), Burkikhan (Geghun), Richin (Kerensky), Koshan and Fitinsky, and each rural community spoke a separate dialect, sometimes unintelligible to its neighbours.

Language policy of the USSR 97

In the 1920s Aguls, Rutuls, and Didois independently raised the question of creating written languages in their native languages before the DASSR authorities. But "due to the small number of native speakers of the Agul language, as well as native speakers of the Rutul and Dido languages, due to the lack of trained personnel and for other reasons, this issue has not received a positive solution" [8]. However, progress was made with the creation of a written language Aguli.

From the academic year 1952–53, the Agul schools from the first grade switched from the Russian language to Aguli language. There must have been confusion between two different bureaucracies for "at the same time, the Rutul and Tsakhur schools switched to the Russian language of instruction." A further confusion occurred in the Tabasaran schools of the Khiv district, where teaching in primary grades was in Lezgi. This was all done by administrative orders and, as justification, it "proved that the national identity of certain nationalities of the USSR rose to an understanding of the objective necessity of self-assimilation" [9].

Since 1992, teaching in the primary grades of Agul schools has been conducted in the Agul language, the same as the regional newspaper *Agularin Khabarar* (Agulskiye Vesti). Agul was taught at the Derbent Pedagogical College and the Dagestan Pedagogical University. "With the creation of written Aguli there are wide opportunities for the cultural and spiritual expression of their speakers," [8] wrote the authority on Aguli.

Since the mid-1950s Communist national policy has a clear bias towards narrowing, and in certain areas (paperwork and teaching in native languages) curtailing the social functions of national languages. Unlike the SSR (All-Union republics like Azerbaijan or Armenia), in the 'autonomous' republics ASSRs which had far less autonomy than the SSRs there was no national language education as such. National language schools were those where primary school education was conducted in the native language, and from the 5th to the 8th grade, the native language and literature were taught as a subject.

Legislation of national-language policy changed again during Soviet and post-Soviet periods. The social, economic and legal protection of languages was replaced from the 1970s by the ideological and political aim of breaking the 'national shell'. Soviet support for language assimilation (especially among the peoples of Dagestan where small minority languages were assimilated into the main languages i.e. Avar, Dargin, Lezgin) had gone so far that the legislators were forced to respond. They recognized the natural rights and requests of these small minorities. These artificial measures did not affect mixed ethnic Russian-speaking children who were not in favour of their mother tongues and voluntarily chose not to learn it at school.

Since the 1980s, the transformation of schools to solely Russian language of instruction began, which was a change from Soviet policy, first with multi-ethnic and then with mono-ethnic cohorts of students. This resulted in a drop in the level of teaching of native languages and literature.

Interethnic conflicts raged in the first two decades after the collapse of the USSR. In 1990, B.N. Yeltsin half-joked "take as much sovereignty as you can swallow." The law "On the Languages of the Peoples of the Russian Federation" (amended on 24

98 *Dagestan – History, Culture, Identity*

July 1998) reduced socio-political tensions around ethnic-language problems. The law proclaimed the equality of languages, the status of the Russian language as the state language of the RF throughout the country, and the right of national republics to establish their state languages. From the 1990s a number of federal laws directly or indirectly governed the national-linguistic lives of Russians. M.M. Magomedov first head of the Republic of Dagestan from 1992 to 2006 kept Dagestan manageable. He further confirmed their loyalty to the ideals of Russian unity and Russian statehood.

The number of state languages was controlled by laws and regulations. For example as well as dominant Russian there are two state languages in both Karachay-Cherkessia and Kabardino-Balkaria. According to the Constitution of the post-1991 Republic of Dagestan, the state languages are Russian and those of the peoples inhabiting the Republic. The numbers of indigenous speakers range from 800,000 Avars to 1,000 Archi.

The Soviet laws were superseded by The Federal Law on state language of the Russian Federation (RF) (2005, amended 2013, 2014) which included:

"4. The state language of the Russian Federation is the language promoting mutual understanding, strengthening of international communications of the people of the Russian Federation in the single multinational state.
"5. Protection and support of Russian as state language of the Russian Federation promote enhancement and mutual enrichment of spiritual culture of the people of the Russian Federation."

The legislation focuses on terminology, omitting that the right to education is guaranteed by the provision of instruction in schools in the native language. It seems to be implicit that teaching in their native language is a necessity for preservation of that language.

It appears that there was no continuity in these general articles that conflate mutual understanding and cultural enrichment. They appear to have been drafted by different people with their own ideas.

Republics did not have the right to establish their own state languages and influence local language teaching and literature. The maximum guaranteed by the Constitution of the Republic of Dagestan is "the right to preserve the native language, the creation of conditions for its study and development." The Republic guarantees the right of citizens to "preserve" and "create conditions", but does not undertake to provide "education in schools in their native language". There is a gap between the objective of preserving native languages and the scope of the legislation. In addition, the existence of the law and its adequate interpretation and enforcement are two different things.

Several laws relating to the language of office work and court proceedings are purely cosmetic, since Russian has been used for over half a century.

As well as language rights, there are supposed to be no legal restrictions for the development of mass media in any languages, for receiving state support for

Language policy of the USSR   99

printing and publishing literature in the local languages and for conducting research into their study, development and preservation.

Moscow appreciates the importance of the full-scale functioning of the Russian language for cultural integration and political consolidation of the regions. That Russian faces the "threat of the cultural-linguistic, and then the political disintegration as a multinational state with a Russian cultural core" seems groundless. Thanks to the Russian lingua franca, in spite of the Soviet deportations and hardships, language barriers have not disturbed the North Caucasus for over a century. Quibbles about linguistics must have been like asking a starving man what language he would like his menu in.

Dagestani and Russian media debate whether the Russian people should gain a new identity instead of the old collective "Soviet people." Meanwhile in the RF language problems of self-identification and assimilation are misused by 'national elites' for autonomy, 'full sovereignty', and separatism.

Realistically almost all languages of the peoples of Russia, except Russian, are functionally stagnant or near-extinct. For example, nearly half of the Karelians, more than a third of the Bashkirs, Komi, Mordovians, Udmurts, and up to a quarter of Mari and Chuvash people consider Russian as their native language. Between the censuses of 1970 and 1989, the proportion of people who did not speak their native languages among Karelians and Mordovians increased one and a half times, and doubled among Buryats, Komi, Mari, Udmurts, Chuvash and Yakuts.

Measures to improve the linguistic life of the peoples of Russia started since the early 1990s announcing state languages, along with Russian, of the so-called 'titular' peoples, and adopting republican language laws. They are cosmetic since mechanisms for their implementation are not stipulated. Nowadays, language loss, particularly in Dagestan, has become irreversible.

References

[1] Stalin J.V. National questions and Leninism. Soch. Vol. 11.
[2] Ed. Gol`strem V. Muslim publishing in Russia in 1910. Oxford. 1987. pp15, 42.
[3] Ismail Bey Gasprinsky. Russian Islam. Oxford. 1985. pp44, 55–8.
[4] Rasul-zade M.E. On pan-turanianism and its links to Caucasian problems. Oxford. 1985. p66.
[5] All-Russian congresses of Muslims, and Dumas of 1905 to 1906. Political life of Russian Muslims before the February revolution. Oxford. 1987.
[6] Communist party resolutions and decisions, seminars, conferences and plenums of Central committee 1898–1986. Vol. 2. 1917–22. 9th ed. Moscow. 1983. p366.
[7] Eds. Krasoviczkaya T.Y. and Tishkov V.A. Ethnic and religious factors in foundation and evolution of the Russian state. Moscow. 2012. p200.
[8] Suleimanov N.D. comparative-historical research on Agul dialects. Makhachkala. 1993. p8.
[9] Kholmogorov A.I. National relations in a socialist society: Problems of scientific management. Kiev. 1982. p66.

13 Schools, literacy and publishing under the Tsar and Soviets

Tsarist policy towards the 'enlightenment of foreigners' which included Dagestanis had as its goal their 'moral Russification', instilling 'the principles of citizenship.' Russian schools and gymnasiums were opened to satisfy these goals. In 1911 the Baku newspaper *Kavkazets No. 9* reported, "the opening of schools, all educational activities among the population, are so constricted that any undertaking of the already few intelligent forces is completely paralyzed." Pre-revolutionary Russian schools did not ban the observance or teaching of Islam to the children, which should have been an attractive policy for the highlanders. But the schools' initial reception by Muslims was ambiguous and often hostile.

Tabulation of percentages from the All-Union Census of 1926 (Table 13.1) showed that the Soviet cultural revolution was not dealing with non-literate peoples and complete illiteracy, as they claimed. Of a total population of 767,243 about 11.7% were literate, literate men outnumbering women by about 3 to 1.

The 1897 census (Table 13.2) shows a similar level of overall literacy (9%) in broad-brush terms, but other than confirming little change in literacy in the first 30 years of the XX century, or possibly indicating that female literacy had improved markedly (from about 2 to 6%) to the betterment of the overall figures, they are more corroborative than permitting useful comparison. To start with, the total population shown is about only two-thirds of the 1926 figure; if we assume a fair degree of stasis in the actual numbers of people (as is reasonable for this period of history), this suggests the 1897 either missed a third of them, or the areas under review by the two censuses were significantly different.

Then, the 1897 count was divided into administrative *okrugs* (regions) which sometimes carried the name of a single ethnic group. Many smaller ethnic groups were included in larger groups, different from the 1926 figures that included all ethnic groups.

Finally, the tsarist statistics allowed knowledge of Arabic to count towards literacy, whereas the Soviet census did not count the Arabic script as writing.

The 1926 census then would appear to be more complete and informative, especially as it also included information about the language of literacy. It is even possible to calculate a breakdown of polyglots:

DOI: 10.4324/9781003388579-13

	speaking	*reading*
national language only		60.8
national+Russian	4.8	5.3
national+Turkic (except Kumyks, below)	0.9	11.7
national+T+R	0.5	2.3
national+other		13.7

The balance were non-Dagestanis.

It follows that about 33% of the literate population of the peoples of Dagestan was literate not only in their native languages but in at least one other.

The first decades of the XX century saw exciting new literature, new national theatres and non-traditional professional arts, influenced by Russian Arts and Crafts, revitalized Arab-Muslim culture and the new generation of European-Russianized Dagestani intelligentsia. During 1907–1917, 80 books in Avar were published in the printing houses of M. Mavraev in Temir-Khan-Shura and A.M. Mikhailov in Port-Petrovsk (now Makhachkala), as well as 34 in Dargin, 132 in Kumyk, 33 in Lak, 15 in Chechen and 25 in two or more Dagestani languages. Two foreign language books were published in Azeri, five in Karachay and five in Kabardin, and one each in Ossetian, Adyghe and Balkar. A.A. Isaev, who catalogued all pre-1917 publications in the languages of the peoples of Dagestan noted that "along with the spiritual and religious books and foreign books were numerous textbooks of mathematics, geography, history, grammars and bilingual and multilingual dictionaries, calendars and medical guides. Also works of fiction and poetry and history of Dagestan, astronomy, philology from the ulama. The relatively large print-runs were from 1,000 to 1,500 copies" [1].

To assess the current state and prospects of national languages one must study the Soviet period, when ideological pressure and radical politicization polluted almost all spheres of life. The ethnic/national policy of the Bolsheviks was based on the subjugation of national movements and cultures to the class struggle and proletarian culture. According to Lenin, [2] " 'No to national culture' is written across our banner, signifying international merging of all nations into the highest socialist unity . . . socialism will have to fully internationalize the entire economic, political and spiritual life of peoples." "The withering away of national differences," called *otmiranie*, would cleanse peoples who presented with symptoms of national 'sickness'. Neither languages nor even nationalities were considered of any existential or spiritual value. On the other hand, the undoubted successes in industrialization, collectivization, the cultural revolution and a sense of social equality inspired the communist future and engendered Soviet patriotism and internationalism [3].

"A fair approach to the phenomena of natural assimilation," a central state publication of 1987 mused [4], "is incompatible with the imposition of preserving identity even if this imposition is undertaken with the best humanistic motives, the desire to ensure that some ethnic groups or their separate parts have not disappeared from the ethnic map of the world."

102 *Dagestan – History, Culture, Identity*

For decades, the same definitions were repeated of 'socialist and capitalist nations' and 'feudal and socialist' nationalities. "Prosperity through rapprochement, rapprochement through prosperity", the development of "socialist in content, national in form" cultures was always subject to interpretation. Any hint of promotion of ethnic/national interests was called 'bourgeois nationalism'. No one asked what was not bourgeois nationalism. According to Marx, 'Proletarian nationalism' could not exist, by definition. Nationalistic manifestations were condemned by obscure concepts ". . . as the 'national shell', isolation, stubbornness, egoism, resentment and 'falsely understood national values'" [5].

A radical shift in view was heralded in 1985 by a Georgian philosopher whereby the opposite of homogeneous Socialism was proposed as a worthy objective, where "the true and perfect being of mankind is not in indifferent uniformity, but in the unity of different, individually distinctive nations" [6].

Academician G. G. Gamzatov noted of the *zastoy* (stagnant) years that "familiar ideological warnings sounded about vigilance against the loss of social-class positions . . . . As if before 1917 our peoples knew only wars and feuds, predatory raids and ethnic strife, as if our ancestors could neither read, write, nor enjoy poetry and music. A stronger truth was that the cultural revolution indeed gave many 'small nations' the opportunity to become self-aware of their national culture by discovering the spiritual wealth to their uncharted past" [7].

From their first years, the Soviets ensured equality of languages throughout the country, as in the Decree of the People's Commissariat of the RSFSR on schools for non-Russian peoples of the republic No. 31 of 18 October 1918:

"1) All nationalities living in the RSFSR enjoy the right to organize instruction in their native language at both technical school and in higher education.

"2) Schools of national minorities to open where there are a sufficient number of students," though the minimum class size of 25 students of the same age group was often prohibitive.

The Tenth Congress of the CPSU 8–16 March 1921 condemned the tsarist policy towards non-Russians "in killing among them the rudiments of all statehood, mutilating their culture, hampering their language, keeping them in ignorance, finally if possible to Russify them." The USSR was given the ambition of "helping the labouring masses of non-Great Russian peoples catch up with central Russia that had gone ahead, helping them: a) to develop and strengthen Soviet statehood in the national living conditions of these peoples; b) to develop their native language courts, administration, economic authorities, local leaders who know the life and psychology of the local population; c) develop the press, school, club, business and cultural and educational institutions in their native language; d) to establish and develop native language courses of both educational and vocational character . . . for accelerated training of the native cadres of skilled workers and Soviet-party workers in all areas of government and foremost in education" [8].

Schools, literacy and publishing under the Tsar and Soviets 103

State and local policies vacillated throughout the XX century from promotion of solely Russian to encouragement of local minority languages, with varying understanding of the implications. After the November 1923 Plenum of the Dagestan Regional Committee, which decided to make Turkic the state language, "no one took local languages seriously. There were too many of these languages which were treated not as foundation stones, but as an evil to avoid ... In schools it was in theory impossible to study Arabic in the era of revolution, as it had no roots in Dagestan. They did speak about Russian to a wary population. Local languages were generally not taken into account – the Turkic language of neighbouring Azerbaijan was easily digestible and the natural solution." "For all Lezgins," said I. Gaydarov, of the State Duma, "Turkic-Tatar [i.e. Azeri] is considered the common language" [9].

In practice during the early Soviet years parents had the opportunity to give their children a popular elementary religious education, to learn to read and write. Most large settlements had a mosque, a parish school, or a synagogue. "Dagestan [had long] supplied the east Caucasus with Arabic experts, readers, mullahs and kadis. This pile of rocks was perhaps the most literate place in the Caucasus. In any self-respecting family boys were taught to read Arabic. Islam literally fed a good share of the population and was respected, unlike in richer Chechnya and Kabardia, where Muslims ignored the primitive beliefs of the masses. In poorer Dagestan theological disputes on the *tariqa* commonly occurred at home" [10].

Arabographic writing was used by all Muslim peoples of the North Caucasus. The ratio of numbers of schools to students from 1924–1926 was calculated by Magidov Sh.G [11]: Dagestan with 50,000 of 56,068 students had 2,000 Muslim schools i.e. 25 per school; and 10,721 students at 151 Soviet schools i.e. 71 per school.

As tentatively observed in comparing the 1897 and 1926 census information above, female education may have improved over the period. It was reported in the St Petersburg *Muslim newspaper* in 1914 that in Dagestan, unusually, the mullahs were not hindering women's education. Indeed some encouraged their daughters to attend segregated secondary schools. However the problem of poor women's education continued. In 1931, one of the activists of the cultural front reported: "There are cases that even individual communists do not let their wives into educational programs."

In censuses since 1939, fluency in native languages was ignored in determining literacy, but used to confirm ethnic identity. Significant discrepancies between census data and the actual language situation were revealed in the 1980s after countrywide surveys.

Since the 1960s the CPSU restricted national languages in paperwork and teaching, curtailing their social functions; the rôle of national languages as the means of cross-generational transmission of ethno-cultures decreased. Soviet Man was to believe in class solidarity, proletarian internationalism and the language of Lenin; lingering traditions and ancestral feelings were to be relegated. Slogans inculcated the merging of nations and languages. Ethnicity was suppressed, though this had the unintended result of increasing nationalism and chauvinism.

There was a drop in the level of teaching native languages and literature as Russian was substituted. As a white-wash, academic and journalistic articles and other

104 *Dagestan – History, Culture, Identity*

portrayals of national languages and cultures were promoted. The public was gradually 'introduced' to the idea of the superfluity of native language. For model USSR citizens it was impossible to practice communism while retaining faith in God, 'remnants of the damned past' and 'tribal languages.' Today few adhere to such views and many Russians feel responsibility for preserving the native languages and actually talk with the natives. "In a bilingual society, a person. . . may have a great desire for his children to speak their native language, learn the best traditions of the people, but, for employment prospects, he believes in the kindergarten and state school" that teaches Russian [12].

Encouraged by inter alia changes in education, after the 1970s steady development, interaction and mutual enrichment of the national languages and cultures of the Soviet peoples ceased. Modern Russian ethno-culture faces a narrowing of the traditional household culture, and modernization of everyday life through 'mass culture' threatening the functional death of some languages. Up to a half of the Karelians, more than a third of the Bashkirs, Komi, Mordovians, Udmurts, and up to a quarter of the Mari and Chuvash today consider Russian as their native language. Between the 1970 and 1989 censuses the proportion of people who do not speak their native languages among Karelians and Mordovians increased by one and a half times, and doubled among Buryats, Komi, Mari, Udmurts, Chuvash and Yakuts.

Since the early 1990s measures to improve the linguistic life of the peoples of Russia were essentially cosmetic. This became evident in the announcement in the republics of the languages of the so-called 'titular' peoples as the state languages and the adoption of republican laws on languages. There were many other reasons for the erosion of ethnic languages including urbanization, apparent irrelevance to modern life and careers and homogenisation of cultures.

As of 2012 Dagestan's urban dwellers made up nearly 45% of the 3.1 million population. Their modern lives and ways naturally leads to ignorance of ethnic languages; the effect is felt more in Dagestan, members of whose 30 nationalities rarely form viable populations on transplantation, than, say, in the Chechen Republic and Ingushetia which are mono-ethnic.

It has been noted that the absolute number of the rural population is not decreasing. The apparent survival of the villages, as supported by urban relatives, suggests they might preserve local languages and culture. However this apparent steady state of rural population disguises an imbalance between the lowlands, where numbers are increasing, and the highlands, which are reducing. The foothills near the Primorsky region and from the Samur river to the borders with the Stavropol Territory and the Republic of Kalmykia appears to be a continuous zone of interethnic mixing, and so are like the urban areas as far as the smaller languages go. It is the highlands that are the preservers of localised culture; and they are under threat.

Finally, about a million Dagestanis live outside the Republic within the Russian Federation, Azerbaijan and other Former Soviet countries.

With such a fragmented demography the prospects for preserving Dagestan's ethnic languages are bleak.

Schools, literacy and publishing under the Tsar and Soviets 105

Table 13.1 Information about the literacy of the ethnic population of the Dagestan Autonomous Soviet Socialist Republic according to the data of the 1926 All-Union Population Census [13].

Nationalities	Population		Literacy (%)	
	male	female	male	female
Avars	65,840	72,909	14.1	0.9
Dargins	51,484	57,442	9.0	1.2
Russians	47,308	50,889	57.2	30.0
Lezgins	44,488	46,021	8.3	0.9
Kumyks	44,595	43,365	17.8	4.3
Laki	14,706	25,118	15.9	3.6
Tabasarans	15,871	16,044	3.1	0.1
Nogays	14,684	11,402	9.5	0.6
Turks (Azerb)	11,733	11,695	9.7	1.9
Chechens	11,134	10,717	7.3	0.0
Kaitags	7,199	7,225	3.8	0.2
Mountain Jews (Israelites Montagnards)	5,582	6,010	32.6	8.2
Rutuls	5,342	4,991	7.6	0.6
Andis	3,607	4,074	6.8	0.1
Aguls	3,902	3,751	2.3	0.0
Armenians	2,989	2,934	58.6	46.9
Karatins	2,630	2,675	7.5	0.3
Tyndals	1,881	1,931	8.0	0.0
Akhvakhs	1,748	1,893	8.7	0.5
Tsakhurs	1,837	1,694	1.9	0.0
Chamalals	1,702	1,736	9.8	0.0
Botlikhs	1,626	1,728	21.0	3.9
Didoans	1,623	1,653	0.2	0.1
Bagulals	1,430	1,624	15.0	0.5
Jews (Israelities)	1,462	1,568	64.1	38.7
Germans	1,294	1,257	47.7	39.1
Kubachians	922	1,435	11.0	0.0
Kapuchins (Bezhtins)	722	725	14.3	0.6
Godberins	550	875	16.2	0.2
Khvarshins	491	528	14.5	0.0
Archies	403	451	9.2	0.0
Hunzals (Hunzibs)	38	60	10.5	3.1
totals m/f	370,823	396,420	17.9	5.9
overall		767,243		11.7

106   *Dagestan – History, Culture, Identity*

Table 13.2 Literacy of the population of the districts of the Dagestan region according to the General Census of the population of the Russian Empire in 1897 [14].

Okrug:	*Population*		*Literacy (%)*	
	Male	*female*	*male*	*female*
Avars	65,840	72,909	14.1	0.9
Kurin	37,687	38,145	12.1	1.0
Temirxan- shura	36,795	36,044	11.6	2.5
Dargin	31,269	41,058	17.2	1.9
Kaitag-Tabasaran	35,923	35,259	9.0	0.9
Gunib	18,233	28,314	30.1	7.2
Andi	20,373	24,156	14.8	1.4
Kazikumukh Lak	13,108	25,669	26.7	4.4
Avar	13,366	17,494	25.8	2.5
totals m/f	206,754	246,139	15.9	2.6
overall 1	452,893		8.7	
*additional	30,910	34,525	. . .	. . .
	237,664	280,664	17.0	1.6
overall 2	518,328		9.2	

overall 1 – totals calculated from ethnicities with known m/f literacy rates
overall 2 – totals and rates cited by source, including . . .
*additional – additional headcount to reach cited totals, unknown literacy rates.
It will be noted that the overall rates are substantially similar, whether one limits the figures to those listed ethnicities with specified literacy or takes the totals previously calculated on the larger population.

References

[1] Isaev A.A. Catalogue of printed books and publications of the peoples of Dagestan. Makhachkala. 1989.

[2] Lenin V.I. Complete writings. Vol. XXIV. 1976.

[3] Lenin V.I. Complete writings. Vol. XXIII. 1976.

[4] Issues of improving national processes in the USSR. 1987.

[5] Ed. Desheriev Y.D. Mutual influence and mutual enrichment of the languages of the peoples of the USSR. 1987; and his earlier works: Ed. Desheriev Y.D. National language and national culture. 1978. Desheriev Y.D. and Protchenko I.F. Development of languages of the peoples of the USSR in the Soviet era. 1968.

[6] Kakabadze Z.M. The problem of human beings. Tbilisi. 1985.

[7] Gamzatov G.G. Dagestan phenomenon of rebirth. XVIII–XIX centuries. Makhachkala. 2000. pp9, 14–15.

[8] CPSU in resolutions and decisions of congresses, conferences and plenary sessions of the Central Committee. (1898–1986). Vol. 2. 1917–1922. 9th ed. 1983.

[9] A. Tahoe-Godi. The problem of language in Dagestan. Revolution and Nationality. No. 11 (69). 1935.

[10] Pokrovsky M.N. Diplomacy and war of tsarist Russia in the XIX century. 1924.

[11] Magidov S.G. Implementation of Lenin's national language policy in the North Caucasus. Makhachkala. 1979. p18.

[12] Bgazhnokov B.K. The foundations of humanistic ethnology. Ms.

[13] All-Union Population Census of 1926. pp104–5.

[14] First General Census of the Population of the Russian Empire in 1897. No. 62. M. 1905. pp12–27.

Additional Bibliography

Agaev A.G. The function of language as an ethnic attribute. Language and Society. 1968.

Baziev A.T. and Isaev M.I. Language and nation. 1973.

Caucasian deputies in the Third State Duma. 1912. p71.

Gadzhiev A.S. The role of the Russian people in the historical fate of the peoples of Dagestan. 1964.

Kaltakhchyan S.T. Leninism is about the essence of a nation and the way in which an international community of people is formed. 1969.

Khanazarov K.K. Rapprochement of nations and national languages in the USSR. 1963.

Language problems of the Russian federation and laws on languages. 1994.

Tishkov V.A. Conceptual evolution of national politics in Russia. Series Research on Applied and Urgent Ethnology. No. 100. 1996.

14 Poems written in Avar and Archi languages

To paraphrase Moshe Gammer obm [1]: from the XI century to the 1920s, Dagestan was a major centre of Islamic learning for the entire Caucasus and beyond. Graduates of its madrasahs found employment all over the Islamic world. Its closest ties were with the centres of the Shafiʻi school – Egypt, Syria, and especially Yemen. In the XIX century the Naqshbandi networks in the Ottoman Empire and Central Asia also became important foci of contacts.

This tradition of learning survived well into the Soviet period. Rukiya Sharafutdinova, who took part in field expeditions in Dagestan in 1960–68, met "excellent Arabic speakers, who could recite classical verses for hours without remission." Respect for learning and for the written word has survived in Dagestan until today. Manuscripts were "kept with reverence from generation to generation . . . Everyone, without exception, cultivated a relation of piety to the Arabic word and of respect to anyone who knew the Arabic script – it is as if this was in their blood, so I felt" (pers. comm. RS).

Libraries were hidden during the Stalin years, when both books and manuscripts in Arabic script and their owners were in danger. And it was with pride in their heritage that after Stalin's death owners allowed scholars and students from Makhachkala to see, record and catalogue these manuscripts. This assemblage was inspired and led by the late Amri Shikhsaidov, whose annual field expeditions to villages also provided generations of students with practical training.

While Arabic was by far the major literary language in Dagestan for more than a millennium and accounts for the overwhelming majority of the country's literary output, it was by no means the only language used in writing. Pre-Islamic texts were in Pahlavi Persian and the Albanian scripts. Hebrew and Aramaic were the languages of the Jews, who remained the only non-Muslim minority in Islamized Dagestan until the Russian conquest. They used the Hebrew alphabet for both the Hebrew and Tat languages until the Soviet authorities banned Hebrew and created a Cyrillic alphabet for Tat [2].

Poems written in Avar and Archi languages   109

Peter von Uslar a Russian officer, an early historian and ethnographer of the Caucasus and a philologist who co-authored the first Avar grammar, wrote in 1863: "I presume that not a single word has ever been recorded in writing in the Archi language" [3]. Yet there are works of religious-educational nature in this language that were written in the early XIX century in prose and verse. Mamaykhan Aglarov discovered XIX century texts in his language of Andi [4]. It is most likely that texts in other 'scriptless' languages exist too. It is true, however, that such early attempts did not develop into a writing tradition. Apparently, this was a function of the actual need to possess such a script. Speakers of so-called 'scriptless' languages were not at all 'without script'. The needs of their religious-ceremonial, cultural and artistic life were satisfied by the use of a script that served the languages of more numerous peoples.

Six unpublished poems in the Archi, Arabic and Avar languages are presented below. These illustrate the range of pre-Russian-conquest XIX century works in Arabic script by authors belonging to the Archi (Rochi) community, written in Archi, Avar and Arabic.

Less highbrow texts known as *'ajamī*, written in the Arabic alphabet, are also of interest here as further literary representations of 'unscripted' languages.

Clumsy and rough expressions, deviations from the Russian prosody rules and other stylistic deficiencies are due to the obvious difficulties that arise when translating into languages with completely different grammatical structures. Moreover, the aim of preserving the original meaning unfortunately meant it was sometimes impossible to combine this with the poetic neatness of the Russian word. There were also issues to overcome in the transcription of poems into an 'alien' script. Therefore the English translation is as far as possible a literal one of the Russian. The translations from Archi to Avar, and the translations to Russian are Magomedkhan's.

Although Soviet writers' presumption that 'scriptless' languages lacked culture, these texts show otherwise; during the XIX and early XX century the Archis enjoyed a full cultural life in wider Dagestani society. The names of Khazakhilaw, Kharda and Mamma-Dibir are familiar to those acquainted with the history of the cultural life of the Dagestani peoples. These three sheikhs, as well as many other ulama, were natives of the Rochi community.

Sheikh Mamma-Dibir al-Rochi (1778–1878) taught the sciences of Islam – both theocracy and science in Arabic writings – to such distinguished educators as hajji-Muhammad al-ghachadi, Ramadan-hajji al-Bukhti, Da'ud al-Khurukhi, Muhammad 'Umar al-Doroni, 'Umar-Apandi al-Baghini, Budaychi-hajji al-ghumuqi and 'Undal-hajji al-'Uradi. The renowned religious activists, who later became sheikhs of the Naqshbandi, the Shadhili and the Qadiri tariqas, Sayfullah-Qadi al-Nitsovkri and Shu'aybAfandi al-Baghini were also among his students. Within the boundaries of the present Lak, Kuli, Agul, Zakatal and Belokan districts virtually no

110 *Dagestan – History, Culture, Identity*

settlement could be found which did not employ an Archi as a mullah, qadi, or teacher at a *maktab* or madrasah.

Nazim of Durghili, ʿAbdurrahman al-ghazikumuqi, hasan al-Alqadari and others name Kharda al-Rochi, the author of the third poem below, as one of the most excellent alims (theologians and Islamic scholars) of Imam Shamil's time. Kharda al-Rochi's life has not yet been studied. It is known that he was born in the village of Khilikh belonging to the Archi community, in the family of the "scrupulous theologian" Muhammad-Paqir. There are stories that Kharda was so popular as a teacher (*mudarris*) in the Arab lands that he rarely visited Dagestan at all. He died in Egypt at an unknown date, but probably in the 1820s.

1.   The song of ʿAbd al-Mutallib, 'ho, people, hear ye my story'

from Archi, original in Avar.

After his death, the song was discovered in a niche carved into the wall of his room. It is said that with the song there was a note saying that if the song were performed too often, it might become a nuisance; nevertheless, he asked that it be sung once or twice a year.

> ГӀенекке гӀадамал хабар бицизе,
> ГӀин тӀаме бахӀарзал, къисса рикӀизе,
> Хираб дунял тарав цо гъаримасул.
> МагӀардаса гӀазу гӀедерлъун бугин,
> Дагьлъулел ратиа дий хъварал къоял.
> Харида бараб тӀегь щущалеб буго,
> ТӀагӀулеб батила дий хъвараб къисмат.

> Ho, people, hear ye my story,
> Listen, ye men, and I shall tell you
> Of he who has resigned of this world.
> The snow is thawing on the mountain tops –
> Those are the days of my life being summed up.
> The mountain flowers have withered and fallen –
> The time set by fate has arrived.

First two of twenty irregular length verses mainly of four lines, with a final flourish:

> Хӏукму-патваялъе Ибрагьим-Дибир,
> Аллагьасул вали дов Хъавлу-Мама,
> Сиррупан цӀаларав дов Хъазахъилав,
> ИхӀягӀ- гӀулумалъе дов Гӏумар-Дибир,
> Гӏелмуялъе цӀакъав Магьди-МухӀамад,

Динalge мухIканав МухIамад-Пакъир,
КiицIул хIаж борхарав ХiажимухIамад,
КагIбаялда хварав МухIамадхIажи,
ГiакълуялЪе цIакъав дов Мусадибир,
Балагъат, пасахIат Аллагьас кьурав,
ТадрисалЪе цIакъав дов МухIамадхан
Дунял рехун тарав бичасул загьид,
Гьижра гьабун хварав я дов МухIидин,
Халкъалда цIар арав ХъардахIажияв,
ТiолазулГо устар дов Мама-Дибир.
Гьелги къанабакье араб мехалда,
Къадаралде щведал щибха гьабилеб,
Бакъияв къадимав къадим цо вуго,
БакъилЪун вижарав инсанго гьечIо,
СагIаталде щведал щибха гьабилеб,
ПалхIукмулиллагьи гIалиюл кабир.

In rulings and fatwas – Ibrahim-Dibir,
The saint – hawlu-Mamma, [Muhammad]
The discoverer of mysteries – Qadikilaw,
The reviver of sciences – ʿUmar-Dibir, [Ihya' ʿulum al-din 'Revival of the
   religious sciences' by al-ghazali (1058–1111)
The most learned of the learned – Mahdi-Muhammad,
The scrupulous theologian – Muhammad-Paqir [Faqir]
A pilgrim, twice – hajji Muhammad, he who died at the
   Kaʿbah – Muhammad-hajj.
The wisest of the wise – Musa Dibir who was blessed with perfection and an
   eloquent tongue,
The strongest of teachers – Muhammad-Khan,
The Lord's ascetic, who rejected corporal life he who perished
   in the muhajara,
the one Muhyi al-Din,
The praised one – Kharda-hajjiyaw [Kharda al-Rochi]
The guide of the faithful – Mamma-Dibir
Even they were not spared the lot.
And if my time has arrived, why should I be sorry?
For only he is eternal and present, yet immortal is no man.
My time now has come. What is to be done?

2. A Qasida by sheikh Mamma-Dibir al-Rochi

Dedicated to his *ustadh*, the sheikh of the Naqshbandi tariqa, Jamal al-Din
al-Ghazighumuqi.

112 *Dagestan – History, Culture, Identity*

Preface:

These are the qasidas. The first is by ʿAbd al-Qadir [al-Ghilani] Muhammad, May Allah exalt him. Following are [the qasidas by] Mamma-Dibir al-Qeseriyyi and [by] Jamal al-Din al-Ghumuqi, May Allah pour light on their tombs and may Allah unite us in heaven. Ho, those who read these wonderful qasidas! Do not forget [to mention me] in your outstanding prayers. (May) Allah have mercy [on us]. And I am – Hamid [. . .], who has command of Arabic, Lak, and five other languages.

Worthy verses I shall not find,
I seek them where they aren't.
I ask for blessing for God's people
And for everyone else! . . .

Who are pure and outstanding.
They are God-fearing
And they are among the Noble.
He who addresses them with a request
Shall greatly benefit,
They grant reward and victory,
They are among the Noble.
In our wish, in our desire,
From the depths of our souls, Without sharp, unclean words
We grant them our love.

3. Kharda al-Rochi, 'A torment-relieving elixir'

from the Arabic original.

Poems written in Avar and Archi languages   113

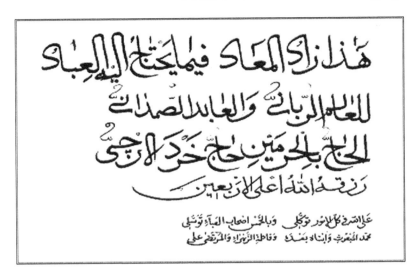

A torment-relieving elixir, which people need for discovering the Lord's Universe and [for] serving [Allah] the Eternal, by Kharda al-Rochi, al-Hajj (pilgrim) to the holy cities of Mecca and Medina, may God grant him the highest Degree of the forty [martyrs?].

Dedication:

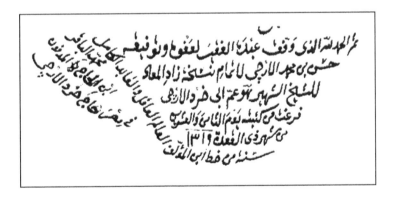

May Allah, who empowered his humble servant with his forgiveness and infused him with will, be exalted. [I], Hasan, son of Muhammad al-Rochi, has completed copying the 'Torment-relieving elixir' by the celebrated sheikh, my father's uncle, Kharda al-Rochi. I completed the copying on the

114   *Dagestan – History, Culture, Identity*

28th day of the month Dhu al-Qaʿda 1319 AH [9 March 1902]. I copied the manuscript prepared by the author's son, the learned, wise and excellent servant of God, Muhammad Paqir, son of the hajji who died in Egypt, the author hajji Kharda al-Rochi.

Excerpts:

People fall into different social categories, such as: women, men, cattle-raisers, land-tillers, merchants and the like. It is obvious that the latter, the same as the former, regardless of their ancestry and the length of time they have followed the Sunnah, are chaste [that is, equal before Allah]. The special among them are the learned ones. There is no doubt that it is they who are the most senior in observing the Sunnah during the ages and in guiding on the righteous path. However, if we turn our attention to the current age, all of them, except for those saved by Allah, have given in to innovations. A few of them – that is those who devote themselves to studying the book of Allah the Supreme, follow the Sunnah of the Prophet (may Allah bless him and give him peace), understand their meaning according to the Arabic originals and trustworthy commentaries – speak not of what these texts gloss over and do not immerse themselves in what they do not comprehend. Those are the true Sunnis and saviours. [. . .] It is them who shall at a time foretold (by the Lord) be made equal to and join those (and they are extremely numerous), whom the Lord wishes to distinguish for their knowledge and pure intentions, to distinguish those who did not spare their own lives in order to extol the *umma*, the ancient and current peoples of the Lord [. . .] he who declares the lawful, such as trade or marriage, to be prohibited; or he who declares the prohibited, such as wine, fornication, homosexuality, murder, prayer with no ablution and out of time, to be lawful – has no say. [This is] against the law both for a Muslim and for a Jew or a Christian being under [*dhimmi*] (Muslim protection). [. . .]

Jealousy is the desire of the soul to gain what has been granted by Allah to another person from among the spiritual or material goods. It is the wish that these goods be granted to the jealous person with no objections, regardless of this person's lack of right to them and regardless whether it would be attained by agreement or by law. If you gained this by agreement, it shall not bring you happiness. An ugly trace shall remain in your heart. [. . .] You must know that jealousy will cause you harm in both worlds [. . . my] guidance, *nasiha* (advice) is wishing the good of another person.

A hater is the one who experiences an internal need to quarrel with someone, feels enmity towards him, wishes him ill. It is a sin, given that it does not arise from oppression and violence. [. . .]

Poems written in Avar and Archi languages 115

An eager desire for power and position, self-aggrandizement, self-admiration [. . .] the bearer of these characteristics is furious for he has not the full right to command over everything that he fancies, he squanders his gift of speech and jealousy in order to attain it. Yet it is a malady of the heart and a lack of reason.

4. A Qasida, 'I was enchanted by this transient world'

with nineteen more verses mostly with the refrain: 'ho, the bitterness of this death!' (redolent of the Latin *timor mortis conturbat me*, fear of death disturbs me).

Translated from Avar to Archi in the XIX century.

Дунилу эз ххарра этти,
Черхин гьавалис хир веӀрхъуӀ,
Амро-нагью имма акъу,
Я ят кӀвимкӀмулин балакул.

I was enchanted by this transient world,
Followed the flesh's desires,
Chose the prohibited, abandoned the prescribed,
ho, the bitterness of this death!
The time has been lost in cruel deeds,
I've spent my life oppressing others,
having served the Lord less and less,
ho, the bitterness of this death!

5. An anonymous Qasida, 'ho, untamed body'

About 59 couplets depending on how they are counted, original in Archi.

Гьай гъапуллуб гӀаси черх,
КӀвимкӀмул икӀма итӀиттуб,
Ссар вас икӀмас экотӀу,
МахӀшар икӀмас эбкотӀу,

. . .

Аллагьлин цӀоб эблълъуна
НентӀу хусдар овхъиттиб,
Я, рабби, ун цӀоб белъа,
ЦӀоб рахӀмулинну, Аллагь!

ho, untamed body, You have forgotten death,
You remember not the grave,
And neither hell nor heaven,

. . .

116   *Dagestan – History, Culture, Identity*

Then God's grace will be given to us – We shall be redeemed.
ho, my Lord, have mercy,
Ye Allah, the all-compassionate!

6.   A Qasida by Sulen Muhammad, 'This transient universe'

About 26 'verses' of various length, original in Archi.

Ят панаттут дунил Панакер ихъна,
Мурад ризауллагь, ХIасул а Аллагь!
ИгIапат кулахъмул –
Ваттиш тIалаб ар,
ИстигIмар лаIхх'IиITIи –
Ватиш и, Аллагь!
. . .
Къабул а, я Аллагь,
Нен овттут дугIи,
Мустажибу дагIват МагIруплин бана!

This transient universe – It is scorched forever,
ho, Allah, make my dream come true,
The dream to make you happy!
Because help and care
I seek only with you,
My existence and life's call –
All comes from You, ye Allah!
ho, the Prophet, I am tormented
By pains of the heart, help me!
. . .
As the oath
Of Ma'rup, [Ma'ruf]
Accept, ye Allah, Our prayer!

'Ajam literature merits a separate heading

'Ajam is awaiting full research [2]. The bulk of the works in Arabic were addressed to intellectuals, while 'Ajam was intended for *'avam* a broader readership, interested in lifestyles, mindsets, customs, and folk morality.

Sirazhudin Oboda (1868–1914) in Bustan Avaristan/Rim versified:

Don't say it is 'Ajam
This is pure moisture from useful books,
It is written in 'Ajam for people who do not know Arabic literacy
in order to teach them knowledge.

Ismaildiber Shulani (1867–1930) called his poems 'A small gift to the young ignoramuses':

> Writing 'Ajam is not very important,
> And scribble does not exhaust science
> And yet, realizing the well-being of the people,
> I decided to write, let it heal.

References

[1] Ed. Gammer M. Written culture in Dagestan. Introduction. 2015.
[2] Gazikumukhi Abdurakhman (abbr. AG). Book of Memoirs. Chapter 9. 1869.
[3] Uslar Peter K. Ethnography of Caucasus: Language knowledge. Lak Language. Vol. IV. 1890. p6.
[4] Aglarov M.A. Andis: Historical-ethnographic researches. 2002. p247.

15 Re-Islamization of public consciousness

For a long time, the historical role of Islam in Dagestan was denigrated by Russian authors as a branch of Arab-Muslim spiritual culture. While writing about the rebirth of Islamic life in Dagestan, authors did not address the ethno-cultural consequences of Soviet 'secularization' on spiritual life. On Judgement Day a person will be asked if he is a Muslim, and not his ethnicity. Ethnicity does not affect the observance of *farsh* (adherence to the Sunnah, sharia standards or the Ummah). Islamic identity can be expressed through religious consciousness and religious feelings, adherence to prescriptions and their attitude to themselves and to people of other faiths.

"On the question of the need for anti-religious propaganda among Muslims, not only in Russia, but also far beyond, we Communists do not allow any disputes and disagreements" wrote a prominent Tatar and Islamic Communist theorist in 1921 [1]. He established that Islam is like a religion (!) and whether those methods of propaganda that are founded on revolutionary practice for other religions are suitable for it. Since the problems of inter-confessional relations are caused by the very existence of religions, the cardinal solution to these problems, according to the logic of scientific communism, was to overcome the religious differences that in their eyes were obscene. Atheistic propaganda was identified with 'international education' and elevated to the rank of state policy. It seems that the desired separation of church from state in many respects was a fiction.

During the years of Soviet rule in Dagestan, "about 12,000 people were repressed (chapter 11), of which more than 5,000 were clergy. Thousands of religious buildings were destroyed along with 670 libraries from mosques and elsewhere, and mountains of spiritual literature and valuable manuscripts were burned. Some 165,000 mosque carpets, rugs, and *arbabash* (ox-cart covers) tapestries were confiscated. Removing tombstones and monuments the Socialists used the stone for 'houses of culture', libraries, and livestock barns." On the establishment of Soviet power, more than 2,000 mosques and 700 schools were functioning. Almost all of them were closed by 1931 (chapter 13). During the War of 1941–1945 there was some relaxation in the fight against religion. From 1941 to 1951, the authorities allowed registration of 26 mosques, 5 churches and several synagogues. In 1944, the Spiritual Administration of Muslims committee was established in Buinaksk.

DOI: 10.4324/9781003388579-15

"At the same time, in the regions where Laks, Lezgins, Nogais lived, there was not a single mosque" [2].

So-called 'official Islam' in the USSR was represented by four religious departments, two Islamic educational institutions and a 'decorative minimum' number of mosques. The 'political trustworthiness' of the muftis and imams representing 'official Islam' was tacitly monitored, and their activity was limited to ritual functions relevant to 'construction of communism.' Muftis distributed occasional fatwas criticizing pilgrimage to *ziyarats* (holy shrines) and even against observing one of the five Muslim canons, sunset, as this is destined for the poor, who, by definition, cannot exist in a socialist country. The conversion of new adherents, and publicizing Islamic values, was out of the question. Rare speeches of official clergymen "on the identity of Islamic and communist ideologies" and "on the coincidence of the ultimate goals of Islam and communism," previously authorized by the authorities, were immediately criticized. To achieve this, the USSR maintained a large staff of atheists, university departments and specialized journals. Despite the state repression, the spread of rumours of improper behaviour and drinking alcohol and party membership of muftis and imams that crippled 'official' Islam, leaders of hedge-Islam got on with the state-sponsored leaders.

Apologists for scientific atheism criticized Islam as a religion, and Muslims as such for 'poisoning the public consciousness of people,' for emphasizing differences between the 'religious' and the 'national,' for using national feelings, traditions, customs and rites to spread Islam among the younger generation, for supporting polygamy and *kalym* (bride-price), for inciting ethnic hatred and enmity. Parents and teachers were criticized for lack of enthusiasm in atheistic work with their children, and the Party-Soviet bodies were scolded for the lack of militancy and intransigence in the fight against 'fanatical obscurantism.' Curiously the Dagestani preachers of 'scientific atheism' focused exclusively on Islam, while ignoring anti-Christian or anti-Semitic propaganda. The atheists had a successful policy of recruitment where anti-Islamic propaganda was reserved 'work' for Dagestanis, so avoiding involvement of even a single ethnic-Russian of Dagestan.

In the early Soviet years the activists, as another slur on Islam, campaigned for the liberation of the Goryanka (mountain woman, chapter 11) from polygamy, bride kidnapping and child marriage. The activists attracted local media and fiction, even though they were not many and not widespread in Dagestan or the North Caucasus. "Religion, clan and family turned the Goryanka into a most meek and conservative creature, legitimized by the adats and sharia" [3]. The People's Commissar Alibek Takho-Godi's 1924 speech for their emancipation is quoted in chapter 11 [4]. The March 1926 decision of the Central Executive Committee and the Council of People's Commissars of the DASSR adoption of equality in divorce was great propaganda. "In order to involve women, traditionally enclosed within the family, public campaigns were conducted called 'Goryanka-coat!' and 'Down with the *chukhta*!'" (the black headdress worn by married women, snug around the forehead with a snood behind for their long hair) [5].

120   Dagestan – History, Culture, Identity

In novels and on the stage, the emancipated Goryanka was propagandized as aspiring to freedom and light to defy the 'dark forces of society', take off the chukhta, become a student, enter the Komsomol and, contrary to her cruel parents' will, elope with a beloved worker or agricultural machine operator [6]. There were hundreds of propaganda publications about how the life of the 'dark Highlanders' had changed beyond recognition, about the escape to a new Soviet life of the unfortunate woman bitter at adat, sharia and the "age-old oppression of the patriarchal-tribal system" [7].

In the Islamic movement of Russia in the 1990s the All-Russian Centre for Spiritual Administration, the Union of Muslims of Russia, the All-Russian Social and Political Movement 'Nur', and the All-Russian Islamic Cultural Centre were created. The offices of these organizations were located in Moscow, with limited influence on the North Caucasus.

The revival of Islam, coinciding in time with the collapse of the USSR, was extensive [8]. In spite of 70 years of state-promoted atheism the Dagestanis had continued to follow their spiritual traditions. With the newly permitted religious freedoms, most of the population quickly and pointedly re-asserted their religion.

In the 1990s the increase in the number of mosques and religious educational institutions was accompanied by organizational disintegration of Muslims, especially in the North Caucasus. Slogans about the Muslim brotherhood of the time might have suggested a united revival but the nationality of religious activists and their deep-seated ethno-political beliefs in fact turned out to be more significant. The disintegration of the former Spiritual Administration of Muslims of the North Caucasus into 12 'ethnic' Spiritual Administrations and the unrest among believers in 1991 coincided with the aggravation of inter-ethnic relations in the region.

In the late 1980s- early 1990s the population of the North Caucasian republics, confused by the problems of survival in the crisis of economy and power and the growth of crime, did take seriously the emergence of Wahhabis and the danger of their ideology to political stability and peace. At first the Wahhabis themselves did not go beyond theological disputes, demonstrating by wearing distinctive white trousers shortened to the ankle joint, a long beard, and the absence of a moustache and *papakha* (hat). Clergymen, deprived of higher religious education during the Soviet period, did not immediately or fully comprehend the destructive threat of the Wahhabis.

At the All-Russian Conference "Actual Problems of Combating Religious-Political Extremism" in Makhachkala on 6 June 2007, M.G. Aliyev summed up, "along with factors of external influence, one of the main reasons for the spread of extremism is the whole range of our internal socio-economic, managerial, socio-political, spiritual, moral and other problems that have accumulated over recent years." He also pointed out that "for the most part we are fighting, as it should be, not with the social reasons that give rise to extremism, but with its consequences, that is . . . with extremists" [9].

In the crisis of the 1990s, the policy of Dagestan as a subject of the Russian Federation was to preserve the unity of the Dagestan peoples, to oppose the use of force in resolving interethnic disputes, and to satisfy ethnic interests [10].

The integration of Russian Muslims in the socio-political and cultural life of the country was such that their engagement with the development of ideas, programs and actions from the Muslim world outside was regarded with unease, as was directly expressed in a Naqshbandi text in Arabic: "And it is good for our standing, as the people of *Aglu-Dagistan* (Dagestan) that our Dagestan has humanity, dignity, philanthropy, conscience, and hospitality, unlike the Arab countries [where] they have more love for worldly goods than Dagestanis" [11].

The postulate: 'All Muslims are brothers' means brotherhood by faith, not cultural identity. In this regard, the strengthening of religious identity observed since the collapse of USSR did not lead to the suppression of the ethno-cultural and ethno-psychological characteristics of the Dagestanis.

When the USSR collapsed, the Wahhabis received mob support in their exposure of how ignorant of rites and rituals were the official Islamic Communists. Unemployed youth amongst the crowds were easy recruits. Despite the appeals of Sufi clergymen warning of the destabilizing consequences of Wahhabis' propaganda, the attitude of the majority of believers towards the Wahhabis in the initial period of their activity was indifferent or even sympathetic as they were rebuilding mosques in Dagestan that had been forbidden during socialism. Wahhabi ideas were spread not only by the local Dagestani converts who had been trained at Wahhabi universities in Saudi Arabia, but also foreign emissaries from Middle Eastern Muslim countries.

Among the reasons for the appearance of radical Islam in Dagestan, researchers reasonably note unemployment, low wages, and corruption in government. However Kadar, Kizilyurt, Tsumadin and other areas where Wahhabism spread did not suffer from these social problems. In Soviet times, their population differed from the rest of the Dagestanis by their commercial activity, not by piety.

It must be admitted that some of the Wahhabi leaders had excellent command of rhetoric and knew, quoted and interpreted the verses of the Qur'an and the hadiths of the Prophet in their own way. Many of them had higher secular education, some had experience working in the Komsomol or public organizations and some were charismatic. The Wahhabis showed complete indifference to both the ethnic affiliation of the members of their 'community' and their cultural characteristics. This seemed attractive as it aligned with the traditional Dagestani rejection of any kind of ethnic segregation.

However, these Puritans of Islam denied the cult of saints and divine rewards for visiting the ziyarats. They banned the veneration of ancestors at Uraza Bayram (festival picnics in cemeteries). They were intolerant towards the Tariqat sheikhs and their followers. The Wahhabis pursued their exclusive dogma even against their relatives, fellow villagers and tukkhum. They put themselves outside the

122   *Dagestan – History, Culture, Identity*

folk-traditional civic and kindred obligations. Those who did not recognize their so-called 'pure Islam' were insulted by Wahhabis as *kyafirs* (disbelievers) and their worship called *shirk* (polytheism).

In the late 1980s the USSR policy of legalizing religious life, publicity and pluralism allowed local Wahhabis to strengthen ties with foreign Islamic organizations and to receive financial support from abroad. Until August 1999 the Dagestani authorities did not obstruct the Wahhabis, puzzlingly distanced from localized armed insurrections in 1986. They promoted Wahhabi ideas and views often distributed in printed and video formats. They opened Wahhabis' madrasahs, build Wahhabis' mosques, and sometimes took over traditional mosques as in the village of Kirov-Aul, Kizilyurt region. In Chabanmakhi and Karamakhi, Buinaksk region, Wahhabis introduced 'their own' sharia. They gave press conferences and were preferred by the Dagestani audience to the 'traditionalists' interviewed by Russian and foreign journalists. Wahhabis had relatively little traction in Dagestan but attracted extremists who engaged in a long violent war against the authorities who described them as bandits and terrorists. It was hard for the authorities to distinguish between ordinary Salafi mosque worshippers and their more violent co-fundamentalists the Wahhabis. An estimated 5% of young Dagestan males converted to Wahhabism compared to 20% to 25% of Chechens, their western neighbours.

Dagestan is a secular republic as enshrined in the Constitution of the Republic of Dagestan. The social structure, educational and cultural level of Dagestan are all comparable with the advanced regions of Russia. As background, in the 1990s the Russian Federation experienced shocks caused by the crisis in and the subsequent transformation of the political system and socio-economic system, the demoralization of public consciousness, increased crime, theft of national wealth and the consequences of inter-ethnic conflicts. Most of the North Caucasus conflicts were caused by inter-ethnic territorial claims and dissatisfaction with the existing political status within the Russian Federation, but not by separatism [12].

Apart from the rare eulogies of individual clergy about a particular candidate during the election campaigns of the 1990s, the Spiritual Administration of the Muslims of Dagestan did not intervene in state policy or oppose the existing secular authorities. This position of the official clergy was attacked by Wahhabis, convinced that only they, as champions of monotheism and 'pure Islam', could eliminate social injustice, corruption, banditry, drunkenness, drug addiction, debauchery and godlessness. To achieve their goals, the Wahhabis needed a revolution to replace the secular Constitution with sharia and shura, and the republican system with the Caliphate.

In Dagestan and Chechnya from the early 1990s the confrontation between traditionalists and Wahhabis went beyond theological disputes, and street brawls became an ordinary occurrence. There were armed clashes between Tarikatists and Wahhabis in Gudermes in 1996. In August-September 1999 there were military operations in Tsumadinsky, Botlikhsky and Novolaksky districts, and in the villages of Karamakhi and Chabanmakhi in Buynaksky district. The Wahhabis were defeated and their destructive potential dealt a major blow. The President of the Republic M.G. Aliyev stated that the Islamization of Dagestan and the rest of the north Caucasus was a real continuing threat and fighting it remained the urgent task for the authorities and society.

Towards the end of the 1990s, the Salafi fundamentalist movement began to spread throughout Dagestan, returning to what they call pure original Islam, bringing religious conflict between Sufis and Salafis who are often branded as Wahhabis by the authorities. They began converting young Dagestanis and Chechens when the hajj (pilgrimage to Mecca) was permitted in 1990 – the first time since the 1920s [13]. By late 1996, the official religious establishment, dominated by Sufi leaders, grew openly hostile to Salafi adherents. Said Muhammad Haji Abubakarov, then head of the pro-government official Muslim Spiritual Board, made a speech in which he said that "any Muslim who kills a Wahhabi will enter Paradise" [14]. Some heeded the call though it was never imaginable in the 1980s that there would be suicide attacks within or from Dagestan; such conduct was against tradition, very un-Dagestani.

It is confusing that the rebels/terrorists are usually Sunnah or Ahlu Sunnah Wal Jamaat or Salafists and not Wahhabi Muslim. As background, 'Ahlu Sunnah Wal Jamaat' is applied to some Muslims in Dagestan. In 2017 I asked my co-author "Please can you explain who are Ahlu Sunnah Wal Jamaat? Can you describe them as Salafist? I see that they are from Somalia." He replied: "Simple explanation is that Ahlu Sunnah Wal Jamaat (people of Sunnah and 'society', meaning 'unity') are those who refer themselves to or identify with the beliefs of the Prophet Muhammed and his companions. The key point of discussions is around the Prophet's hadith which says that "my community (*ummah*) will be divided into 73 groups (parties) but only one of them go to paradise."

According to all Islamic scholars the last group is called '*ahlu sunnah wal Jamaa*'. Every Muslim society or sub-division, Sufis or Salafis who also call themselves Sunnah, claim that exclusively *they* are ahlu sunnah wal Jamaa, but not the rest.

In some mosques there are Salafi imams and in others Salafis pray alongside Sufis and Sunnis, so it can be difficult to tell them apart.

The democratically elected Chechen president Maskhadov repeatedly denied links with Bin Laden and Al-Qaida but repeatedly failed to control independent Wahhabi warlords such as Basayev and Khattab and was assassinated by Russian forces in 2005 [15].

Russian reports have often lumped both Salafi and Sunni rebels as 'Wahhabi', portraying Wahhabi international terrorists as the only forces opposing the Russians in Chechnya. For example, the Chechen Ruslan Khachaburov, involved in the Beslan school siege of 2004, was described as a Wahhabi in an article by IWPR the independent London-based NGO, an unintended inaccuracy. This was denied by Musa Arapkhanov, his cousin: "When Ruslan Khachaburov was here last year, he faithfully went to the mosque and did the *zikr* (traditional Sufi Sunni Chechen prayer ritual), which the Wahhabis don't do" [13, 16].

124 *Dagestan – History, Culture, Identity*

The Russians attempt to broaden their terrorism beyond Russian borders in order to gain foreign support against their 'fight against international terrorism.' Their objective is that if foreign countries accept their argument, they will ignore human rights violations in Chechnya or Dagestan by Russian forces.

Dagestani and Chechen rebels (as opposed to Chechen Wahhabis) had always targeted Russian forces and co-nationals in retaliation for Russian invasions of Chechnya and human rights abuses. Even the Chechen Wahhabis, who have promoted inexcusable suicide bombings and attacks on civilians, have always operated against Russians, with one alleged exception in 1992–3 when they reputedly fought against the Georgians on the Abkhaz side.

The first example of a Dagestani involved in an overseas terror attack was Dzhokhar Tsarnaev a Kyrgyz-American of Chechen descent whose family live in Dagestan. He was convicted of terrorism in bombing the Boston Marathon on 15 April 2013. Tsarnaev's brother was also involved; he died in a police shootout after the attack. Tsarnaev remains in prison.

In 2009 a police wanted poster was published for members of NVF Buinaksk region part of Dagestan. There were pasted-in photos of mainly men but some women [17]. NVF stands for the Chechen for *Free Ickheria* [the Chechen name for Chechnya] who are militia rebels apparently also operating in Dagestan as well as Chechnya. Russian authorities claim that NVF has been taken over by Wahhabis, with reason, since Chechen rebel leader Umarov declared a North Caucasian Emirate in 2007 [18].

The word *Vakhabism* is merely the Russian transliteration of the English Wahhabism. Contact with Wahhabis is deemed to be aiding terrorism chargeable under anti-terrorism Article 205.1, which carries a sentence of 8 to 20 years. Other anti-terrorism criminal Articles include 208, 210, 222 and 226 and carry similar sentences [19, 20].

The criminal Articles are broadly drawn, and, combined with poor intelligence and the determination of the Russian state to be seen to be doing something, can lead to evident miscarriages of justice. For example, a doctor who worked as part of a mobile surgery to treat inhabitants in mountain villages treated a man who was brought to his surgery, who he later found out was an alleged terrorist. He was accused of assisting terrorism and put in detention from December 2012 to December 2013 when he was acquitted. The case was reopened in September 2014, and he was again found innocent but the decision was reversed on appeal [21, 22]. There was a similar unreported case in 2015 (pers. Comm.) where a dentist was put on a 'wanted' notice, described as a member of NVF and accused of terrorism for treating a patient.

The Caucasus Emirate was a terrorist Jihadist organisation active in rebel-held parts of Syria and previously in the southwestern region of the Russian Federation. Its intention was to expel the Russian presence from the North Caucasus and to establish an independent Islamic emirate also called Caucasus Emirate. Partially a successor to the secessionist Chechen Republic of Ichkeria, it was officially announced on 7 October 2007, by former President of Ichkeria Dokka Umarov, who became its first emir. By late 2015, the group no longer had a visible presence in the North Caucasus region, as most of its members defected to the local IS (also known as ISIS and the Arabic acronym *Daesh)* affiliate, Vilayat Kavkaz in Dagestan, one of the four districts of the Emirate.

It is unclear if the Caucasus Emirate made a deal with IS. A video of 27 November 2014 where it appears that the Dagestani emir of Vilayat Dagestan had sworn allegiance to IS was claimed to be a fake to smear the rebels [23]. Numbers of Chechens and Dagestanis who have joined IS in Syria were estimated between a few hundred and 1,500. It is also not clear if any have officially returned. Bearing in mind that Russia is Syrian President Assad's most important ally, any suspected IS returnees could expect harsh treatment. Any Dagestani and other north Caucasian returning from abroad, especially Turkey and the Middle East, are even now also at risk of being accused of links with IS.

On 16 February 2015 the new Jihadist leader in Dagestan, Said Arakanskiy, denounced any former colleagues who had sworn allegiance to IS, emphasizing that the rebel Caucasus Emirate had nothing in common with IS which he condemned [24]. 'Wahhabi' attacks peaked about 2012 and in March 2019 state security press releases claimed that all rebel/terrorists had been eliminated.

Modern assessments of the Islamic identity of Dagestanis are hardly positive. Dagestan as the most Islamized region of Russia 'endangers its security'. Legal, social, economic and other issues are allegedly regulated not by secular structures, but by 'Muslim communities' and 'ethno-clans.' During the XX century academics quoted elsewhere in this book held conflicting theories. Aglarov thought that earlier communities in Dagestan were seen as civil structures, rather than the tsarist historian M. M. Kovalevsky and M. O. Kosven's (fl. 1940–1960s) tribal frameworks or Soviet historian A. G. Agaev (fl. 1960–70s) and the modern historian of the Islamic revival V. Bobrovnikov's tribal and ethnic clan and religious-communes. Misunderstandings of the complexity of theoretical structures remain today. The terms 'Orthodox community', 'Jewish community', and 'Muslim community' are only correct in a confessional context; they are not ethnic identities.

Valery Dzutsev, a respected commentator, wrote in 2014 that state interference in religion was seen as destabilizing Dagestan and ironically to recruiting for Wahhabi extremists and ISIS [25]. The best solution is to give young men hope in their future, opportunity to work and make a living and a path to engagement in a good civil life. But this solution is flawed for example in UK where there are much better opportunities for young men, yet a small number of graduates and students continue to be radicalized. There must be other new factors that would avoid radicalization. But that is for another book. The next chapter describes contemporary culture that can perhaps point to replacements for extremism.

126 *Dagestan – History, Culture, Identity*

References

[1] Sultan Galiev Mir Said. Life of Nationalities. Methods of anti-religious propaganda among Muslims. 1921.

[2] Kurbanov R. and Kurbanov M.G. Religion in the culture of the peoples of Dagestan. Makhachkala. 1996. pp18, 20–1.

[3] Daniyalov G.D. The construction of socialism in Dagestan. 1988. p99.

[4] Isaev A.A. The scientific heritage of A.A. Tahoe Godi. Makhachkala. 2007. pp14–16.

[5] Ed. Tishkova V.A. The Russian Caucasus. Book for Politicians. 2007. p64.

[6] Magomedkhanov M.M. The image of an emancipated bitterness in ideology and popular consciousness. Gender relations in the culture of the peoples of the North Caucasus. Makhachkala. 2008. pp101–4.

[7] Karpov Y.Y. Female space in the culture of the peoples of the Caucasus. St. Petersburg. 2001.

[8] Magomedkhanov M.M. The revival of Islam and Islamic publishing. Demokratizatsiya. Vol. II. No. 3. Boston. 1994.

[9] Aliev M.G. Actual problems of counteraction to religious and political extremism. Makhachkala. 2007. pp17–24.

[10] Ibragimov M.-R.A. and Magomedkhanov M.M. Some aspects of religious extremism in Dagestan. Dagestan Ethnographic Collection. Vol. II. Makhachkala. 2008.

[11] al-Bagini, Tabakat al-Hwajakan al-Naqshbandiyya wa sadat mashayih al-Khalidiya al-Mahmoudiya. Dimashq: Dar al-Nu‘man lil-l-Qulum. (in Arabic) . . . Damascus: Dar al-Nu’man ms. 2003.

[12] Tishkova V.A. Society in armed conflict (ethnography of the Chechen war). 2001.

[13] Chenciner Robert. Daghestan Tradition and Survival. Curzon Press, GB. 1997. pp96 photo of shrine, 215, 245 photo of Goryanka propaganda, 286 photo of zikr (hedge religion).

[14] Anon. Human rights watch. Document 305566. 18 June 2015.

[15] Fuller Liz. Chechen president Maskhadov denies links with Bin Laden. RFE/RL Caucasus Report. Vol. 4. No. 35. 11 October 2001.

[16] Aliev Timur, Dadayev Aslanbek and Zhadayev Ruslan. Confusion surrounds Beslan band. IWPR. 23 September 2004.

[17] Anon. Members of NVF of Buinaksk administrative region. February 2009.

[18] Tumelty Paul. The Rise and Fall of Foreign Fighters in Chechnya. Terrorism Monitor. Vol. 4. No. 2. 31 January 2006.

[19] Article 210. Organization of a criminal community and article 205. Russian Federation Criminal Code NO. 63-FZ of 13 June 1996 (UK). Legislationline. 2004.

[20] Article 208. Organisation of an illegal armed formation, or participation in It. Russian Federation Criminal Code NO. 63-FZ of 13 June 1996 (UK). Legislationline. 2012.

[21] Kommersant newspaper. The Supreme Court believed Zakhar Prilepin. 16 September 2014.

[22] Radio Free Europe Radio Liberty. Dagestan's Supreme Court overturns medic's acquittal. 17 September 2014.

[23] Anon. Caucasus emirate casts doubt on video of 'Dagestani emir' pledging to IS. 27 November 2014. www.chechensinsyria.com.

[24] Joscelyn Thomas. New jihadist leader in Dagestan denounces Islamic State defectors. The Long War Journal. 16 February 2015.

[25] Dzutsev Valery. Lack of conflict resolution mechanisms and state interference in religion seen as destabilizing Dagestan. Eurasia Daily Monitor. Vol. 11. No. 186. 21 October 2014.

16 Pre-Soviet and contemporary cultures

The history of the Caucasus may be observed as a continuous dialogue of cultures and civilizations.

The inability to change ancient and strong religious, cultural and ethnic identities, and the futility of interfering in the living communication of Caucasian and Dagestani peoples were realized to their cost by a succession of empires, which periodically captured parts of the Caucasus or, as with the Russians in 1864, the whole Caucasus. The borders were always open between the Caucasian regions, both when they were part of the empires, and during the Soviet period. However after the collapse of the USSR, the new borders and the physicality of the Great Caucasus Mountain Range as the watershed between the north and south Caucasus became significant. During the second half of the XIX and early XX centuries, Tiflis capital of Georgia became the Russian administrative, cultural and scientific capital of the Caucasus, and Baku capital of Azerbaijan the economic centre, with no rôle for Dagestan.

In the post-Soviet period there has been an increasing confusion and debate about national-ethnic identities, that is arguably linked to increasing political support for populist leaders. In contrast the following presents an inclusive approach to deal with the multi-ethnic Caucasus where nation-state-ism is often questionable while the need to preserve ethnic identity is a given.

The current ethnic situation in the Caucasus cannot be characterized as positive for two significant reasons. There are first the foreign policy consequences of old and recent historical events that led to administrative-territorial changes. Secondly, inter-republic nation-state conflicts-of-interest, related to the requirements of various ethnic groups in relation to their social status, linguistic and cultural needs. In the Caucasus, it was not acceptable both to point the finger at the nationality of a person, and to restrict his or her rights to follow his/her ethnic traditions.

The history of the Caucasus from 1900 was shaped by development of new types and forms of art and culture, through the new generations of Russian-educated ethnic intelligentsia. However, the foundations of the national culture were actually formed by the large number of local Caucasian written languages, unintelligible to virtually all Russians. The autochthonous languages included those which used

DOI: 10.4324/9781003388579-16

128   *Dagestan – History, Culture, Identity*

Arabic transliteration, and so were part of the Arab-Muslim transnational cultural tradition (chapters 13 and 14).

During the Soviet period radical changes were imposed on socio-cultural life. According to the communist ideologists, human development would naturally lead to the fact that "the nation will be convinced in practice of the advantages of a common language over national languages." The 'supreme values of humanity', a condition of human progress, were not derived from the peoples with their traditional cultures and writings, but from the class struggle for a new life.

In Dagestan's cultural sphere this struggle featured the destruction of centuries-old manuscripts, as well as everything else written in Arabic script. A complementary part of this policy was the elimination of traditional Arab-Muslim education and Muslim scholars (religious and language teachers in madrasahs). Arabic was declared to be a tool of the exploiters and a means of oppression and enslavement of the working masses. Otherwise, if more coincidental, perhaps it must be admitted that from 1920 to 1960 unique conditions were created for the extension of social and cultural functions of local languages, for raising the prestige of these languages, and for raising the level of national artistic consciousness. This compared well with the fate of minority languages elsewhere in the world.

Since the 1960s the trend toward diminishing the everyday social functions of the native languages in contrast to the national Russian lingua franca became more and more obvious. The rôle of the national languages in the transmission of ethnic cultures, in the appreciation of national-linguistic forms of folklore and traditional arts were gradually reduced. At the same time there was a decline in the teaching of native languages and literature. The omission of the local ethnic language from the education syllabus, which started in the 1970s, was the main cause of cultural stagnation and the gradual displacement of the national languages from functional life outside the family. In contrast to this reality, scientific and journalistic literature propagandized the aspiration towards full development of national languages and cultures over the generations.

The extinction of national differences also implied the process of transforming "one of the most advanced international languages . . . into a single world language" [1]. As Rasul Gamzatov, the national poet and leader of 'the Dagestan and Caucasus idea' mused "For me, the languages of peoples are like stars in the sky. I would not want all the stars to merge into one huge, half-sky star. That is the Sun. But let the stars shine too. Let each person have their own star" [2].

In the conviction of orthodox Marxist-Leninists, since the history worthy of humanity began with the establishment of Soviet power in 1917, any real or mythical obstacle on the 'main road of human history', that is, on the road to communism, was to be overcome, destroyed and eradicated. Alternative thoughts about the prospects for the development of peoples and cultures were regarded as anti-Soviet, and dissent as dissidence. Yet in Soviet society there were people who dared to talk about the inhuman essence of the idea of the merging of nations. For example,

Pre-Soviet and contemporary cultures 129

the Georgian philosopher and poet Zurab Kakabadze (d.1982) – posthumously published – wrote: "The awakening of national consciousness observed throughout the world today indicates that the process of merging nations is contra-indicated to human nature, because a person wants to be, first of all, but to be is to be something definite, i.e. to have your own individual person . . . If humanity has a future, then in the future it will certainly abandon this idea of merging and levelling . . . the true and perfect being of humanity is not in indifferent uniformity, but in the unity of individually peculiar nations" [3].

The CPSU did not declare assimilatory attitudes in national policy, but confusingly adhered to the idea of progressive natural assimilation. The attitude to the growth of ethnic (national) self-consciousness was twofold. On the one hand, it was acknowledged as the achievement of the national policy of the CPSU, which was concerned with the development of the material and spiritual culture of nations and nationalities, and on the other, it threatened to undermine the larger transnational union.

The reduction of the basic characteristics of an ethnos (for example, language, customs, traditional etiquette) does not necessarily lead to a loss of ethnicity or a decline in popular morality. As noted by leading researchers [3–6] ethnic consciousness consists of compensating functions, as expressed in ethnic actions and campaigning. This encourages social self-affirmation and achievement of success in business, education, science, artistic creation, public service, or sports.

Today in Dagestan, cultural identity with one's people, knowledge of one's mother tongue or adherence to traditional ethics, generally has far less value than the demonstration of material well-being, ostentatious piety or loud mantras of concern about the 'fate of the people.'

Sometimes deviations from popular traditions are presented by 'socially advanced' or materially prosperous sections of the population as a kind of standard of behaviour which (consciously or unknowingly) the rest of the inhabitants are pressured to aspire to.

In political life, ethnicity is often clothed in the form of the 'will of the people', although the spokesmen usually come from socially and/or institutionally organized groups with power and wealth, in a position to use the intellectual, creative resource of the personnel serving them. In public life, ethnicity can be actualized in both creative and destructive ways.

The media, social media (chapter 18), fiction, movies, direct communication, rumours, anecdotes, sarcastic humour, and pseudo-scientific writings are often mixed up in the creation of ethnic stereotypes. These serve as a psychological mechanism for the regulation of human behaviour and inter-ethnic relations, identifying persons who are 'not their own' or 'the other'.

But ethnic prejudices and stereotypes are formed not only on the basis of rumours or distorted images of peoples. A Dagestani individual objectifies himself and his

130 *Dagestan – History, Culture, Identity*

life purpose in joint activities and communicating with other people. And in this sense, the reputation of a particular nationality, its prestige in the eyes of other nations is created by people belonging to it.

Increasing use of the latest electronic media keeps the population in 'tense awareness' of current affairs in the country, magnifying small incidents at the risk of inter-ethnic relations.

Caucasians, for example, in recent years have a much more complete picture than before the web, not only of how they themselves relate to individuals of certain nationalities, but also about how they are treated in various cities and regions of the country.

The objectivity which foreign researches can bring to the study of ethnicity and identity is nevertheless often compromised by their prioritisation, albeit unconscious, of their own ethnic, national and religious affiliations. In this regard, they cannot claim objectivity or sociological accuracy of their description of the 'national spirit'.

To paraphrase Rasul Gamzatov, one can say that every Caucasian has his own Caucasus. The description of Caucasian identity in the form of some generalized, identical image of Caucasian peoples is apparently both a labyrinthine task, and a useless one. The very concept of 'Caucasian identity' contains the ideas of unity, coexistence, and community, which form the foundation of its fundamental reality and manifests itself in real social practices, expressed in worthy deeds and actions of decent people who feel as Caucasians.

The fact that Caucasians are one people with many languages, but with a similar national character, clothing, folklore, dances, and traditions, which can be attested by any traveller in the region, was confirmed by Prof. Abaev I. Vasilij the Soviet and Russian philologist, linguist, and cultural historian of the Caucasus: "With all the impenetrable multilingualism, in the Caucasus, there was a single essentially cultural world" [7].

Caucasians are interesting as creators and subjects of history, and not just because they have ethnic fragmentation, ethnographic quirks and the ability to establish the prominent role of their fellow tribesmen in the world-historical process.

Caucasian identity is not a modern neologism, but an historical reality, testified by Leontij Mroveli, Georgian historian of the XI century, Bishop, one of the compilers of *Kartlis Tskhovreba* (Life of Georgia, ancient Georgian chronicles, gathered into a single book between the XII and XIV centuries) in his wonderful story about the forefather of the Caucasian peoples namely Targamos, the grandson of Yafet, and great grandson of Noah [8].

Caucasian identity is unthinkable without the understanding that the Caucasus does not accept the division of peoples into 'rulers' and 'subordinates'. Nor do they accept the distinction between 'courageous' and 'not courageous' as signifying good versus bad.

The traditional identity of the cultures of the peoples of the Caucasus is based on the similarity of moral values, and domestic and gender stereotypes, based on a Caucasian perception of human dignity. Otherwise, Caucasian identity is just a myth.

References

[1] Hanazarov K. The rapprochement of nations and national languages in the USSR. 1963. p225.
[2] Gamzatov Rasul. My Dagestan. 1985. p36.
[3] Kakabadze Z. The problem of human existence. 1985. p245.
[4] Bgazhnokov B. The foundations of humanistic ethnology. 2003.
[5] Guboglo M. Identification of identity. Ethno-Sociological Essays. 2003.
[6] Tishkov V. Ethnology and politics. 2001.
[7] Abaev V. Ossetian language and folklore. 1949. p89.
[8] Mroveli L. Ed. by Metreveli Roin Life of Georgian kings. History of Georgia. 2008. p14.

17 New traditions in urban weddings

Dagestan's population of 3.1 million contains 30 indigenous peoples living in over 700 villages and 10 cities: urban population is just under 45%.

Approximate populations of the cities:

Makhachkala, capital,	750,000 [1]
Khasavyurt	140,000
ancient Derbent	123,000
Kaspiysk	113,000
Buynaksk	64,000
Izberbash	58,000
Kizlyar	49,000
Kizilyurt	47,000
Dagestanskiye Ogni	29,000
and Yuzhno-Sukhokumsk	11,000

Each city has a different polyethnic configuration [2].

Until the 1970s city weddings were celebrated by only urban-dwelling Russians, Armenians, Jews, Azeris and Kumyks, while the rest married in their home villages, even if the newly-weds would then leave the village for the city. Many of the rural young, both sons and daughters, headed for the cities anyway seeking further education and then work, and the village wedding has virtually disappeared. Since the 1990s villagers have come to town for weddings, having blessed their children leaving the village. City-dwellers stay attached to their jamaat (rural community) and observe family customs back in their community, celebrating weddings, funerals, and *Eid al-Adha*.

The Caspian lowlands, from the Azerbaijan border in the south to the northern Stavropol Territory *krai* and the Republic of Kalmykia, are polyethnic and mixed ethnic. Thus, modern urban weddings are increasingly based on confabulated rural models.

Conversely the new rural wedding halls show the cities' influence on the village.

In Dagestan marriage is understood only as a heterosexual alliance, between a couple of marriageable age, for their common life and procreation, observing tradition, religious and state (secular) law.

DOI: 10.4324/9781003388579-17

New traditions in urban weddings   133

Traditional marriage was by 'conspiracy' or mutual consent of the parties. Marriage by abduction was rare and punishable by death. Marriageable age for a girl was 15–16 years old and 17–18 for a boy, but pronounced signs of puberty were sufficient. Parents tried to marry off their son quickly if he showed signs of becoming a rampant hooligan or debauched. Forced marriage of a youth was justified if he was not interested in girls because of his age or physical immaturity. Daughters rarely married earlier but the parents wanted her married before she was 20–22 years old. Dagestanis viewed celibacy with regret, as well as childless marriages.

Prior to official matchmaking, an uncle or other relative, and then the parents, found out from the potential groom which of the suitable girls he liked. Selecting new family relations required careful consideration. The choice depended on her piety, sweet temper, *lamus* (shyness), beauty, neatness, health, diligence; the nature of her mother and the reputation and wealth of her parents.

Piety was associated with obedience; sweet temper with peaceful family relationships; diligence with material well-being; and beauty and health with good, strong offspring. If her mother was grumpy, gossiped, involved in scandals, greedy, deceitful, or thievish it was hard to find someone who wanted such a vicious woman as his mother-in-law. It was believed, with some justification, that her shortcomings were somehow transmitted to the daughter, who would take after her.

The parents' initiative in the choice of a bride implies that they already have a dossier on her, which is not difficult to do in both rural and urban Dagestan where villagers frequently visit the cities for shopping or other regular business. Part of the research is to confirm that ideally her mother has high morals, is hard-working and a hospitable mistress of the home, implying that her daughter is the same, as in the popular proverb "a rose will never blossom from nettles."

The last word rested with the parents; the bride's family valued the groom's ancestry, courage, masculinity, honesty, diligence and, not least, health and constitution. The parents were supposed to take the girl's wishes into account, but any expression of a positive desire was thought shameless. Girls had to limit themselves to what they were allowed to refuse.

Then there was collusion; first between close relatives of the bride and groom, and then between their parents. A positive answer to the request of a daughter's marriage was subject to delay. During matchmaking gifts were given to the future bride and 'response' gifts to the future bridegroom; any violation of the collusion had serious consequences, in addition to bad feelings between those who had proposed the match. The ceremony of matchmaking was prepared in advance and the formulaic sponsors avoided haggling. On a Friday evening, the groom's matchmakers, including his uncle, aunt, sister, mother and an elderly respected paternal relatives visited the bride's parents' house, but only when they knew the expected answer, the day of the planned wedding and much more. The men mainly discussed funding the wedding and further support for the couple. In parallel conversations, his relatives learned which cow and which calf the bride would receive from the

134   *Dagestan – History, Culture, Identity*

groom's mother, considered as preliminary gifts of the bridegroom's side. Most of the bride's gifts were exhibited at the departure ceremony from the bride's house and solemnly brought to the groom's house before the wedding. Sharia (Islamic legal) marriage took place only with the consent of the couple – although sometimes it appeared that the girl did not have an equal say – and was concluded the day before or on the day of the wedding.

When the boy proposed, the girl especially was restrained from showing her true desire for the match. The tradition was that she had to reply to the proposal with the formula that she must follow her parents' decision. Boys were only slightly less restrained about showing any enthusiasm. For the future couple, a walk in the park, sitting in cafés or European-style dates were all prohibited. To avoid unnecessary rumours and disappointments the potential partner must promptly pass on the parents' intentions either personally or via a close relative.

Nowadays the girl's prospects are enhanced if her brothers and sisters are respected and have well-organized lives. It is preferable if the bride's family is financially secure, but less important if the groom's family is comfortable.

The current requirements imposed on the bride and groom depend on their upbringing. For the daughter of wealthy people, the groom had to be socially acceptable, and that he fitted in materially, that is, he was successful in his own or the family business, and knew how to make money, so that he was able to maintain an apartment, car, and an annual vacation abroad. A highly-educated groom with remunerative public employment and prospects of career growth was also acceptable. In contrast, for average-income families the groom was expected to provide an apartment and have a trade such as a builder, tiler or plumber to service the local construction boom where good master tradesmen earn well.

While these traditional forms are still usually followed, urban youth increasingly disregards the traditional norms about what is allowed or forbidden. Apart from the pressures of urban life the majority of the young are simply ignorant of their ethnic traditions. Many thought that the city life involved dressing better, receiving an 'allowance', learning to get a diploma or degree, a car, and to teach them to 'take everything from life'.

Since the 2000s attitudes towards the previous compulsory requirements for a groom have changed. He may have a higher education, but family connections do not guarantee public employment, as before. Higher education, though desirable, is not necessary; it is more important that the groom is able and eager to earn money, and keep himself. In many families, as in the past, the groom is also required to be religious and have no bad habits. However, there are difficulties in assembling a complete dossier in an anonymous urban setting. The widespread erosion of traditional moral foundations of the marriage initiative opens the door to base interests. An adventurer might desire to marry a rich bride to usurp her family's property, borrow from them on the pretext of providing a dwelling for the young family, fully intending to leave her. Parents and relatives are extremely cautious for their

New traditions in urban weddings 135

daughters' futures, knowing of women ruined by marriage to religious extremists, drug addicts, drug or sex traffickers. They try to root out any information, more easily concealed in city life, about drug addiction, contagious diseases, mental state, or extremism, to protect their children.

In recent years, wealthy young men are looking for brides who, after marriage, will wear *hijab* and pray. There is little surprise when, after the wedding, a girl who looked European yesterday, comes to work in a long dress with sleeves covering her wrists, and a kerchief tied so that she covers not only her neck and head, but also the forehead and part of the chin. Similar changes are expected from brides even in very wealthy and high status families.

If he has not met her, the hopeful groom researches his bride through friends, neighbours, fellow workers or at her place of study, before dispatching his matchmakers. With the help of friends he sometimes even arranges a moral audit that could be gleaned from conversations with girlfriends especially if one is the sister of one of the groom's friends. If parents do not know each other, fellow villagers will find out the other family's pedigree, as was customary and is preferred, and still important for many families.

After completing his inquiries the man tries to get acquainted with the girl to gain her consent to proceed, which is difficult unless an 'accidental' meeting is arranged by her friends or relatives, so that he can speak to her about his intentions. The main thing is to find 'common ground' – a degree of mutual understanding and agreement after which one of the close relatives of the bride (most often an aunt, usually from the mother's side) visits the girl's parents with customary gifts of good tea and sweets. Her job is to assess their attitude to the possible union and to see the living conditions for the bride after the wedding, the sources of income of the groom's family and the groom himself. But increasingly everything is secondary if the girl is smart and beautiful and the more so if the boy is in love with her.

If the girl's family are positive, they agree to think it over and discuss the proposal with relatives. Shortly after, the girl's family also makes inquiries about the groom; even if they know the family, they need to be sure. Inquiries include both the groom and his whole family and if a father or uncle's bad behaviour would be a bar to being worthy parents-in-law. It is better to be safe than to learn too late about any skeletons in the cupboard of the future son-in-law, such as bad habits, an intractable nature, or irregularity of work with frequent changes.

In cities people do not differentiate the engagement from matchmaking, which if successful is considered an engagement, and few associate the day of presenting gifts with the betrothal. The pre-wedding script is a) 'they took a word' (gave their word), that is, negotiations concluded positively; b) they 'got stuck', that is, parents of the bride and close relatives of the groom became close to the bride's family; and c) 'carried the suitcase', that is, gifts for the bride. Only women participate in 'showing the suitcase', where it would be unworthy of a man to exhibit interest or be present. The showing marks the final consent of the bride's parents.

136 Dagestan – History, Culture, Identity

Nowadays thanks to social networks (chapter 18), the boy and girl can discuss the decision taken by their parents, without meeting. If the message is positive he can get his supporters to make a preliminary visit to her parents, bringing only sweets, fruit, and if the families do not adhere to religious traditions, two bottles of cognac or Scotch whisky.

At this meeting, where the bride's family have been pre-warned about the questions, the terms of the official matchmaking are proposed. Since the bride's family is hosting the party and is committed to significant expenditure, they need to know the number of groom's guests and the quality of gifts. Since about 2013, many well-off families prefer to conduct matchmaking in a café or restaurant (which costs more, but is less trouble), and so they choose a suitable place. Deciding the wedding date is just a practical matter of allowing for necessary preparations and ensuring the availability of all involved.

Since gifts should be prepared according to the degree of kinship, they also agree to exchange lists of extended family members and close friends who wish to take part in the matchmaking. Men from the groom's side are supposed to be given a beautifully packaged shirt as a present. Until recently women were given a fashionable scarf or today, beautifully wrapped rugs, tablecloths or bed linens.

Importantly it is necessary to delay the groom giving gifts to the bride on the day of matchmaking, to keep them for later, but to give her a family heirloom diamond ring. Recently girls choose new diamond rings and the price is limited by their parents. In return the bride gives the groom a silver ring, because Islam forbids a man to wear gold.

The ring is presented in an envelope with a beautiful bow, and her parents are given a similar envelope with, as agreed, money for buying a mink coat or a sheepskin coat, several pairs of shoes, clothes, linens and accessories. Naturally, the amount of money and the quality of the clothes depend on the wealth of the groom and the social status of his parents, since it is her side that dictates the conditions. This ranges from 100,000 to 300,000 thousand roubles (~1,500 to 4,500 euros, in February 2018). Usual gifts for the parents and extended family of the groom are expensive shirts (for the father, grandfather, brothers), a fashionable expensive scarf usually showing an international logo, a dress, a suit, or their money equivalent (for the mother), expensive scarves (for grandmothers and sisters), and not very expensive scarves for the aunts.

In addition, the groom's party must prepare at least three large trays with traditional sweets such as walnut halva, flour and noodle halva with almonds or hazelnuts. The trays are wrapped in transparent wrapping, usually with red bows on top. Matchmaking sweets include three or more different pies in one beautifully packaged box, a huge basket with exotic fruits, and another with beautiful boxes of tea, coffee and sweets. If alcohol is permitted in the bride's family, a box of champagne and good vodka will be among the presents. At the appointed hour, an elegant procession drives up to the house or café and the groom and his sisters or supporters bring in all the sweets and gifts and bouquets of flowers. All the men in the procession have agreed their contribution to the bride, usually less than 3,000 roubles each. Everyone gives money to the mother of the bride, either in person or handed to the mother's female relatives in charge of collecting, in envelopes with a list of contributors.

The matchmaking ceremony begins with the presentation of the groom, his parents and his guests, close friends and senior representatives. Then the bride's side presents her family. When the bride is presented, the groom comes up and puts the ring on her finger. Sometimes in observance of traditions, the groom does not attend this ceremony, and on his behalf the groom's ring is worn by his paternal uncle. During the feast, people get acquainted, and the young have fun. In Dagestan, no such feast can be prepared without fried chicken, *dolma* (minced meat wrapped in vine leaves), *khinkal* (flour dumplings eaten as the staple meal throughout Dagestan, flavoured or plain, of different shapes and sizes depending on ethnicity – Avars have the largest, a four-inch long solid cylinder, down to babies' little-finger-size in Archi) and kebabs, although there is no prescribed list of ritual dishes. If the matchmaking is in a café or restaurant, it is now fashionable to order meat or chicken cooked according to French or Arab recipes. International dining trends include winter salads with olive oil, beet salad with prunes, crab, and in summer 'Caesar' or 'Greek' salads, all traditionally garnished with sliced raw vegetables and copious fresh greens.

The civil registration of the marriage, introduced during the Soviet period, can be carried out as soon as the wedding date is fixed; many couples prefer to do this before the wedding itself, so as to not overload the busy day. Having exchanged gifts, the relatives go their separate ways. The bride and groom are now allowed to see each other, go to the cinema, café and other public places. In most cases the interval between matchmaking and the wedding is reduced to a minimum; in rare cases it might be a year but most often it is two to three months. The longer the interval the greater the expense, for on every holiday it is expected to exchange gifts with the bride and her parents.

Even before choosing the date, the style of the wedding, religious or secular, depending on the families will have been determined. The venue for the day is chosen accordingly. The New Millennium banquet hall is almost a palace complex, designed for weddings, concerts and other events. All the rooms are decorated in European or Oriental styles. There is virtually nothing Dagestani in the design or names of these venues. The most prestigious, popular and expensive are designed for 850 and more people, costing from 150,000 to 200,000 roubles a day. Slightly more modest banquet halls for 500–650 rent for 90,000 to 120,000 roubles a day. Rental includes the provision of crockery, and in good rooms they are expensive and beautiful. For breakages in the so-called post-war battle of utensils, the agreed advance is 7,000 to 10,000 roubles.

Other beautiful venues have been created for those wishing something less secular. Religious weddings, 'wedding-*mawlid*', ban alcohol and the food must be cooked by Muslim chefs observing religious canons and of course serving halal food – even if the menu is the same otherwise. There are no traditional dances, but they listen to the preaching of an alim and sing hymns. Women, including the bride and girls over seven, must cover their hair, arms to the wrist and feet to the ankle. In addition, men must be served by waiters, and women by waitresses. Wedding preparations of the bride and groom are different. Nowadays Dagestani grooms have adopted the European tradition of a bachelor party or stag-night in cafés or restaurants. In addition, they must buy their wedding dress and shoes, which by tradition, was paid for by the bride's parents.

Figure 17.1 Inside a wedding banquet hall

The bride, on the other hand, needs to buy clothes for her 'suitcase', paid for by the groom's parents. In addition, they must buy the dowry of bedroom, kitchen, and living room furniture and a chest of drawers and everything else for the groom's new apartment or house. Sometimes the more modest groom's parents buy bedroom furniture or hall furniture with a carpet, or kitchen furniture and a TV. The dowry may include bedding, a washing machine with powder, crockery, kitchen appliances, chandeliers and a sewing machine, even needles and thread.

To help with the expense, most Dagestani women tastefully, modestly and seriously assembled their daughters' dowry from the first years of their own marriage, as it used to be. The cultural stereotypes of Dagestani women would indicate that all this is unnecessary excess. Indeed, why give 100-year-old soap, out-of-fashion women's handkerchiefs or a set of slippers? But a more careful look reveals that it is a French soap from tsarist times, kept in grandmother's *sunduk* (chest); that the shawls are Persian silk, bought by their grandfather's great-grandmother's bride in Tabriz; that the very elegant slippers are a present from an aunt in Milan. Soap and handkerchiefs are heirlooms to be cherished, and the slippers can come in handy for an unexpected visit of several guests.

As soon as the bride and her mother finish buying clothes for the suitcase, they pass it to the groom's parents and wait for their invitation to display the wardrobe. A week before the wedding, usually on Thursday or Friday, girlfriends of the bride and two or three close female relatives are summoned; and the groom. Everyone surrounds the suitcase for the showing. At the same time the groomsmen's gifts are shown – usually gold or an envelope with money. In the past, the bride's status in her new family was determined by the number of gold items she brought with her. Today, it is the amount of money given for matchmaking and

New traditions in urban weddings   139

the wedding ceremony. After the showing of gifts, the bride is offered exquisite dishes. Next, several relatives of the bride, young and old, deliver her dowry to the groom's house on a truck-transporter, where they are met by the groom's relatives. The furniture and household appliances have already been sent to the groom and now the carpets, crockery and linen arrive. All is neatly arranged, the apartment is put in order and the wedding-bed made. After tea-drinking, all the girls and women who came with the dowry are presented with small kerchiefs or scarves.

The wedding preparations can be put in train as soon as the hall is rented; but there is always more to be done, by both families, in the final days beforehand. In recent years wedding organizers have appeared with their ideas of how things should be done. With their involvement the cost is increased by another 200,000 to 300,000 roubles, which not everyone can afford.

The bride visits several wedding salons to choose her wedding dress and accessories, which might cost 20,000 to 150,000 roubles to rent, depending on its label and quality. The bride must return the dress within five days.

On the morning of her great day, a specialist hairdresser and a wedding make-up artist go to her house with their equipment. Hairstyling costs 1,500 to 2,500 roubles and maquillage from 1,200 to 2,500 roubles.

Every day wedding menus become more luxurious, and are served by more and more waiters. The popular glossy magazine for newlyweds *Wedding Legend* under its motto "With the help of our magazine, your wedding will be legendary!" published since 2009, carries ads for all these specialists. Another part of the expanding market is the twice-weekly local television half-hour program *Wedding Planner*.

Most people use both the help of relatives and private services, but the latter are expensive, more and more so with the trend or competition to larger and fancier affairs. The head chef oversees his team of cooks and a head-woman her team of waitresses. The cooks are contracted two to three months in advance, to fit into their tight schedules. Famous wedding chefs are booked up like hot cakes, for the whole of Dagestan competes for them. The chef is paid 35–50 roubles per guest. The cook and his assistants charge separately.

The number of waiters depends on the number of guests; according to banquet convention, one waiter should serve from 25 to 30 people. Each waiter is paid from 1,200 to 1,500 roubles, and the head-waiter from 1,500 to 2,000 roubles. All the brigade should be given new kitchen towels, and on the eve of the wedding, the chef with his two assistants are given tea, coffee and sweets. The number and set of prepared food dishes is determined by the chef, depending on the number of guests and the pre-negotiated menu of the hosts. The chef's raw ingredients are ordered by phone from butchers, fishmongers, and green grocers. The cost of washers-up and cleaners is included in the rent, but detergent must be provided.

140 *Dagestan – History, Culture, Identity*

It takes two hours to lay a table with flowers and the specialist decorators are paid 2,000 to 3,000 roubles. In the centre of the wedding table, there is a great white tiered marzipan cake, costing 10,000 to 20,000 roubles. The bride's parents pay for the expensive floral decoration of the couple's limousine, hired by the groom from 35,000 roubles a day. A gold-plated wedding Mercedes is available for 50,000 roubles and beautiful carriages drawn by three horses have recently appeared. Some seven years ago the bride's friends would decorate it with colourful ribbons, artificial flowers and silk handkerchiefs. The length of the wedding cavalcade depends on how many friends and relatives with presentable cars come to an agreement.

On the wedding day, the bride and her friends arrange a video/photo session as they leave her house, costing from 1,000 roubles per hour. Photo albums with individual covers cost from 2,500 roubles. A professional video of all that happens in the banquet hall, the heaving wedding tables, welcoming each guest, the wedding itself, the bridegroom's farewell leaving the house for his bride, the cortege, and the bride's departure from her house starts at 8,000 roubles.

The waiters arrive at seven in the morning, set the tables and begin serving. From noon (at the bride's house) and from 2:00 pm (at the groom's house) visitors start to gather. The exception is Derbent evening weddings starting about 6:00 pm, a surviving tradition from the time when the main population were Mountain Jews and Azeris.

By 11 in the morning, the groom accompanied by an adult relative-mentor and friends arrives for the bride. If they do not need to go to the registry office, he takes the bride with her female *yengue* 'big friend' and her girlfriends. Before leaving the bride's house the mother gives her a vase or porcelain jug filled with sweets or sugar, for luck, which is kept prominently but untouched for a year. As soon as the wedding procession departs, led by the bride and groom's car, the customary bucket of water is thrown after them, so that the bride will not return home, that is, be divorced. The procession circles the city, stopping for the photo session, which lasts about an hour, and then to the banquet hall, where the wedding begins. The *tamada* (toastmaster, who charges 15,000 to 30,000 roubles) announces the arrival of the bride and groom. All stand and they are welcomed with songs and dances. The groom is seated at the head table and the wedding begins, led by the toastmaster. If he is a relative or a fellow villager his services are paid with a gift, not money. Several invited people give speeches.

At the appointed time, the tables are revealed for the guests to marvel at the perfectly prepared foods and even rare Kamchatka caviar in small short pastry vol-au-vents, complemented by fresh fruit juices and beautiful bottles of quality non-alcoholic and alcoholic drinks (if permitted).

When the guests are seated, they start serving hot dishes. In addition to the obligatory national dishes such as *chudu* (a kind of pizza) and *kurze* (a dumpling filled with meat or cottage cheese), khinkal from corn and wheat flour with dried sausage,

New traditions in urban weddings   141

dried or fresh lamb and beef, Caucasian dolma stuffed with minced Bulgarian pepper; and eggplant stuffed by minced meat, kebab, *manti* (the Kazakh version of kurze), all types of shish kebab, and sweet *pilaf* (sweet rice with raisins or chicken). European cuisine features 'French meat' (grilled meat with potatoes, cheese, tomatoes, mushrooms, onions, garlic, mayonnaise, olive oil, pepper, spices, and herbs all served together *à la Française*) and pancakes with meat, chicken medallions in foil, chicken in a nut crust, sturgeon in batter, and *tsarskii losos* (tsar-style salmon). Waiters periodically bring trays with tea.

Surprisingly the traditional division of males and females has survived in the banquet halls – male relatives on the right, women on the left. The only tables where men and women sit together are for non-family work colleagues, neighbours, family friends, or classmates.

Traditional live wedding music played on the zurna, *agach-komuz* (three-stringed fretted lute), *chungur* (four-stringed, plucked), *chagana* (four-stringed, bowed) and clarinet by well-paid senior musicians (chapter 27) has been expanded to, or replaced by younger generation pop and well-known Soviet-period songs, dividing the guests into two age groups, unlike traditional weddings. The climax is a well-known celebrity singer loudly performing solo his or her best-known song amplified through powerful speakers. The singer's ethnicity does not matter, but they must know how to light up the wedding. Singers who accompany dance tunes are preferred. Though most singers sing to their own DVDs, nevertheless they still charge 15,000 roubles an hour.

It has also become popular to invite dance groups in national costumes, especially to greet the bride and groom as they enter the hall. During the early 2000s belly dancers performed at weddings, but they went out of fashion. Parents invite all relatives, including the elderly, however the loud wedding entertainment is for the young so senior relatives, normally respected, are marginalized as passive observers or ignored.

Collective dances are the rule. The bride and groom watch the dancing until the end. When the bridegroom invites his bride to dance, his friends surround them and throw money at her. As soon as the bride and groom dance, everyone understands that they are going to the private part of the wedding at the groom's house. One of her girlfriends collects the money and gives it to the woman behind the table, who puts it in a bag for the bride. Next, the tamada invites all the groom's close male and politely invites the bride to start the next part of the dancing on her own. In the villages she had a decorated 'stick of love' occasionally in the form of a *knut* (whip) or even a kebab which she passed on to a male relative to dance, which he then gave to his chosen woman and so on. Sometimes the bride picks all the males to dance one by one.

The bride's wedding obligations last a maximum of three hours and the bridegroom's wedding duties go on longer. The bride, her friends and her relatives leave the groom with his friends, going to the threshold of another room, where her mother-in-law meets her with a cup of honey so her words will always be sweet. The bride's closest friend, the groom's friend and the female mentor escort the bride and groom to a table with food from the wedding set by two or three close relatives, as they have not eaten at the banquet. The bride and groom change out of their wedding finery into their home clothes, drink tea and chat with friends, who soon leave. The bride and groom are left alone for their wedding night.

Early next morning the bridegroom must meet the female mentor, who will divine his mood. If he is satisfied, she should inform the bride's mother for which she receives a gift, usually a good scarf. No one makes a traditional 'show' of the sheets confirming the bride's chastity, although some modern young Dagestan men still take it seriously. If she honestly confesses, the bride can conceal her perceived sin for up to six months or a year so as not to disgrace her parents' status, and then be divorced.

The day following the wedding the First Visit to the bride's parents takes place, when her mother gives her an expensive present, followed by a return visit to the groom's relatives. Visits to relatives can be postponed for many months, until their often exhausted hosts can cope with their symbolic visit representing joining the family with formal greetings and seating arrangements.

In a gradual erosion of traditions urban couples ignore several post-wedding rituals such as walking the path to the village spring, the introduction to the household or respecting the hearth.

City weddings have become an expensive and profitable business involving numerous wedding halls and salons, cooks and waiters, musicians, singers, dancers, photographers, video cameramen, hairdressers and toastmasters. The host family, usually of the bride, have to bear most of the costs of the wedding in advance; if they can't afford this, they can borrow funds from a close relative or bank for a few days. They hope that guests will pay for the wedding: signed envelopes are dropped into an ornate urn in the banquet hall, guarded by two or three women. Ordinary guests contribute 1,000 to 2,000 roubles, though depending on kinship, larger contributions can reach 30,000. The urn is handed over to the hosts at the end of the wedding.

Weddings roughly pay for themselves in a round-robin, because the parent-hosts will go to weddings of all their guests, and make similar contributions. Each contribute to their abilities above a lower limit, in an effective traditional social mechanism.

The wisdom of such a risky 'investment' has been debated in recent post-Soviet decades promoted by the magazines and TV shows.

Other issues are reducing expenses and removing alcohol from wedding tables; or what to count as a dowry or wedding gifts. The new wedding-mawlids cause further division between religious and secular weddings, but both forget their ethnic customs and traditions, eroded by modern culture and behaviour.

As well as a claim to the new couple's social status, the extravagant wedding is a sort of social hostage, to avoid reproach or the suggestion that they might lack confidence. Some traditions which provide a positive life experience over the generations are used in modern urban wedding ritual, but other new habits are problematic. Modern weddings are increasingly materialistic. Increasing materialism is good in so far as it indicates general growth in prosperity, but is corrosive in replacing traditional values with other competitive attitudes.

Almost no old wedding ritual songs are heard from the beautiful repertoire. Older people recall that rural weddings were much more interesting, that the entertainment was richer and brighter with jesters, jokes and singing competitions; they believe that the rejection of wedding traditions is not justified. Some thirty years ago, when city residents celebrated weddings in the yards outside their apartment blocks, there were special ushers, often brandishing a knut, who respectfully greeted every guest, and personally took them to their table. Great attention was paid to keeping the rules of each part of the wedding ritual. Modern urban weddings have dropped the colourful theatrical folklore and ritual that survived the Soviet repressions (chapter 11) and little remains.

The modern Dagestani marriage is recorded in a civil ceremony and the wedding is optional. By tradition the wedding enshrines the exuberance of youth and the joy of parents, relatives and friends, as symbol of the unity of generations and the continuation of life. New forms are evolving, even while older customs are lost. The ethnographer hopes to record enough of the latter to allow revival if they should seem, with hindsight, better after all.

References

[1] Dagestan permanent population. Dagestan Statistics. Rosstat. 1 January 2017.
[2] Ibragimov M.R.A. and Magomedkhanov M.M. Ethnographic aspects of the formation of the urban population of Dagestan (second half XIX- beginning XX centuries). St Petersburg University Messenger. History Part 1. 2009. Pp247–59.

18 Social media – the XXI century

In memory of Dr Ramazan Khappoulaev (1943–2003), our friend and head of Dagestan ASSR's librar-
ies and museums who in the 1970s anticipated social media with his hugely popular TV series where he
interviewed Dagestani veterans.

Until 2003, when a mobile network was rolled out, the only methods of communication were in the hands of senior communists, the KGB or FSB – a few land-
line phones, telexes and fax machines. On our expeditions we had to check before
our arrival if we were acceptable to the party administration as some places were
unpredictably 'closed', so we stopped at a town as we approached our destination to use their official phone. Often the lines were down or people were out, so
communications were slow. The phones available for foreigners, in a few Intourist
hotels, were usually bugged or the numbers didn't work or couldn't dial out or
couldn't take calls. A red passport-sized *spavochnik* (directory) contained all the
party people's numbers; it was like gold-dust.

The new mobile network led to a relative explosion of communication and the
use of new ways to do this; it was later than elsewhere, but social media came to
Dagestan. There is little research into social media in an authoritarian republic like
Dagestan, which was largely rural but rapidly changing to urban. Social media is
also altering the meaning of 'rural'. Russia has been severely criticized for abuses
of internet freedom but Dagestanis have their own ways of coping. Videophone
(WhatsApp/Zoom/Skype) is now the norm. As soon as they were available, mothers and grandmothers, especially in mountain villages, insisted that they saw the
faces of their children when they spoke. An estimated 700,000 to 1,000,000 Dagestanis live in the Russian Federation because of their employment, outside the
north Caucasian republics which are of course also part of Russia, so many families now live apart where earlier generations lived near each other. The sense of
identity with home, otherwise eroded by distance, can be fostered by regular video
communication.

By 1961 a Russian Leonid Ivanovich Kupriyanovich increased the range of his cell
phone to 80 km. It was developed for military, political internal security and medical purposes. Early developments in mobile telephony from the 1950s were limited

DOI: 10.4324/9781003388579-18

in the USSR for Party and intelligence uses; eventually, the public gained access when in 1994 a joint venture between Moscow City Telephone Network, T-Mobile and Siemens offered Russia's first mobile phone service in Moscow.

Mobiles

The Russian public started using cell phones in a big way from about 2000. Dagestanis' adoption of the new technology took off from about 2002; today, mobile and smart phones are used throughout the country. A phone signal and data connection is available throughout almost all the mountainous region, which suggests a serious infrastructure investment in mountainous regions.

There are three providers: 'Megafon' PJSC owned by Alisher Usmanov's USM; 'Bee Line' part of Veon a Dutch-domicile international digital conglomerate; and 'DagTelecom' subsidiary of MTS owned by privately owned Sistema Venture Capital, is a Dagestani mobile communications company. The table gives comparative information in about 2020:

Name	Parent	Operating since	Subscribers, '000	Base stations	coverage, %
Megafon	USM	2002	400	100	95%
Bee Line	Veon	2003	125	112	80%
DagTelecom	Sistema Venture	2003	100	92	99%

In the competitive struggle, DagTelecom went for the lowest tariffs for network calls and the largest territory coverage, including the mountains.

Internet

In 2000 the Yandex.ru search engine was incorporated by Arkady Volozh, a Russian. By 2004, Yandex advertising sales increased to $17 million, up 1,000% in two years. It expanded exponentially into all sorts of apps from state information to news, to estate agency, gps maps and weather. Yandex Zen Dagestan online platform, an extension of Yandex to train new Dagestani content creators had a local audience of 200,419 as of mid-August 2020. As well as Russians, Dagestanis also use Vkontakte (VK/vk.com) the second largest social networking service among Russians after Yandex.

Odnoklassniki (OK) is the Russian equivalent of LinkedIn, originally an alumni network. 600,000 Dagestanis are registered with OK in their social network, half of them in Makhachkala [1, 2]. At an OK seminar in the capital on 2 June 2017 the Minister of Press and Information Rashid Akavov admitted, "if you don't deal with the Internet, then the Internet will deal with you," and hoped to control its "negative enemy attacks" – Russian state xenophobia seeing all perceived oppositionists as the enemy funded from abroad. Alexander Volodin representing OK on their first visit to Dagestan said that it was a key region for the company, since

146   *Dagestan – History, Culture, Identity*

social networks were very popular there. OK were marketing their recent techno-logical innovations. 71 million people use OK every month. It is the third largest social network in Russia after Vkontakte and the second after YouTube for watching video on social networks.

By the end of 2015, it was estimated that internet use and data subscriptions in Russia represented about 70% of the population on average, with broadband at about 55%. However this was particularly concentrated in urban areas, with some regions lagging far behind, for example Chechen Republic and Ingushetia had less than one broadband connection per 100 inhabitants. Dagestan, while not the lowest, only had two such connections [3–5].

Dagestani identity is strengthened on the web, with minority language sites, posts, blogs and chats; Muslim affairs including *Minder* dating; the existence of criticism of local government corruption, the creation of an opposition and Salafi news; family news of births weddings and deaths; traditional and Dagrock music, and rapping; art and design; farming and shepherding; car accidents and medical emergencies; and business.

Instagram has a growing niche in the digital ethnography of Dagestan. Audience involvement attracted blogs on beauty, food, family life, celebrities, and humour and information, as in this snapshot of the most-followed blogs as of 2020, together with a representative selection of others:

- Khabib Nurmagomedov (@khabib_nurmagomedov) the mixed martial arts champion has 19.7 million worldwide followers. In 2019, he became the most popular Russian citizen on Instagram and in 2020 he reached the top three most popular people in Russia (chapter 24).
- Murad Osmann (@muradosmann) has 4 million followers. The self-taught photographer and filmmaker became famous through "Follow Me To" link www.instagram.com/explore/tags/followmeto/?hl=en.
- While studying civil engineering in London, his first famous photo-image was accidental. His girlfriend was annoyed at him forever stopping to take pictures and would pull him away; this time in Spain he captured just that 'follow me' moment. It inspired his project. Murad, born in the mountains of Dagestan, is now settled in Moscow. Last year, he ranked 58th in the list of Russian Instagram users by advertising revenue, and is always faithful to his roots.

The most popular food bloggers in Russia nowadays are frequently Dagestanis:

- Raisa Alibekova (raisa_foodblogger) has 2 million followers and now lives in Moscow with her family. Educated as a physicist and programmer, in 2016 she was awarded 'Best Food Blogger of the Year'. The family blog began with an argument with her husband. Raisa decided to post a photo of her dinner, which her husband mocked: "Who needs your cutlets?" Raisa replied that in a year she would gain 365,000 subscribers: she succeeded.

Social media – the XXI century   147

- Zarema Saypudinova (recepti_zaremka) has 1.6 million followers. She started blogging her original Russian recipes at 21 four years ago. Her USP is feedback with subscribers.

Social bloggers include:

- Elmira Ilyasova (elle_happy_mom) has 1.8 million followers. Young mothers daily watch the Dagestani-nuanced life of the mother of five, interested in how she copes, as well as looking after herself. Elya, from Derbent, now lives in Moscow.
- Malvina Magomedova (Malvina_makeup) has 1.2 million followers. One of the most celebrated make-up artists in Dagestan gained popularity before Instagram, with the wedding boom (chapter 17). After Instagram allowed monetization in 2012, the beauty blogger began to upload on that platform and in eight years welcomed her millionth follower. She posts daily makeup master classes.

Comic blogger:

- Khadzhimurad Nabiev (khadzhimurad_nabiev) Insta KVN has 581,000 followers. The popular comedian from 'Makhachkala tramps' expanded on Instagram with solo video blogs and cartoons, ridiculing everyday topical problems. Last year he starred in the film Thank you grandfather for the victory.

Dental blogger:

- Ali Bayrambekov (dr.bayrambekov) has 307,000 followers. Following the internet success of cosmetologists and stylists, Ali the dentist quickly gained 105,000 subscribers and a long waiting list, charmed by his humorous dental treatment videos.

Smaller blogs: A shepherd in step with the times:

- Abdurahman Kadinaylo – though he only has 47,000 followers, his content is unique in Russia. In England *The Lakeland farmer* has a similar nostalgic blog. The shepherd and his friend Zelimkhan, a veterinarian, began an occasional blog about life in the Kulinsky district in the uplands of southern Dagestan, to attract tourists and discuss the infrastructure needs of the village. The blog lured some travellers and reporters to Kuli. Having no internet domain does not prevent a Dagestani from creating a blog and talking about the life of the highlanders. His blog is translated from Lak into Russian. He is definitely the most popular shepherd in Russia.

From a number of useful sites:

- Dagestan online (https://dagestan.online/) – an independent but cautious information channel that publishes only reliable news from Dagestan. The account

148   *Dagestan – History, Culture, Identity*

was created from the Dagestan Online web page. The page follows the events unfolding in the republic and gives an assessment independent of local and central government's narratives of what is happening. In addition, you can find out about where to go, where to spend the weekend and what's on.

- Mikail Mikailov (mikailmikailov) has 31,000 followers and is better known as a YouTube blogger. The channel *Разворот на 300* (spread 300) @razvorot_na300 shows films about Dagestani, life and interviews with high profile people such as Salman Dadaev, appointed mayor of Makhachkala in 2019, Murad Aliskerov CEO of LaRiba Islamic Finance, and Gadzhimagomed Huseynov first deputy chairman of the government of Dagestan. Mikail's film I came, I found, I am happy is about Dagestan's recent immigrants.
- Rustam Makhmudov based in Connecticut www.linkedin.com/in/rustammahmudov got a BSc in IT from Samarkand University in 2004. He has a wide variety of IT expertise that he shares with his 10,000 followers in Dagestan from IT beginners to masters. His account was created by Programming Laboratory, a digital developer.

Ethnic culture appears in smaller sites:

- Dagestanis@DaghestanR: Group Information about the culture and traditions of the peoples of Dagestan and news of Dagestanis has 1,800 subscribers: https://web.facebook.com/DaghestanR
- Avars Facebook *Magĺarul matzĺ, tarikh wa madaniyat*: Closed group with 7,800 participants under the stylized coat of arms of the Avar Nutsals (Khans): https://web.facebook.com/groups/avarmillat
- Avars all over the world: Public group has 6,000 participants: https://web.facebook.com/groups/555864708479256

Former groups of rural communities complement the 'ethnic' pages:

- Unkrak: Public group with 6,800 participants: https://web.facebook.com/groups/1477432202536798
- МагIарул мацI, тарих ва маданият Avar highlander: Private group with 8,100 members, over 100 posts in November 2020: www.facebook.com/groups/avarmillat
- Andalal: Era, events, and people; a public group with 398 participants. https://web.facebook.com/groups/Andalal
- Archib: Closed group with 113 participants https://web.facebook.com/groups/103409116718267
- Ahvakh Edin: a religious site with 5,000 friends, https://web.facebook.com/ahvah05
- Young Ahvakh: public group with 1,400 participants, created by Patya Magomedsaygidova in March 2018, https://web.facebook.com/groups/1488593394586602. The site warns that Ahvakh ethnicity must not be considered as an excuse for ethnocentric nationalism and such content will be removed.

Or other sites feature famous personalities of any ethnic group:

- Umakhan Andiyskiy, editor of the main Avar state newspaper "Hlakikat", on Facebook since August 2017, with 5,000 friends https://web.facebook.com/profile.php?id=100021746013308

However, regional websites and Facebook pages are monopolized by regional administrations such as Gunibsky District @Gunibrayon Government Organization which has 2,275 subscribers https://web.facebook.com/Gunibrayon

The state authorities, as elsewhere in the world but especially with the Soviet legacy only a generation ago, regard this unfettered torrent of communication askance. Censorship and restrictions on free speech are a matter of shifting boundaries of acceptable behaviour and regulation. As an example of banned posting in Dagestan, on 30 April 2020 the FSB security force with local Interior ministry MIA revealed that the symbols of the banned terrorist group Islamic State had been posted on a private social network [6]. The offender confessed, repented and voluntarily deleted his illegal content. He is liable for a fine under Article 20.3 (propaganda, public demonstration of attributes or symbols of extremist organizations) of the RF Administrative Code up to 50,000 roubles, and up to five years imprisonment under Article 280 of the RF Criminal Code.

Russian regulation

The poor Russian record on human rights cases infers a similar attitude to internet abuses of privacy and right to associate online. As part of the Russian Federation the Dagestan government is obliged to comply with Russia in regulating internet infrastructure and blocking content [7]. The international NGO Human Rights Watch (HRW) report of 18 June 2020 relied on Russian state information and local informants described the growing internet isolation, control, and censorship with which the youth of Dagestan (and all Russia) must cope.

Oppressive laws leading up to the Sovereign Internet (SI)

The 2016 'Yarovaya amendments', named after its leading author of the ruling United Russia party, severely undermined the right to privacy and freedom of expression online, including the 2015 provisions for tech companies to store Russian citizens' user data on Russian territory. From July 2016 telecommunications companies were required to retain and disclose metadata for three years, and for registered internet companies to retain data for one year. From July 2018 companies were required to retain and summarily disclose the content of all communications for six months.

An associated 2017 law authorized the state digital authority *Roskomnadzor* (RKN), as agent of the FSB, to blacklist banned onliners, proxy services, including virtual private networks (VPNs) and anonymisers such as Tor, Opera or Telegram Open Network, and all circumvention of government blocking. In April 2018 RKN

150 Dagestan – History, Culture, Identity

blocked millions of Internet Protocol (IP) addresses in an effort to block Telegram, which had failed to hand over user's encryption keys to the RKN (it did not hold them!). This temporarily blocked legitimate banks, online shopping sites, and search engines services, driving Russian internet users to use VPNs (anonymizing their IP address) to bypass these disruptions. RKN reacted by blocking 50 anonymizers and VPNs. In March 2019, RKN required VPNs, anonymizers, and search engine operators to block sites on its blacklist.

The SI law, calling for all internet traffic to be routed through servers in Russia, making VPNs ineffective, allegedly protects the Russian Internet from threats to its security, integrity, and sustainability. In reality, it further expands state control over the internet. From November 2019 internet service providers (ISPs) were obliged to install "the technological means [equipment] for countering [external] threats". Deep packet inspection (DPI) technology was required, allowing the government to track, filter, and reroute internet traffic. DPI has nothing to do with the decision to actually *block* websites – it merely gives the user information about the data packet. The policy decision to block a website is taken by some committee; DPI can then help *effect* the block.

In June 2019 RKN threatened to block 9 out of 10 VPN services for failure to comply. Kaspersky Secure Connection, the only Russian service out of the 10 registered, complied. Another, Avast SecureLine, left the Russian market.

Several VPN and internet anonymizer services still operate in Russia and provide access to blocked websites. By mid-November 2019, some of the Russian ISPs had installed and tested the DPI equipment in the less populated Urals where five of eight operators reported slower internet speed, weaker signals, and local disruption of internet services. Theoretically users in the Ural test were prevented from accessing any banned content; however, Telegram messaging continued.

ISPs were obliged to store data on Russian soil, which would necessarily be subject to Russian regulation. In December 2019, public procurements of foreign data storage were banned for two years. The RKN list of firms not complying included 237 internet services, such as Yandex services, Telegram, the Mail.Ru Group, and Sberbank-online. Inexplicably, Google and Facebook services, including WhatsApp, had not yet been ordered to join.

Even with DPI technology only partially functioning, as at June 2020 some 85,246 websites have already been blocked by several state agencies.

In December 2019, Russia's consumer protection law was amended to oblige all smart phone, computer, and smart TV manufacturers operating in Russia to pre-install specified Russian apps on any devices sold in Russia. Apps include messengers, browsing services, maps, news readers, and email providers. There is a fear that surveillance apps and traffic decryption devices would be installed at the same time. Andrei Soldatov co-author of *The Red Web* (2015), the first book on the Russian internet, commented that "the idea is to make Russian customers use Russian developers' applications, which can be more easily controlled than foreign apps" [8]. The Covid pandemic caused postponement of the implementation of the amendment from July 2020 to 1 January 2021.

Continued use of VPNs and other proxies to bypass governmental blocks is a matter of further study by the RKN, who seek to reduce the permeability of their digital curtains.

The state's intention is to monitor and if necessary control access to material from outside its territory, an obvious parallel with China. The regulatory squeeze on the physical infrastructure is being tightened at all possible levels. The NGO HRW warned that "state interference with ISPs potentially affects the market and forces smaller ISPs to leave. The variety of internet actors and interconnections is what actually ensures internet security." RKN's mandate spans shutting down networks within certain areas of Russia, to cutting Russia off from the World Wide Web. During 2018 and 2019 the Russian government blocked mobile internet services during protests in Moscow and Ingushetia.

Summary

There are many positive social effects of the internet in Dagestan as exemplified by burgeoning use and the sample blogs above. However the recent laws limit space for public debate on topics the government deems divisive or threatening, such as LGBTQ rights, political freedoms, or most recently, the Covid pandemic. These developments allegedly are in breach of the International Covenant on Civil and Political Rights and the European Convention on Human Rights, to which Russia is a party. But it is unlikely that any penalties would be effective.

References

[1] Chundaev Shamil More than 600 thousand Dagestanis are registered in the Odnoklassniki social network. RIA Dagestan. 2 June 2017.

[2] Odnoklassniki social network will sign an agreement with the MFC multifunctional centre of Dagestan. AiF-Dagestan. 5 September 2017.

[3] Nikolaychuk Alexander. Digital. Report (Belarus). Russia: State of Affairs report. April 2018. https://digital.report/russia-state-of-affairs-report/.

[4] J'son & Partners Consulting. The development of the Russian corporate cloud and web services market, 2016 results. May 2017. https://json.tv/en/ict_telecom_analytics_view/the-russian-mobile-phone-and-smartphone-market-results-of-2016.

[5] Deloitte CIS Research Centre. Media Consumption in Russia. Key trends (based on 2015 Comprehensive Survey). ND 2016. https://www2.deloitte.com/by/en/pages/technology-media-and-telecommunications/articles/russian-telecom-market-2015.html.

[6] Dagestan residents fined for publishing extremist materials on social networks. RIA Dagestan. 30 April 2020.

[7] Russia: Growing internet isolation, control, censorship. Human Rights Watch. 18 June 2020.

[8] Interview with Andrei Soldatov on Digital Rights in Russia. Human Rights Watch. 19 June 2020.

19 Surviving Covid and traditional medicine

"Bob, my dear brother!" MMM emailed on 2 December 2019: "My uncle, people's doctor and chief cardiologist of Dagestan, Gamzat Javatkhanov, for cancer treatment recommended dry wine with the entrails of young heifers. I understand that you have wine, but please ask Marian to add the entrails."

His seemingly folk-based prescription for cancer patients speaks of his ancestry but is hard to reconcile with him being chief cardiologist in Dagestan. Gamzat has not been with us for ten years, but his ideas are alive and more important to us than the ideas of Lenin or Zhirinovsky.

You remember talking to him sitting in his courtyard late at night. He was fluent in Archi and Avar, Azeri, Dargin, Kumyk, Lak, Lezgin and even Mountain-Jewish languages. As you know, Avar is native in western Dagestan, and before the nationalism of the 1990s knowledge of Lezgin and Azeri was usual for the Agul, Tsakhurs, and Rutulites in the south.

In his department of cardiology (rheumatology), it was exceptional that he could talk to almost every patient as a fellow villager in his native language. It is a great compliment if the person who speaks with you in your native language is not of your ethnicity and of course if he was also the chief doctor with the title 'Narodniy vrach Dagestana' (Peoples' Doctor of Dagestan – a rare honorary title)!

Really, he was adored throughout Dagestan. He had guests almost every day. I learned a lot from Gamzat. Before serving in the army, when I was a student at the Dagestan Medical School, I indignantly complained to him about the misbehaviour of one twat/mouflon. Gamzat said: "Let him do what likes, but you and I and those for whom we are responsible will do what is necessary." During the Soviet times of stagnation that was an unusually courageous position to stick to.

Today's Dagestani doctors seem to have inherited his courage when they spoke out in the face of state-controlled under-reporting of the Covid pandemic, as their colleagues died about them.

DOI: 10.4324/9781003388579-19

COVID

Novoye Delo Dagestan joined the doctors and extracted the following admission from the state: "Due to the recognition of the leadership of the Federal Service for Supervision of Consumer Rights Protection and Human Welfare in the Russian Federation, delays in the analysis of tests for 4–5 days, information in the federal resource stopkoronavirus. rf may not be relevant. For all questions, we recommend contacting Rospotrebnadzor."

On 22 May 2020 the total deaths were officially 65. After several public letters from doctors working in hospitals asking why Putin and the Russian Federation had ignored Dagestan, Putin unexpectedly seized the initiative: Russian troops, who usually wear black balaclavas, arrived in white masks to disinfect Makhachkala the day after his speech. Competent locals reported an actual increase in help. And with this help arriving from Moscow, the local authorities began to be afraid of lying about the real human costs of the pandemic.

Comparison of the Federal Information Resource Government of Russia figures of 22 May 2020, 7 December 2020 and 16 February 2021 respectively indicate the progress of the infection but not their true size:

	22 May 2020	7 Dec 2020	16 Feb 2021
Current infections	3,855	19,810	29,169
Current hospitalisations	908	1,164	1,157
Recovered (to date)	2,882	17,641	26,711
Deaths (to date)	65	1,010	1,301

Actual figures are of course estimated to be much higher. As background, on 3 October 2017 President Putin appointed Vladimir Vasilyev Acting Head of Dagestan. The half Russian half Kazak retired police chief was entirely unknown in Dagestan. It presaged an increase in repressive direct rule from Moscow [2]. By October 2018 he had brought in his cronies from Kazan and many Dagestani officials had been sacked and arrested.

Dagestan, among the poorest Republics in Russian Federation with over 80% of its state budget coming from Moscow, was seriously hit by Covid which by May 2020 had spread to almost every village where often half the families were infected. The main city hospitals and regional centre polyclinics were barely equipped and became centres of infection. On 21 May 2020 the main hospital in Makhachkala had to be quarantined for five days. The doctors pleaded in vain to Putin for protective equipment, tests, breathing equipment, oxygen, medicines and hospital beds. Desperate young men drove long distances to refill oxygen cylinders for their sick relatives. Even Vasilyev, who had disappeared for several weeks, questioned the official Russian figures.

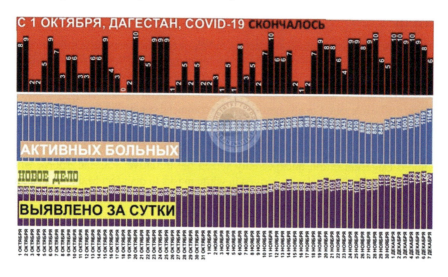

Figure 19.1 Covid-19 as of 7 December 2020 [1]. The top section represents deaths; the middle section currently ill with Covid-19; and the lower section daily infections

RFE/RL reported on 17 May 2020 that Dagestan's top health official Dzhamaludin Gadzhiibragimov (a Tabasaran) has said more than 40 doctors had died from either the coronavirus or 'community-acquired pneumonia' – official newspeak's name for the disease so as to obfuscate the actual effects of the virus. He supported the many questions raised about the accuracy of Russia's reported cases and deaths from Covid. In another interview with a blogger the day before, reported in the RFE/RL article, he contrasted the official figures of 3,280 cases and 29 deaths with his informed estimates of 13,000 and 657 [3].

In the Russian Federation many Covid deaths are counted as pneumonia and home deaths are not counted at all. On 21 May 2020 Tatyana Golikova, vice-president of the RF and Coronavirus spokesperson, announced that during the first three months of 2020 the overall death rate had *decreased* by 21,000 people [4]. To community-connected Dagestanis on the ground she was from a different world.

The highest-profile Dagestani is Khabib (The Eagle) Nurmagomedov, the fearsome world MMM champion who symbolizes the national hope for the future (chapter 24). On 19 May on Instagram he reported that hospitals in Dagestan are "running over capacity" as his father continued his final battle against coronavirus, one of more than 20 relatives who had spent time in intensive care, with several dying. "We have a very difficult situation. A lot of people have got sick, and a lot of people have died." Khabib also supported "Islamic scholars [who] are telling us to perform [Eid Uraza Bayram] festival prayers at home [during 24–26 May 2020]. Do not go to visit others, and do not accept guests" [5]. Eid usually involves mass picnics at the graveside of ancestors.

There are many factors in traditional Dagestani life that increase the risk of viral transmission. The poor economy means workers often have to take several part-time jobs, increasing their exposure. Migrant work abroad requires queuing for long periods at airports and border controls. Village food is produced in a family-group system. Village architecture is close-packed in medieval clusters along narrow alleys; three or even more generations live in the same house. Outside, respectful greetings include handshakes and embraces especially for *aksakal*, white-bearded elders, who will meet on a *godekan* (bench) to discuss village matters; weddings and funeral visits extend to days or weeks; frequent guests and hospitality are social essentials.

Folk medicine in maternity rites

'Clinical medicine' is what we think works now, according to our current knowledge and the principles of scientific process – critical observation, collection of evidence, testing and repeatability. The overwhelming nature of the Covid outbreak means that much more has yet to be learned about the virus and its hydra-like mutations. The urgency of care needs, particularly with the lack of resources from which many systems, including the Dagestani one, suffered in 2020, meant that hope and belief often had to be pressed into service. Folk medicine and ritual may be seen as no different, making the most of what resources were to hand – or are still to hand.

The maternity rites of Mountain Jews, recorded in detail in 2003 [6], are similar to those of other ethnic groups in Dagestan. Folk medicine has a long history in Dagestan, served by a vast variety of local herbal medicinal plants in which the alpine flora transmits medically-useful minerals. Dagestan is reputed to be second only to Tibet with regard to the variety of such plants.

To ensure a safe birth and strong development of the child, people developed actions and rituals to help protect the future mother and child from evil forces. The following unwritten rules were strictly followed by both rich and poor.

The general belief is that the child's soul is in the pregnant mother, and interacted with her and other forces; her behaviour influenced its future. Difficulties arising in pregnancy could be traced to this relationship. A sure protection against evil forces was for the mother to keep her pregnancy and the expected birth date secret for as long as possible. Therefore, no matter how joyful the expected childbirth, she let her husband and mother-in-law know only when it could no longer be hidden. Like other peoples of Dagestan, the pregnant Mountain Jewess carried on working for the family, but was excused heavy exertion: moderate labour was thought good for her health. However her life changed dramatically, circumscribed by prohibitions, actions and manipulations believed to ensure a successful pregnancy. The system of fantastic rituals was handed down from generation to generation, supposedly to protect the mother, although perhaps it was rather that the other women insisted on following the customs whatever the result.

Similar prohibitions and actions can be found in other cultures worldwide, due to the ancient mystery of reproduction [7, 8]. At the root of many of these is the principle of sympathetic magic, 'like happens from like' [9]. The original basis of these rules and taboos may no longer be clear, but some seem more rational than others [10].

156   *Dagestan – History, Culture, Identity*

Physical deformity and undesirable character traits in the child are most feared. The mother-to-be should not look at ugly people or some animals. Examples are a hare to avoid a cleft palate; a wolf to prevent infection with its wicked characteristics; a frog to avoid a big mouth or bug-eyes at birth; and a snake to prevent dribbling. She needs to be protected from fright when she sees these animals. It is taboo to stare at anything for too long or the baby will be cross-eyed and gloomy. If she sits in the corner of the room or at the table the baby will have a bad character. If she flushes water over the threshold it will wet its bed. She is not allowed to knit as the yarn will symbolically wrap around her baby's neck, or sew else the child will be needle-thin.

Her baby's morals also need cultivating. If she takes something secretly, the baby will become a thief. Excessive frugality makes a child greedy. Sloppiness will be imitated by the baby who will be snotty and lousy. But if she wants her child to be virtuous, she tries to look at beautiful people and things, such as the full moon or the sun. 'Moon-like' and 'sun-faced' are descriptions of great beauty in a person. She also washes her face with snow and milk so that her child, especially a daughter, will be born white-skinned. Her good mood and peace of mind have a positive effect on her baby.

During pregnancy she often refuses to eat certain foods for physiological reasons, but follows specific nutritional recommendations as well: not to consume buffalo milk which makes the birth overdue; goat which makes the baby smell; or unripe fruits which causes premature birth. In the distant past Mountain Jews generally held the same superstition as all the other peoples of the Caucasus [11] that many virtues or vices can be passed from meat.

Pregnant women are vulnerable to harmful spirits, Shaitans or the evil eye (chapter 2), and so never go out in the dark, when evil powers emerge; or unaccompanied from a house. She always carries a piece of bread for protection.

The spirits of the deceased can infect the pregnant woman, so she must avoid a cemetery. If she has to attend a funeral, she should bring a piece of bread, sulphur as in matches, a small knife and a safety pin on her left side with the clasp down. After the funeral, she has a thorough wash.

In her final three months of pregnancy, if she is alone in her home, she fears the mythical *Vechekhur*/ Eating-the-chick, which can abduct a baby from the womb while she sleeps unless she leaves a piece of bread on her window sill. The demon-woman named variously Absally, Albasty, Sutkyatyn, Ayuli, Hal, Alpab, Budallaba in Dagestan (chapter 2) also threatened the health of women in labour [12, 13].

Those she meets have to follow specific rules, treating her with emphatic politeness. In a public she is offered a warm place, as if emphasizing her 'uncomfortable position.' Relatives try to satisfy her food fads because they fear the child will have birthmarks imitating the berries and fruits. It is indecent for her to have luxury foods, non-seasonal fruits or other treats.

Unlike most Caucasians who considered a pregnant woman 'unclean' the Mountain Jews of Dagestan did not, and were only afraid of offending her [14, 15].

The expected confinement date was determined by the lunar calendar, and boys were supposedly born one to two weeks later than girls. "Girls are always in a hurry," they used to joke, "although it should have been the other way around, for God first created man and then woman."

A pregnant woman is particularly sensitive to people, trees and pets, and as a fertile woman, if she eats the first fruit from the tree, then good harvests will result and she will have many children. When a woman becomes a mother she gains a higher position in her family and more generally in the village community, as a contributor to the commonweal of the family. Better still, the birth of the first-born boy further strengthens her status.

Mystery surrounded the appearance on earth of a new man. A woman with only daughters feels guilty before her husband and his relatives, little better than if she is barren, and either can lead to a divorce or justify her husband taking a second wife. Reproached by her husband and mother-in-law, and ridiculed by neighbours, she is insecure in every new pregnancy. So she tries to determine the gender of the unborn child in advance. If her belly is round she expects a girl; if it is convex and she can move easily, she expects a boy. Moreover, if she becomes ill, with age spots on her face, with swollen lips and legs, then the women about her expect a daughter because she steals half the beauty of her mother. Heartburn, especially in late pregnancy, is caused by long hair and means the baby is a girl.

During her first pregnancy she did not prepare a layette for her child, which her mother did for her, and if she was not alive, then her aunt or sister. The future grandmother first acquired a *guofer* (a deep wooden rocking cradle with a baton connecting the two high arched headboards) made by local craftsmen and sold in the bazaars. The flat base had a hole in which a right-angled tube carved from a single piece of wood was inserted, different for baby boys and girls. This catheter allowed the baby to be left unattended for a long time. Such cradles are found in many countries of the world where there was an early settled farming society [16]. The mother's 'birthrights' – essentials – are prepared for her baby's cradle, including a *challah* (mattress) stuffed with hay or wool; two wide thick swaddling bands tapering towards the ends, where ties are attached; a small soft pillow for the knees and a flat pillow under the head. In addition to the cradle and bedding her mother prepares two caps, kerchiefs, and diapers.

Generally the birth takes place in the house of the husband who leaves during childbirth. As soon as labour began, they call the *mama* (midwife). Experienced midwives, like the famous Sarah-Lie from Derbent, are at a premium, so they are booked in advance. Most midwives know if necessary how to change the foetal position by manipulation or massage to facilitate birth. They also try to stop bleeding with nettle decoctions.

158 *Dagestan – History, Culture, Identity*

The birthing room is swept, washed, and covered with hay, clean rags and felt. Alternatively the custom of giving birth in a stove-heated room outside the home was common in the Caucasus [17–19], recognizing the purifying power of fire. In addition it lessened the risk of catching a cold when weakened by childbirth. During childbirth, one or two other women – neighbours and relatives – were assistants to the midwife.

Other family gathered outside the birthing room, waited for news. People were not specially invited, as with other folk of the Caucasus [20], but if someone came, the family welcomed their solidarity. Childless women were excluded. A known lazy woman and the mother of another woman in childbirth were banned because their presence could cause the birth to be harder. Close relatives who were canny avoided the birth, since it was believed that the birth pangs would fall on them. A woman in labour could jinx both relatives and strangers, especially unmarried girls and childless women, hence the idea that "the less people know about the birth, the easier it will be and the faster it will pass." It was fear of the evil eye, rather than ethical standards, that caused older women to justify concealing labour and even to hide during childbirth, though this was almost impossible in the confines of a mountain village.

Apotropaic metal amulets, axes, sickles, and naked daggers are laid on the threshold of the birthing room. The Jewish woman in labour, in common with other folk, has to wear *ovungez* (gold jewellery) [21]. And of course in the birth-room a Torah is kept, and a goatskin decorated with *mishiravi* (the hand of Moses) as talismans against evil spirits and an appeal to God to protect the woman and her child through childbirth.

Preparing for the birth of a child includes mystical openings of chests, cabinets, and locks to facilitate or release childbirth. Women also braid wool before birth, while others present untie knots and belts and unfastened clothes, chanting "let the contractions ease." If childbirth is delayed, or waters do not break, then various obstetric measures come into play, founded on centuries-old empirical experience of midwives. Women most often give birth on their knees or squatting, grappling a heavy chest or a thick strong rope hanging from the ceiling, which contribute to a lighter and faster birth. Between contractions, the midwife makes the woman in labour walk around the room, giving her warm foot baths, a circular massage to her stomach and rubbing oil into her back and lower back. Some anesthetized contractions are possible because many midwives know the pressure points which relieve pain. Even if the woman in labour is weak and suffering, she is not allowed to sit or lie, and especially not to fall asleep. When the child is in the wrong position the midwife can correct it, and in extreme cases extract the baby by hand. Other effective methods of moving the baby are making her jump, leading her around the room, and getting her to swing on the curtains. During a long labour the woman is forced to go for a long walk on the bridge across the river or a ditch filled with water, because the movement of water will get the birth going. With prolonged and difficult births the blend of psychic warding against 'corruption' and *sadan* (unclean forces) with empirical physical methods is particularly striking.

The midwife tried to stop haemorrhages by washing the woman in labour with cold water in summer, or laying snow compresses on her belly in winter. Unfortunately, in the absence of clinical facilities, even time-honoured techniques were not always able to avoid the death of newborns or prevent their mothers from catching fevers or worse. The high mortality was ascribed to the will of *Yahweh* or the evil eye. If there was a choice, they usually tried to save the mother, not the baby. 'Died in childbirth' was a leading cause of mortality.

The postpartum customs and rites consisted of numerous prescriptions and prohibitions governing the mother's behaviour and treatment of her child, protected by rituals and religious-magic. For 40 days after the birth, she is considered unclean and as the baby is constantly with its mother, they both represent an easy target for evil supernatural powers.

As soon as the newborn cries out, it is held upside down by the right heel and patted on the back, while the umbilical cord is cut leaving enough length of it to knot. The knife is cleansed and disinfected over the fire and the knot is secured with silk thread from the midwife's bag.

The midwife follows this process for the newborn: she examines it for defects. To give the head a 'regular shape' she slightly squeezes it on all sides. Next she cautiously bathes the baby in spring water, warmed with a hot coal as a remedy for evil spirits. Water is poured down the midwife's elbow onto the back of the baby on her lap. The baby is greased with fat or butter, and its navel is sprinkled with corn flour. A clean rag, soaked in creamy oil, is rubbed on its navel and the top of its head. The baby is tightly wrapped and after touching its lips with honey, laid to sleep, with a longitudinal strip of cloth stuck onto its forehead with soot, against the evil eye.

It is important to wash the 'unclean' birth-room(s) thoroughly and throw into the fire a pinch of salt as a symbol of imperishability for further protection. Postpartum, the midwife carefully massages the mother's stomach and lower legs. To prevent a hernia, her abdomen is tightly bandaged for two to three weeks. Nettle broth, chamomile and hypericum are given as anti-inflammatory and haemostatic agents. To treat mastitis the mother drinks less than usual and steamed flaxseed and plantain compresses are applied to her chest and then covered with a lambskin.

Lula (the afterbirth), as part of the baby's spirit or the soul of its father, is treated solemnly. The shrivelled *nof* (umbilical cord) is washed, dried, wrapped in a cloth, put in a calico bag and hung on the crossbar at the foot of the cradle, following the universal belief in the integrity of the body [9]. Indeed when the child has a stomach ailment, it is given crushed cord dissolved in sweet warm water. In Dagestan, if a woman wants to stop having children, her final afterbirth is secretly buried deep in the earth, out of reach of dogs.

After birth the mother is ordered to lie in bed for a week and excused from housework. Female family care for the mother and baby. First the exhausted woman needs food and is given *cough*, nutritious warm liquid porridge sweetened with honey, to cleanse her body and increase the fat content of her milk. Eggs fried in

160   *Dagestan – History, Culture, Identity*

animal fat with honey help too. After her hearty lunch, her baby is brought to feed, having sucked on a finger greased with honey and creamy oil.

The important first feeding starts with the right breast to ensure that the child is right-handed. A trickle of first milk colostrum anoints the baby's skin especially a girl's, repeated before washes for its first 40 days. If there is a lot of milk, it is kept quiet, to avoid the jinx of milk 'burn out' or drying up. Excess milk is never poured into an unclean place likely prowled by a thirsty cat, to stop her milk disappearing. When the milk is insufficient or there is none, the mother-in-law pours warm water mixed with flour onto her right breast, to move or restore her milk. The mother also tries drinking water from three springs. It is more rational to give her dairy products, hot lentil soup with milk and pumpkin and boiled wheat with milk and butter. The same soup with crushed nuts helps increase low-nutrient milk. It is a sacred duty for the mother to suckle her baby as much as possible. If nothing works, the family carefully choose a neat and healthy wet-nurse from a nearby village, forming a 'milk relationship' that safeguards the baby's character, habits and societal traditions, and engaged family marriage taboos. After at most 40 days, the baby is weaned to diluted goat or cow milk, whichever the baby prefers. Close relations with her husband are not recommended for 40 days, during which time it is dangerous for him to touch them.

She is not allowed home until her swollen midriff is down, and then forbidden to pick up a needle and sew, to knead dough, to light the stove, or to go out after sunset. The baby stays with its mother for the 40 days, to ensure its good health by keeping it safe from outside influence. It is not paraded in the village or surrounded with talismans and amulets, so as not to attract the evil eye during this period of uncertainty.

During her isolation the mother keeps a raw egg in a bowl on the windowsill to invoke fertility magic and to protect them both from the evil eye. In addition a horseshoe is hung over the doorway or in another prominent place.

Some believe that hygiene was the original practical basis for the 40 day recovery quarantine that was later transmuted into superstition [15], others that it derived from the idea that postpartum a woman risked infecting every being or object she touched with her weakness [6].

The family try not to leave the newborn and mother unattended, especially before circumcision, because the baby is vulnerable to 'unclean spirits'.

The mother and baby were allowed to bathe on the seventh day, before *milo* (circumcision). Their bath water was left in daylight and poured into a clean place, otherwise angry hiding *sadans* (shaitans, chapter 2) would make "the child numb, and its mother will die." The rabbi and close relatives, normally the men only, were invited to milo. Before the cut ten men surround the baby and, having covering its crown with a cloth, recite a prayer. A limited number of more distant relatives and neighbours may now visit with small pieces of cloth and scarves for the baby and

Surviving Covid and traditional medicine   161

mother, and fresh or cooked food. The baby is presented with gifts and everyone is treated to festive food.

Naming often coincided with circumcision. Girls are also named within seven days, as it was thought that any longer delay could let in an 'unclean power'. The girl's naming is a more modest affair sometimes in synagogue with the rabbi and mostly women relatives, who provide sweets, *cough*, pilaf and dolma.

The ceremonial laying of the child in its cradle involved special textiles: embroidered silks, satins, velvets and soft towelling, used next to the baby, and the base of the cradle is lined in cotton. The baby is usually swaddled tight in the cradle, with its chest and knees held tightly with ribbons, so that it cannot move its arms, legs or head, and covered with a blanket on top of the crossbar. Mountain Jews, like other peoples of Dagestan, believe that the swaddled cradle protects the baby's legs and spine from curvature, and stops it having colds. The cradle disciplines the child, making it persistent and hardy. Special headbands were invented to give its head a rounded shape.

Girls are put in the cradle immediately after naming, and the boys usually two weeks later after the circumcision had healed. Delays of up to three months, the latest for it to become accustomed to swaddling, occurred when a child was premature, weak or underweight. The first laying in the cradle is held at noon on a *Shabbat* (Saturday). The important person who first puts the baby in the cradle is typically a respected mother who loves the Torah and who has her own healthy children, so that her talents and abilities are transferred to the child. If the mother-in-law was considered by the community to be successful, she could fulfil this rôle. A good treat is prepared for the women and children guests.

Before laying the child, they rehearsed the rite with a bundle or another older baby. Dagestan peoples had a different custom of 'warming' the cradle by inserting a besom or iron fire-tongs or, sometimes, a sleepy cat [12] (so the baby will sleep) or a stone (to make the child strong). Ashkenazi Jews cradled a living rooster or dog for a boy, or a chicken or cat for a girl. Others laid a fetish doll in the cradle and rocked it briefly.

The baby is bathed and oiled three times before being laid in the cradle which was garlanded by loving messages such as "Let the cradle become sweet, help her grow quickly and be always healthy." The magic of the Word was recognized by Mountain Jews and others in Dagestan. Great attention is paid to the well-wishers' verses, whether spoken or sung. The Torah, garlic, scissors and *misharavin* are kept under the pillow to shield against bad dreams and the machinations of evil spirits, intensified while the newborn was still weak.

Views on when a child's hair should be first cut varied; some other Dagestanis thought the 'heavy uterine hair' should be cut at 40 days. The Mountain Jews preserved *kekul* (one strand) from the first haircut of the first-born son on his first birthday. The kekul was to be left on his head and not cut until the age of seven in

162   *Dagestan – History, Culture, Identity*

the *sugdo* festival when the child was dressed in everything new with great celebrations. The Nogai had a similar custom with braids [8, 22]. It seems that attaining seven was widely celebrated as a social marker [23].

With the evolution of complex religious cults, hair and nail cuttings were needed for the Day of Judgement (perhaps an explanation of why mountain women placed their relatives' combed hair in a small pillow, which after the owner's death was buried under their head). Nails were left for almost a year before the mother carefully tore or bit them off. She wrapped up the first nails and preserved them in a clean place. Nails getting into the fire risked making the child's hands tremble. Only after a year could the mother cut the nails with scissors. The magic customs associated with cutting the child's hair and nails were widespread in almost all the peoples of the world [9].

It was believed that during the first 40 days the newborn did not see or hear: it was in the balance that its soul would remain in this world or leave, so it was treated as an inferior being. The first stage in becoming human was that teeth should appear after 6–7 months. If lower teeth appeared first, the child would live longer. Early teeth at 4–5 months predicted supernatural mental abilities. It was generally believed that if a tooth appeared at 6 months, then the first milk tooth will fall out in 6 years, similarly for 7 months, 7 years. When the child became agitated and was drooling, it was assumed that a tooth was coming through. To ensure that the child had strong and healthy teeth, a relative with beautiful teeth is invited, who checks the emerging tooth. The mother is not supposed to look for the first tooth for it might mean the child will have bad teeth. When the first tooth appears, *genduma* (porridge) made from wheat grain, beans, and lentils, and cooked in beef leg broth, is handed out to neighbours and relatives, but only to an odd number of houses to encourage the remaining teeth. Many other peoples of Dagestan and the Caucasus shared these customs [22]. Genduma was likewise distributed at the First Steps celebration. When the child first stood on his own, he supposedly saw a circle of fire that vanished after the rite. The first steps completed the apotropaic rites of the first year: naming, laying in a cradle, cutting first hair and nails, and emergence of the first teeth, that made up the symbolic welcome of the newborn into society.

Pregnancy, childbirth and the first two years of life involved many archaic customs and rituals surrounding family events. Ceremonies and beliefs relating to pregnancy seem more conservative than for parturition, partly because it is more intimate and partly because modern medicine has more to say on the actual parturition, eroding traditional behaviours there, while the nine-month period of pregnancy normally requires less intervention.

References

[1] Covid-19. Novoye Delo, Dagestan. 7 December 2020.
[2] Abdullaev Nabi. The murky mechanics of Russia's governor reshuffle. The Moscow Times. 9 November 2017.

Surviving Covid and traditional medicine 163

[3] Dagestan's health minister says more than 40 doctors have died of Covid-19 pneumonia. RFE/RL. 17 May 2020.

[4] T. Golikova mortality in three months decreased by 33 [percent] or by 21 thousand people. Novosti. 21 May 2020. https://ndelo.ru/novosti/tgolikova-smertnost-za-tri-mesyaca-snizilas-na-33-ili-na-21-tys-chelovek.

[5] Monaghan Jen. Deaths mounting in Dagestan – Khabib Nurmagomedov. BBC Monitoring. 19 May 2020.

[6] Musaeva M.K. Traditional customs and rituals associated with birth and upbringing children among the peoples of Nagorno-Dagestan. 2006.

[7] Smirnova Y.S. Family and family life among the peoples of the North Caucasus. 1983. pp67, 72.

[8] Dyakonova V.P. Childhood in the traditional culture of Tuvans and Telechits. Traditional Parenting Among the Peoples of Siberia. pp177, 182.

[9] Frazer D. The golden bough. 1980. pp20, 51–2, 165–9, 237–8.

[10] Koshuba M.S. and Martynova M.Y. Yugoslav peoples. Birth customs and rites. Countries of Foreign Europe. 1997.

[11] Solovieva L.T. Customs and rites of the children's cycle among Georgians second half XIX- early XX century. IES. Vol. 8. 1984. pp168–9, 171, 175.

[12] Gadzhieva S.S. Family and marriage among the peoples of Dagestan XIX- early XX century. 1985. pp237, 278, 283.

[13] Gadzhieva S.S. Kumyks. P325.

[14] Koshuba M.S. and Martynova M.Y. Yugoslav peoples. Birth customs and rites. Countries of Foreign Europe. 1997. p69, 81, 91.

[15] Pokrovsky E.A. Physical education of children from different nations, mainly of Russia. 1881. p270.

[16] Ethnography of childhood. Traditional forms of parenting children and adolescents among the peoples of Western and South Asia. 1983. p9.

[17] Musaeva M.K. Khvarshins. Historical and Ethnographic study XIX- the early XX century. 1995. pp104–5.

[18] Pchelina E.G. Maternal customs in Ossetians. Soviet Ethnography. No. 4. 1937. p99.

[19] Kaloev B.A. Ossetians. 1967. p198.

[20] Ter-Sargsyants A.E. Armenians History and ethnocultural traditions. 1998. pp189, 192.

[21] Gadzhiev G.A. Amulets and talismans of the peoples of Dagestan. 1996. p152.

[22] Gadzhieva S.S. The material culture of Nogais in the XIX- early XX centuries. 1976. p115.

[23] Karpov Y.Y. Dzhigit and the wolf. Men's unions in the sociocultural tradition. Highlanders of the Caucasus. 1996. p15.

20 Traditional medicine of mountain Dagestan

Ethnoecology is "a special area of ethnography that studies the relationship between ethnic communities and the environment, related to the development of their material and spiritual environment and the use of its resources" [1, 2]. The Avar, Dargin and Lak minorities developed ethnically unique cultures during the XIX- early XX centuries in response to their natural environments [2].

The elements of man's habitat, traditional management of nature and his worldview are clearly interconnected; man is a product of nature and his environment. Every ethnic community has its specific aspects of 'traditional' medicine [3], accumulated from centuries-old local empirical knowledge, based on the relationship between human activities and the environment [4], and using uncultivated products for the prevention or treatment of diseases. The striking range of folk medicines described here is but a fraction of mountain villages healers' secret recipes.

The famous tsarist Russian surgeon N.I. Pies wrote, "Most of the military people, even the most educated commanders, are confident in the extraordinary art and experience of Asian physicians . . . The art of treating external injuries in Caucasian tribes is purely hereditary and passes from father to son [5]. Dagestani surgeons never amputated a leg, an arm, or other part of the body, except in an exceptional case" [6]. An imperial Russian Lieutenant General was similarly impressed: "The results of the treatment of Dagestan surgeons can be said to be incredible; there is almost no wound, excepting a purely fatal one, which the indigenous doctors would not have cured, so that the patient did not suffer any bad consequences" [7]. A Soviet Armenian academician went further: "the surgery of Caucasian traditional medicine was almost at the level of scientific medicine, and the folk surgeons of Dagestan even performed operations such as craniotomy" [8].

Thanks to technology and modern analytical techniques, scientific development of treatments and drugs takes less time than empirical medicine. The leading chemist the late Professor George Taylor correctly criticized what I wrote in *Madder Red* about alchemists not being chemists. As he told me, they also conducted large numbers of experiments, and while certainly their theoretical knowledge was different and generated fewer repeatable results, the same cannot be said for many pioneers of chemistry from the late XVIII century on.

DOI: 10.4324/9781003388579-20

The folk doctors realized that a hard lifestyle, malnutrition, frustration and disharmony of spiritual, mental and physiological balances, weakened the sufferer's will, who lost power over the base instincts of the body as the possibility of a contented life disappeared. The most important conditions are mental balance and harmony, reasonable ways of working, relaxing, eating, and knowing how to keep the body healthy.

From the point of view of ethnoecology, Dagestan healers used to successfully treat a wide variety of diseases with only local ingredients, some of which seem most improbable to modern readers.

The healers

The medicine of the Avars, Dargins and Laks was influenced by the experience and knowledge of all the peoples of Dagestan and externally from the rich heritage of oriental medicine, which arrived with Islam and Arab-Muslim culture. The madrasah education ensured a profound knowledge of Arabic language and grammar [9], so that "almost all treatises of medieval medicine were known in Dagestan," often brought back from the hajj. The most popular was the world-famous "The Canon of Medicine" of Abu Ali ibn Sina (Avicenna), which incorporated the medical knowledge of ancient Rome, Greece, Persia, India, and Central Asia. The earliest Canon found in Dagestan dates from 1400 [10].

The healers both translated medieval medicinal texts using Arabic letters ('Ajam) into local languages and "created works themselves in various fields of medicine" [11]. The Hannal Murad (Damadan) medical guide known throughout Dagestan is a translation from Persian to Lak of the medical guide of Muhammad al-Dailami al-Mazandarani, under the name Tukhfatal-Muminin [12, 13]. Lukman al-Hakim's book of medicines was also widespread among the doctors of Dagestan because it presented formulation methods for medical drugs from minerals, plant and animal products, with their methods of use and dosage [14].

The fame of doctors and their knowledge was passed down from generation to generation, creating medical families. Avar, Dargin and Lak healers came from almost every village [4]. Some were women.

Mostly the doctors were universal physicians. General practice included midwives or chiropractors, who diagnosed and cured internal, infectious, skin, neuropsychic and other diseases, and also provided surgical intervention if necessary. The doctors took account of the patient's age, gender and general physical condition.

Paradoxical treatments

The experience of Dagestan doctors and healers formed a unique system of healthcare by a combination of what we now perceive by modern standards as rational methods from traditional folk empirical experience, with irrational religious and magical practices.

166 *Dagestan – History, Culture, Identity*

The lifestyle of the mountaineers, with their simple diet, work, leisure and relationships between people, contributed to a healthy, active old age. A hard-working lifestyle, reasonable nutrition, fasting and treatment with natural remedies prevented most serious illnesses.

Mountaineers observed nature closely and learned from animals. Washing small skin wounds with saliva or stings with urine was observed from prehistoric times and is still significant today. Psychological, physical, mineral and plant treatments were sometimes combined.

Evil spirits

A serious illness arose either as punishment for sins; or as a test of perseverance and faith in predetermined destiny of the Almighty. When a disease penetrated a person, it mystically 'resided' in his body for as long as the patient allowed. Diseases were transmitted by magic to the earth, plants, animals, people and even to sacred domestic objects – the home, grain store and clothing such as a headdress or sheepskin coat, or a cradle.

The common treatment for diseases caused by the 'evil eye' was with talismans and prayers. The healers' magic words and ritual actions punished the objectionable and banished the disease to distant mountains, forests, rivers or steppes. They could even change the weather and inspire love [15].

Infectious diseases

The transmission of a disease by air and wind caused obesity, denoting a 'sticky' contagious disease. Hundreds died from smallpox in the mountains of Dagestan in 1890 [16]. In 1892 cholera infected some 23,000 and almost 10,500 died [17]. Other infectious imports were typhus, tuberculosis, plague and dysentery. As well as fighting the Russians, Shamil created a department in the Imamate to combat epidemics that was more effective than the Russian efforts [13]. For example, the recorded adats of the Tsez regulated everyday behaviour of plague-infected relatives [18] to control epidemics. As warning, a stake covered with a donkey skin was placed outside a plague or cholera dwelling [16].

Fire and water

Fire and water were purifiers, so during epidemics, both healthy and sick walked or jumped over a small bonfire, carrying their babies. Ritual fire was manipulated by jumping, circling or fumigating. Widespread magic healing properties were associated with spring-water, rainwater and dew. Water that washed away dirt and impurities could cleanse diseases.

Plants

Wild plants endowed with supernatural properties were used as food seasoning and in healing magic. Bunches of wild caraway seeds, thyme, oregano and

St. John's wort were hung around the house as talismans, and the vapour from roasted caraway seeds protected the house and barn from unclean forces. Fumigation of patients with burnt rue was a remedy for the evil eye, and, despite it being poisonous, Avar healers gave small doses of a weak infusion of it for haemorrhoids and varicose veins [15].

Trees were also used for magic and medicinal purposes. Fruit and berry trees and berberis or hawthorn bushes supposedly gave protection from the evil eye. Mountain ash offcuts made a reliable amulet against sorcery, spoilage, and the wiles of evil spirits. Avars hung rowan brushes tied with red thread as a talisman in sheds or houses to protect livestock and farm buildings against harmful magic and diseases. Even today, in many villages, girls string red rowan berries and wear them like beads. Similar bracelets made from rowan branches were talismans for children, as was a small piece hung by a red thread on the child's neck or chest [15]. For Avars it was sinful to cut down mountain ash without burning it in the stove. As punishment the perpetrator would lose an arm or a leg or fall ill and die. Other ethnicities protected the quince tree, called *Hawa 'Iech*, Apple of Eve, in Avar. Shreds of cloth or scarves were tied to the branches of trees in sacred groves, where sacrifices were made to transfer their healing power to a sick child or a barren woman.

Dagestani doctors and healers gained considerable experience in pharmacology through the agency of herbal medicines. The distinctive flora boasts some 4,500 species of herbs of which 70% are medicinal [19–22]. Mostly female healers collected the medicinal herbs, which required special harvesting to work. One plant was not to be torn off with a bare hand, others should not be torn apart except by the patient, while others should be entirely avoided. Before gathering herbs, it was recommended to perform *namaz* by reading one of the Qur'an suras, and when collecting some herbs they danced in circles around them reciting ancient quatrains praising their healing properties.

Herbs had to be harvested on the right day in the right season to be effective. Leaves, stems and flowers were gathered during flowering, buds and bark from March to May, roots and rhizomes in autumn or early spring and fruits and seeds when ripe. Some plants were collected only at new or waxing moon – some plants accumulate therapeutically active substances at night, others in the morning, and some in the midday after the dew has dried. Some herbs are cut with a knife, others are dug or torn out along with the root. Leaves, grass, flowers and berries were harvested by hand only in dry weather, after the dew had dried. Especially good medicinal and edible herbs were stored in so-called 'clean' places, far from the village dogs and cats. Herbalists-healers and villagers stocked up for winter with seasonings and teas of dried horse sorrel, caraway seeds, mint, thyme and coltsfoot, which was dried in the sun, while the rest were dried in the shade at home. Dried plants were stored in canvas or cotton bags and wooden or clay vessels. On academic expeditions it was noticed that plants collected immediately after rain or covered with dew did not dry out, but blackened with mould.

Medicinal plants are administered as tinctures, alcohol solutions and mixtures, decoctions, ointments, vegetal patches on a fat base and raw herbal products [15].

168   *Dagestan – History, Culture, Identity*

Powders or juices from freshly harvested plants were convenient to use. Cut, crushed or powdered medicinal plants were popular for teas, infusions, decoctions and external tinctures. Tinctures, solutions and mixtures were prepared with water, vodka (chapter 7) or grape wine. Decoctions not requiring vodka or alcohol or fats were cheaper and simpler to prepare.

Ingredients were measured by the handful or pinch, and infusion times varied from several minutes to several weeks.

Ointments were prepared from crushed dry plants with vegetable oil, sour cream, honey or animal fat. To treat skin diseases, wounds, boils and burns, ointment was applied with patches of dough, tobacco leaf, resinous birch bark or animal skins.

Herbal medicines were administered cautiously because if incorrectly used some plants had an opposite effect. Overdoses caused itching, skin rashes, vomiting, and diarrhoea, such as overdosed yarrow broth which caused skin rashes and dizziness.

Herbs

Vast experience ensured that safe wild plants were selected and poisonous plants avoided. The healer was responsible for any accidents. Gathered medicinal herbs included coltsfoot, yarrow, immortelle, chamomile, nettle, tansy, mint, wormwood, dog rose, marshmallow and madder roots, plantain leaves, water lily, hoofed grass, calamus, blood-crust, valerian, lily of the valley, meadowsweet, marshmallows, large plantain and burdock.

Edible wild plants provided proteins, fats, carbohydrates, vitamins, and potassium, iron, and phosphorus salts.

The healers' recipes were secret. For unusual diseases a larger number of plants were combined, in the hope that one would work. Respiratory diseases were treated with an infusion of coltsfoot, plantain, sage, oregano and mint.

Narcotic and poisonous plants such as poppy, bleached bulbs and 'rabbit cabbage' – probably lactucarium, milkweed, or celandine – were applied externally on humans and animals, as well as small doses for infusions, tinctures or juices. The bulbs and horseradish infused with vodka were a popular rheumatic embrocation.

Highlanders traditionally picked raspberries for colds, blueberries for intestinal disorders and rose hips as a restorative and against flu and colds, as well as diseases of the liver, bladder, gastric catarrh, low acidity, stomach ulcers, anaemia and atherosclerosis. Compotes and teas were prepared from dried rose hips.

The Avars, Dargins and Laks widely used decoctions of flax seeds, hemp oil and hops for medical purposes, as well as *urbech* 'highland chocolate' from apricot kernels. Onions and garlic have long been used as a tasty preventive and therapeutic agent against colds and gastrointestinal diseases. Crushed pepper was both the seasoning for the favourite khinkal and porridges, but also as an anthelmintic against worms and mites. Sucking on a chewed clove of garlic and rubbing garlic juice and vinegar into a healthy body gave protection against epidemics.

Traditional medicine of mountain Dagestan 169

Local edible herbs are widely used in fillings for the delicious chudu thin or thick pies with greens and cottage cheese, broths, stuffed khinkal, fried eggs with greens, but most of all eaten raw by women and children to improve their health and vitamin intake [22]. Regular consumption of wild plants as medicine and tonics, supplementing low-calorie food, plausibly helped villagers to adapt to extreme weather [23].

Heat treatment

Wormwood was heated with hot charcoal in ancient cast-iron cullenders and set alight to make 'wormwood cigarettes', with which the patient massaged himself to improve arthritis, myositis, bronchial asthma, hypertension and gastric ulcers [15].

Honey

Beekeeping was important in the Highlanders' economy. Honey is similar to plants in application and effect, because its properties depended on the nectar the bees gathered [24]. Honey had a universal therapeutic effect, prescribed orally for diarrhoea and cold and externally for purulent wounds, ulcers, dental treatment, to treat skin burns, wounds, and sore eyes. Honey was mixed with oil, salt, baked onions, and decoctions of medicinal herbs. Honey-derived wax, royal jelly and propolis were widely used for medical purposes and bee stings for rheumatism.

Animal products

Milk especially goat and red cow, lactic acid products, cow's butter, fat or lard from goat, bear, badger and other animals, especially *kurdyuk* (fat tail sheep fat), animal skin and organs, birds and insects all had medicinal uses. Bear and badger meat and fat were used for tuberculosis and pneumonia, and their bile for rheumatism and stomach diseases. Bile compresses were used for liver or joint diseases.

Chicken stomachs were a strong astringent for diarrhoea; chicken egg protein was used in plaster for fractures and dislocations; yolks for burns and eggshells for rickets.

If a person did not recover for a long time, Tabasaran villagers in the south killed a cow and wrapped the patient with the still-warm skin up to his throat for several hours [15]. To treat pneumonia or bruises the patient was wrapped in a warm skin from a slaughtered domestic animal, until it dried [25], but the most common cure for pneumonia, then and now, was hot milk or water with goat fat. For tuberculosis local doctors recommended various combinations of badger fat, black dog meat, puppy, fox and hedgehog, and mare or donkey milk [4].

A Russian physician about 1850 wrote that "there are curious methods of treatment [of consumption] that were randomly applied by mountain doctors. They gave the patient plant rot with an admixture of minerals and mould from under large stones. Alternatively they forced him to swallow powdered stone with sulphur from matches in the home, and finally treated him with a patch, smeared with squashed flies. They even resorted to vodka, obviously to the detriment of the patient, and to donkey milk which acted as a cleanser" [26]. A Dagestani researcher noted in 2011 that "plant rot" and "mould from beneath damp stones" are the precursors of antibiotics, in particular penicillin. The "crushed stone" contains trace elements, which became known to scientific medicine only from the 1950s. Donkey milk acts as a diuretic and the "patch" may have had a warming effect like the modern pepper patch [13].

Animal fats were widely used to treat skin diseases. About 1860 a Russian described the treatment for his scabies: "About three months after my arrival in Kumukh [the Lak capital], I got scabies. Big acne spots appeared on my arms and legs and no remedies helped me. At first my comrades did not disdain me, but the more they became infected, the more they openly revealed their displeasure. They seated me at a separate table, and gave me separate dishes . . . I went for a cure to a nearby village, to one kunak [who,] delighted with my wife's arrival, immediately began to make my medication. He took old bovine fat, set it on fire and then poured the ashes and an equal amount of soot and sulphur into the fat. Every morning and evening I cooked it all together and smeared my scabies. After three days, the acne completely dried up, and on the fifth and sixth day I was almost completely recovered" [27].

As well as crushed pepper to get rid of worms, they gave the patient donkey milk, wild boar piglet meat, old ashes of burnt bovine liver in rainwater, fluff from the neck of a pigeon with honey, powdered dried bull bladder or cockerels and eggshells.

Frogs were used to treat carbuncles and inflamed extremities, while leeches treated headaches, radiculitis, hypertension, flux, blockage of veins on the legs, and were used for bloodletting.

Insects

A living spider inside a nutshell was worn on the chest, supposedly to cure fever because when the spider dies, the disease goes away. The spider's web can be stored for years in a humid environment without decomposition. When needed it was swallowed against typhoid, or as a dressing for wounds. Scientists have since identified that the web contains bacteria inhibitors [15], being similar to the lymph gland of the human immune system.

Unusual recipes

The unusual medicines from fauna and organics may cause bewilderment and even horror today, though the effects of many plants long known to Dagestani doctors were verified in the XX century, for example modern science confirmed that honey is bactericidal.

Traditional medicine of mountain Dagestan   171

For scabies the affected area was rubbed with fresh bird droppings, or in Tindi, Khvarshi and Andi the patient had to carry a fresh sheep or ram's bladder on his head. To kill lice back in the 1950s, the Archi shaved the head, smeared it with oil and covered it with well-salted ram meat with warm fresh salted internal fat, tightly wrapped in a white cloth for two weeks. Healing usually followed. Dargins treated lichen and scabies by rubbing-in mare or donkey milk. Laks sprinkled lichen with powdered ash, then rubbed it with silver, and smeared-on wolf blood. Avars treated scabies with lichen infused with an extract of lizard fat and dried chopped snake, as well as a mixture of pine resin with a sparrow egg yolk, and a mixture of wolf fat with the ashes of newly burnt logs. The probability of contracting scabies was high in a crowded mountain village, which explains why in one village, 40 people interviewed had scabies [28].

Minerals

Modern science has established that sodium, potassium, calcium, magnesium, copper and iron in balance are essential for human health, forming part of the cells and tissues of the body, regulating osmotic pressure and fluid distribution and acid-base balance. Minerals also have an effect on the functional state of muscular and cardiovascular systems. They play an essential role in enzymes, vitamins, haemoglobins, all types of metabolism, and the transmission of information in the nervous and endocrine systems.

One way to restore the balance of trace elements in the body is taking them in preparations [15]. In folk medicine, many cures for a diseased digestive system included volcanic soda, as well as salt, ash, chalk, and mercuric chloride. Skin diseases were cured with earth, copper sulphate, iron, ash, soot, gunpowder, salt, clay, tar, sulphur, oil, and amber. Lime, soda, salt, clay, copper, kerosene, dust, grease, earth, sand, ash, yellow arsenic, lapis and amber were used for the treatment of internal organs. Kerosene, stone, pebble, salt, sulphur and camphor were used against infectious diseases. Iron, salt, ash, tin, lead, and copper were used to "cure the evil eye and fright," as were red corals, porcelain, ultramarine and natural silk.

Doctors also understood the healing effect of the sun, spring waters, melted snow, morning dew, natural aromas, sunrise, sunset, and even moonlight.

In addition to plants the doctors used hot springs, sulphur waters and muds and mineral waters, iron ore, silver, mercury, coal, clay, oil, gypsum, soda, bronze and copper. Medicinal mountain springs flowed in Lower Nizhelo and Kwanhidatl in the Botlikh region. Carbonic waters flowed from boron springs in Tindinsky, Inkhokvarinsky and Khvayninsky in Tsumadinsky regions; ferruginous springs were found in Bezhtinsky, Tidibsky and Karadakh. Khvartykuninsky, Untsukulsky, Tlyaratinsky and Gergebilsky springs are close in salt composition to Kislovodsk's Korodinsky's, and Datunsky's *narzans* (healing springs) in Shamilsky district [29, 30].

172 *Dagestan – History, Culture, Identity*

Summary

Medicines and poultices were mixed with talismans; behaviour, of both healer – in spells and rituals – and patient, who might be required to pray or seek repentance, was prescribed.

Successful healing combined plant, animal and mineral medicines with ritual actions. In sacred medicine, supernatural forces and faith in their ability to cause diseases and healing were necessary. Belief in the universal animation of matter served also as the basis for diagnosis. The power of traditional medicine was that the mountaineers realized that their health also depended on the environment, sanitary conditions and the health of their neighbours.

Prior to urban and nationalised medical systems, small ethnic groups depended upon local doctors for their survival. Although many of these healers' cures and methods might have been idiosyncratic and indeed occasionally appear bizarre to modern eyes, the dissemination of Arabic knowledge was widespread; modern science has indeed validated many of the treatments, even if rejecting others. The intersection of the spiritual world with the mountaineers' daily lives is rejected by Western science but is the basis for ethno-cultural understanding of many of the processes described.

References

[1] Alekseev V.P. Essays on human ecology. 1993. pp32–6.
[2] Krupnik I.I. Arctic ethnoecology. 1989. pp14–15.
[3] Bromlej Y.V. and Voronov A.A. Traditional medicine as a subject of ethnographic research. No. 5. 1976. p16.
[4] Bulatov B.B. and Luguev S.A. Essays on the history of the spiritual culture of the highlanders of Central Dagestan in the XVIII-XIX centuries. Makhachkala. 2004. pp113–14, 127, 139.
[5] Pirogov N.I. Report on a trip to the Caucasus. 1852. p69.
[6] Abdurakhman Gazikumukhi. Book of Memoirs. 1869. Repr. Ed. Saidova M.S. Makhachkala. 1997. p129.
[7] Dubrovin N. History of war and Russian dominion in the Caucasus. Ed. 6. Vol. 1. Bk. 1. St. Petersburg. 1871. p586.
[8] Oganesyan L.A. The history of medicine in Armenia from ancient times to the present day. Pt. 1. Erevan. 1946. p188.
[9] Musaeva M.K. and Musaev M.A. Intellectual development and education of children in the traditions of the peoples of Dagestan. Archaeology, Ethnology Folklore of the Caucasus. Tbilisi. 2010. pp497–9.
[10] Saidov M.S. Dagestan literature of the XVIII-XIX centuries in Arabic. Proc. XXV international conference of the East. Vol. 2. 1960. p121.
[11] Shtanchaev S.T. Folk doctors of Dagestan in the XIX century. Soviet Health Protection. No. 7. 1963. pp59, 121.
[12] Akhmedov S.K. History of Lak literature. Pre-Revolutionary Literature. Vol. 1. Makhachkala, 2008. pp45–8.

[13] Many'shev S.B. Hannal Murad – a source on the history of medicine in Dagestan. Lavrov collected Materials XXXIV and XXXV. St. Petersburg. 2011. pp76, 151–3.

[14] al-Hakim Lukman. The book of medicines. Ed. Isaev A.A. Makhachkala. 2008.

[15] Alieva P.S. Traditional medicine of Avars. Makhachkala. 2009. pp78–9, 110, 113,116, 120, 126–7.

[16] Dibirov M.A. Folk medicine of the Avars. Makhachkala. 1984. pp9, 46.

[17] Overview of the Dagestan region for 1892. Temir-Khan-Shura. 1893. pp57–8.

[18] Monuments of customary law of Dagestan XVIII-XIX centuries. 1965. p202.

[19] Chikov A.S. Medicinal plants. 1982. pp20–1.

[20] Lager A.I. Healing plants. Minsk. 1998.

[21] Maxlayuk V.P. Medicinal plants in traditional medicine. Saratov. 1993.

[22] Ordynskij V. Onions and garlic. 1934. p34.

[23] Grigulevich N.I. Traditional nutrition of Azerbaijanis and the problem of longevity. 1989. p111.

[24] Ramazanova Z.B. Beekeeping of the peoples of Dagestan in the XIX and early XX centuries. History Archaeology and Ethnography of Caucasus. Vol. 15. No. 3. 2019. pp485–94.

[25] Alimova B.M. Tabasarans XIX – beginning of XX century. Historical and Ethnographic Research. Makhachkala. 1992. p223.

[26] Piotrovsky S. A trip to the mountains. Kavkaz. No. 71. 1853.

[27] Omarov A. Memoirs of the mutalim. SSKG. Tiflis, 1868. p14.

[28] Musaeva M.K. Rites of inducing rain and sun among the Hvarshins. Makhachkala. 1987.

[29] Chursin G.F. The cult of iron among the Caucasian peoples.Tiflis. 1927. pp4, 7.

[30] Dr. Fekhner. Alphabetical list of treatment places (mineral waters, mud, sea bathing and climatic stations of the Caucasus). Caucasian calendar for 1916. Tiflis. 1915. p184.

21 Dagestan mountain-valley horticulture

Perhaps you see horticulture as small-scale, like gardening, and agriculture as large-scale, like farming. Generally speaking, this assumption is true, but greater differences exist. Horticulture can actually be classified as a field under the umbrella of agricultural science. That being said, they both use many of the same techniques for cultivation and overlap with crop and turf sciences. Horticultural science includes the research, study and practice of plant cultivation, propagation, breeding, production, and physiology. The plants focused on are mainly vegetables, trees, flowers, turf, shrubs, fruits, and nuts. The key difference is that horticultural products have to both taste good and look good! For example, if you are enjoying a fresh, juicy tomato on a sandwich – a horticulturist grew it. If you are dipping French fries into ketchup, a crop science graduate running an agricultural farm grew it [1].

Mountain-valley horticulture has been in a terminal state in market-economy Dagestan, as in other regions of the Caucasus, since the 1990s. Magomedkhan's 2013 expedition to Gergebil, Khunzakh and Botlich districts gathered data on valley-use for plant production. The available land areas, the boundaries subdividing these, and the technology of terracing and irrigation, all indicated decline and decreasing efficiency.

A real threat is the disappearance of local varieties, caused by the privatization of land, the reconstruction of ancient gardens, and the surprisingly large-scale flooding of mountain-valley gardens by changing water basins and artificial lakes for hydroelectric power stations. Fruit varieties such as Arakan Red, Golotlinsky, Dzhir-Haji, Kakhar-ich, Renet Akhtynsky, Dakur Chukhver and Kal Chukhver have almost disappeared; others have been entirely lost.

Dr. Magomed Abdulgamidovich Magomedov of the Mountain Botanical Garden Institute found on expeditions to the mountain-valleys that most local varieties were more resistant to diseases and pests than imports. The fruits, especially apricots and peaches, were distinguished by unmatched taste, large uniform size, marketability and good transportability and storage, even under adverse conditions.

Vanished cereals included mountain-valley corn, frost-resistant bare-grain barley, durum wheat varieties Sary-Bugda and Ak-Bugda. Centuries-old breeds of cattle,

DOI: 10.4324/9781003388579-21

sheep, goats and horses, highly adapted to the harsh mountain conditions, have degenerated or been lost.

The weakness of state support has aggravated the decline. By 2000, the area of orchards was reduced to 2,100 hectares, and fruit production to 45,300 tons. The nursery base practically ceased to exist and the canning factories were left without raw materials and ceased to function and were mothballed, which had secondary effects on the economy and employment. While the former infrastructure worked after a fashion, the return on capital to renew and modernise this industrial base, after a period of disuse, is prohibitive.

Everything is available in Dagestan for growing and processing fruit and berries for local markets, but it is not used effectively. In Soviet times the markets sold only local products, while today imports have undercut local produce. Although there are government regulation to protect local producers, they are not enforced. Fruit and berry products, often tasting inferior compared to local equivalents, are imported from Moldova, Azerbaijan, Iran, Morocco, Israel, Argentina, Brazil and Egypt. Local varieties potentially have higher yields and winter hardiness than others. Development is hindered by bans from Russia's Federal Veterinary and Phytosanitary Oversight Service *Rosselkhoznadzor* on importing seeds, cuttings and trees to Russian Federation on pretexts such as pest-control and doubts about genetically modified (GM) plants. For example in April 2013 a temporary ban on 21,000 tonnes p.a. EU seed-potato imports was allegedly due to pest risk.

Mountain gardening is part of the traditional economy of Dagestan. Terraced slopes are an ancient and large-scale form of engineering. Terracing enlarges the conservation and accumulation of both soil and moisture, and thus increases yields, one of the greatest achievements of the Ancient World. "A person changed the mountain, but in return it also changed the consciousness of the mountaineer. It changed society itself, that had created this culture" [2]. Archaeological finds of fruit seeds in the Irganai and Chirkei settlements of the Bronze Age (second millennium BCE) indicate that Dagestan is one of the oldest zones of terrace technology, whence it spread across the globe.

Since the Bronze Age, the warm mild climate and man's terracing allowed successful cultivation of Caucasian persimmons, peaches, apricots, pears, apples, cherries, plums, walnuts and almonds.

Although the cultivation of grain and the production of meat was of highest importance throughout Dagestan, some mountain societies specialized in one type of production, for example salt mining in Kwanhidatl village; fruit growing in Botlikh; the production of edged weapons and firearms in Harbuk; forging steel in Amuzgi; jewellery in Kubachi. Archi was known for its shepherds; and later Dargin Levashi grew cabbages for Russia. In many mountain valley villages, horticulture was the main branch of agriculture.

Villagers have always sought to benefit from what land they have, however little; and surplus beyond their own needs became the root of economic activity in the

Figure 21.1 Terracing in Dagestan

subsistence landscape. Horticultural products were bartered for grain and meat in the plains and high mountains.

Fresh market garden produce could not be transported far, especially on horse-drawn vehicles or pack-animals; until the railway reached Dagestan at the end of the XIX century, only nuts and dried fruits could be exported.

In all feudal societies of Dagestan, fruits were included in the list of tithes. The Ummah Khan of Avar taxed his subject villages specifically in gardening products, and other cattle breeding villages either feudal or part of jamaats paid their tax in kind. Some of these payments are documented giving an insight into what was produced where.

The mountain-valley jamaats regulated horticulture and winemaking. Adat records from the XVI–XVII centuries show harsh penalties provided for violations, even 'a prohibition on eating grapes.'

Punishments involved material payment-in-kind of land, cattle, copper vessels or textiles, but not fruits and vegetables. While it was possible to pay gold or silver, in-kind fines were more visible as an example to others. Damage to arable fields, the garden or fruit trees was punished severely. In Kudutl village "if someone cuts off an apricot tree, he will pay a measure of grain (*zerna*)." Setting fire to a field before harvest, a hayloft, stacks of straw, or a garden at any time of the year, as well as setting fire to a house, destroying a bridge and killing an innocent person were equated with insurrection, with the most severe consequences. Violation of the legal starting time and date for fruit picking was punishable by a severe fine.

With the accession of Dagestan to Russia c. 1860 and the establishment of a stable peace, cattle breeding and horticulture developed rapidly. A modern Dagestani economic historian [3] noted that "the area of gardens in Dagestan has increased many times over. According to existing data, over 14 years up to 1914 in Khadzhal-makhi and Tsudakhar Dargin villages, the area under garden cultivation increased

Dagestan mountain-valley horticulture 177

5.15 times, in Avar – 3.83 times, in the Andean – 4.55 times, and in Gunib – 17 times. In 1902 Khizri Hajiyev's factory in Temir-Khan-Shura produced 20,000 poods of canned food and 18,000 poods of mashed apricots and plums. His other factories, in Arakani village in the Avar district and Khadzhalmakhi in the Dargin district sold 800 poods of canned puree for 50,000 roubles. By 1914, 45 small handicraft factories were busy in Hindalal, making some 500 tons of products. In the same year dried fruits (apricots 50% and 15% plums) production reached 980 tons with canned foods and mashed potatoes, exported to Nizhny Novgorod and on to Manchuria and China, where they successfully competed with Californian canned foods."

In 1913, out of 208,700 hectares sown, 95.7% were grain crops. Industrial crops used 4,110 hectares, vegetables and melons 2,140 hectares and forage 2,700 hectares. Orchards occupied 4,400 hectares, as did vineyards. Orchards were esteemed for the high value of their produce. In other regions of Russia gardening was not so serious, and was developed later during the Soviet mass collectivization [4].

Climate is vital for productive horticulture, the most suitable in Dagestan is on the southern plains of the Kyurin district, near Derbent and in the foothills of the Kaitago-Tabasaran district, and it flourished in these areas. Especially suitable were the high plateaus of Nizhne Kaitag and Urkarakh villages in northern Tabasaran, and in the northern foothills of Temir-Khan-Shura. Horticulture also developed significantly in the Avar, Andy, Gunib, Samur and part of Dargin mountainous districts [5]. Market gardens were even carved out of areas normally given to arable crops.

The mountain valleys hosted ancient and intensive settlement, taking advantage of the hot summer Mediterranean climate (Köppen-Geiger 'CSA'), the absence of sharp fluctuations in temperature and the numerous springs for irrigation. Mountain-valley gardening exports were more developed than plains and foothill subsistence gardening, which was more suited to grain.

Larger-scale orchards were rare in Dagestan due to topographical constraints and fruit trees are found dotted wherever they could find room. Where ground was cleared from forest, wild root-stock could have cultivated varieties grafted onto them. Grazing cattle on the same ground meant that the fruiting crowns had to be above their reach. Other trees were planted near houses, and in winter pastures; obviously the most open ground tended to be planted with arable crops, but small terraces and gardens could usually include some productive trees too. Gardeners tried to plant trees near their houses and livestock winter pastures.

The highlander-gardener's expertise in breeding created dozens of local varieties of fruits. Successful varieties were transferred to other areas and villages.

During the second half of the XIX century after the Russian pacification, there were separate propagation nurseries with rich prepared soils and the young plants were sold on to other villages. The nurseries and gardens were privately owned. With good care, the young plants yielded crops in seven or eight years. In addition, local gardeners grafted to stronger wild fruit tree stock in hay fields.

178   *Dagestan – History, Culture, Identity*

Winter preparation of the gardens began immediately after the harvest. Usually, by autumn, the soil was carefully dug by hand (i.e. not ploughed). Where there was a need and availability, organic fertilizers were applied. A thorough sanitary cleaning was carried out by pruning dry branches, and by pulling weeds, which were burned. Very often the trunks of young trees were tied with straw to protect them from being damaged by frosts and hares and other rodents. Then they pruned the trees, depending on the species, variety and condition.

In the spring, early watering was carried out, followed by loosening the soil around the roots. Over the summer, five to six more irrigations were completed, depending on the weather that year. Disease control was dealt with from early spring and pests like weevils were collected by hand.

The irrigation system of Dagestan, created over many centuries, has specific features, including a fixed distribution of exact quantities of water in sequence to irrigate the fields and gardens of jamaat members, who ruled on the right to water as a communal property. Private ownership of water is still unknown. They also strictly controlled the maintenance and construction of irrigation facilities. The village foreman and irrigators controlled the punctilious observance of the order, with severe punishments for the slightest violation of the unwritten rules. In one village, a bull was taken from a violator and given to his community, another was sent to the back of the queue, with unenviable consequences for his garden. If an irrigator-inspector discovered on his rounds that a careless owner had let water overflow his garden, then he lost his next turn.

Without the permission of the jamaat, it was forbidden to divert water for other household needs such as the preparation of adobe. In fact the irrigation system self-regulated the watering sequence. Since ancient times, fields were divided into sections. The main water canal was a complex structure with supporting stone walls, and water supply tunnels. A special sluice diverted water from the stream or river into the canal, from which, by means of a distributor, water was diverted from the main channel into the middle channels. In 1901 a Russian agronomist wrote admiringly "In Dagestan, the water is supplied not only in the valleys – I have seen water outlets even high in the mountains. Often a native leads water from one height to another, even through an entire gorge, in wooden gutters, almost hanging in the air, on thin high supports, and sometimes he leads water underground in pipes" [6].

All plots belonging to individual farms were irrigated on the top-bottom principle with first year watering from the top, and the second year's from the bottom, which ensured fair distribution over time. This encouraged observance of the watering sequence between adjacent owners. If irrigation began from the upper section, then the top-bottom principle was also observed between the owners of neighbouring plots. This regulation held for all plots. If the owner of the next plot from below did not appear on time for watering, his turn passed to the next one. Even if he came late, he still lost the right to water. Again, the irrigation system self-regulated the sequence of irrigation. Complex piping systems can still be seen which were used

Dagestan mountain-valley horticulture   179

to avoid water flooding along the terrace, when the increased weight of the wet soil threatened the retaining walls. Naturally, it was easier to water hay fields, and other level fields which did not require retaining walls.

In the old days, watering began after *pervaya borozda*, the holiday of the First Furrow. The main canal was kept in top condition and maintained according to the decision of the elders, informed by regular inspections, as announced in the larger villages by their spokesman. It was repaired and cleaned by the whole village and the secondary channels were kept up to scratch by the owners of the sections through which they passed. The irrigators inspected the canals before the water was turned on. The construction and repair of walls and aqueducts were entrusted to craftsmen. Everyone contributed manual work, like breaking the line and digging the canal. Any repair work shirkers were fined tariffs by the jamaat. During renovation the village was locked-down. If someone needed to leave, he had to pay for a substitute.

The villagers used picks, crowbars, shovels, and hand carts for digging, clearing and maintaining the canals and when necessary the jamaat also built a few reservoirs. Currently the traditional irrigation systems, which were largely neglected during the Civil War (1918–21), followed a few years later in the 1930s by the Soviet anti-kulak policies, have been replaced by spraying.

Fresh fruits, apricot kernels and walnuts were exported to the Russian market. In 1916, ten canneries in Dagestan sold about 4,800 tons of canned fruits, approximately 15% of the total Russian Empire production. Lack of sugar during the Civil War meant canning had to stop; without sales the businesses were bankrupt, and by the time of the establishment of Soviet Power in 1920, they were dilapidated too. In 1921 the total output was 193 tons of canned fruits, only 4% of the output five years earlier [7].

In general Dagestan productivity declined 90% from 1913 to 1921. Cities suffered huge damage; industry, fishing, and handicraft production lacking raw materials and sales markets, all declined dramatically. But agriculture was in an even worse position. The number of working livestock decreased by 60–75% compared to 1913 and wheat area decreased by 54%. Bread produced was 8% of the quantity calculated as necessary for health, and in 1922 there were 200,000 undernourished hungry people [8].

In Soviet times, radical changes took place in the organization of gardening in Dagestan. The first major step was the opening of the Dagestan experimental fruit-growing station in Buinaksk at the beginning of 1931, which studied and developed gardening in the republic.

In the 1930s, the largest proportion of fruit trees in Dagestan – 46% – were planted in the mountainous regions and less suitable highlands of northern Dagestan. (The rest were in the plains.) In southern Dagestan orchards accounted for 33%, of which 18% was in the foothills, 2.4% in the northern plains and 1.3 % in the alpine regions and the rest in the plains [9].

180   *Dagestan – History, Culture, Identity*

The hilly topography of course meant that gardens and orchards still had to be squeezed into narrow artificial terracing. Such little plots required intensive maintenance by the locals.

Gardens in the 1930s mainly grew local varieties. The Fruit Experimental Station had 70 varieties of apple, some 30 varieties of pear, over 40 varieties of apricot, and over 30 varieties of peach. In the 1950s, the champion (the highest Soviet honour) village of Khadzhalmakhi handed over to the state more than 1,500 tons of apricots and 2–3,000 tons of apples and pears in a regular harvest year. Local varieties of pears yielded 2–3 tons per tree. Nowadays there are almost no such trees left, and harvests are estimated at a few hundred tons [10]. In 1939, there were 21 canneries producing about 181 metric tonnes.

From 1946 to 1950 there was radical restructuring by the central Soviet authorities of the horticulture of the republic, with reconstruction of old natural gardens, where old trees were replaced by young trees, supposedly introducing more promising varieties.

The area of commercial market gardens increased especially during 1954 to 1956 when over 13,000 hectares were planted by kolkhoz state farms, complemented by a dramatic increase in fruit processing that enabled an annual output of about 3,290 metric tonnes of canned fruit. In the Tsudakhar, Botlikh, Kaitag, Gergebil, Kasumkent, Uitsukul and Akhti regions, the sale of horticultural produce accounted for 70% to 80% of total income.

The general increase in industrial production of the 1950s gave a powerful impetus to the development of processing enterprises in areas with well-developed horticulture. Thanks to the development of a relatively efficient canning industry, more than 30,000 people found reliable employment. In 1989 a record 149,000 tons of fruits were produced.

From the 1960s in mountainous and foothill Dagestan, after the liquidation of the farm system, many lands were banned from family habitation because they were too far from kolkhoz settlements, so mechanization was abandoned and manual labour was all that was available.

In the 1980s, the area under horticultural cultivation amounted to 65,500 hectares, or 1.6% of the agricultural land of Dagestan, which provided over 6% of gross agricultural output and 16% of crop production. With the collapse of the collective and state farm systems c.1990, in which all economic activity had been planned, even with harvest quotas, collective care of the gardens was discontinued. Unlike most state enterprises, gardens were puzzlingly left without 'new' private owners and were neglected. Abandoned orchards became unproductive and yields plummeted. The mechanization of horticultural production in Dagestan was solved much more slowly than in other industries, hampered by the lack of machines that could be used in terraced gardens. So-called 'small mechanization' of horticulture had increased in Russia, but was of little use in the mountains, so many old decayed

Dagestan mountain-valley horticulture 181

Figure 21.2 Avar Kolkhoz woman with baby, cot and sickle going to mow hay;
photo: Dr Professor of Art Tatyana Znamerovskaya 1958

gardens were uprooted, neglecting the perfect climatic and natural conditions and the sophisticated art of grafting.

Since 1990, the area of garden land, especially in the mountains, has decreased despite extensive research into the technology of gardening. In 2002, a Dagestan ethnographer regretted "Earlier, the mountaineer never created a plot without making it productive. He was immediately planting trees to 'catch on' to the slope and gradually level it. But, by the late 1980s in the mountains, 6,000 hectares of ready-made garden land were empty, not to mention the slopes that could be turned into excellent garden plots" [10].

As the leading Dagestani ethno-agronomist explained, "private traders still felt that gardens were not only of economic benefit for them, but also for their ecology.

182 Dagestan – History, Culture, Identity

A thousand-year hereditary occupation in gardening is their peculiar religion. Accordingly the order and aesthetics of the garden were observed in the private sector." The Soviet alienation of the garden economy from private owners and the creation of large horticultural collective farms led to the degradation of horticulture. "The introduction of Soviet agrotechnical achievements to reconstruct gardens was based on methods that had not been developed in Dagestan conditions." Clearly economic intensification and horticultural culture are not the same thing. Although "the modernization of agriculture was inevitable, it needed to be introduced gradually, modified by a comprehensive scientific and practical rationale" [11].

Market conditions are inefficient in Dagestan where horticultural products are either sold below cost or not at all. For example in 2019, apricots fetched a paltry 5 roubles each at the Tlokh canning factory and 6 roubles at the Gotsatlinsky cannery.

To address such anomalies and encourage the restoration and development of horticulture the republican program "Development of gardening in the Republic of Dagestan for 2011–2016" was adopted by the state. Unfortunately its implementation is yet to come. The traditional experience of mountain-valley management remains dormant.

References

[1] NC State Horticulture Science, NC State University. Agricultural Science and Horticulture. 23 January 2017. https://horticulture.cals.ncsu.edu/online/horticulture-vs-agriculture/.

[2] Aglarov M.A. More on agricultural terracing in Dagestan. 2016. p. 30.

[3] Yakhyaev M.M. Economic effectiveness of the mountain-valley horticulture of Dagestan. Makhachkala. 1974. p17.

[4] Agriculture of Dagestan. 1946. p10.

[5] History of Dagestan. Vol. 1. Nauka. 1967. p235.

[6] Nadezhdin P.P. Caucasus region: Nature and people. 1901 Repr. 2010.

[7] Dagestan Industry in the five-year plan 1920–1925. Buinaksk. 1925. p48.

[8] History of Dagestan. Vol. 3. Nauka. 1968. pp145–6.

[9] Dagestan agriculture. 1946. pp121–2.

[10] Osmanov M.-Z.O. Economic and cultural types (regions) of Dagestan in the Soviet era. 2002. pp149, 200.

[11] Aglarov M.A. Khindalal. Avars of the mountain valleys Central and Western Dagestan. Essays on traditional culture and ethno-economics. Makhachkala. 2018. p31.

22 About Mountain Jews

The Mountain Jews had an integral role in Dagestan's culture yet they are rarely written about. Their identity is interwoven with the other ethnicities contributing to Dagestan's mostly cherished plurality.

Some Mountain Jews, self-named Dzhugyur, Dzhugyurzho call themselves 'Tat', as does the official press. Their language Dzhuguri belongs to the southwestern subgroup of Iranian languages, influenced by Azeri and Kumyk languages.

In Dagestan, 98% of the Mountain Jews live in Derbent and Makhachkala. Until the 1970s, rural residents were scattered in traditional locales in Derbent, Kaitag, Magaramkent and Khasavyurt districts of south Dagestan. Outside Dagestan, Mountain Jews live mainly in cities – in Azerbaijan (Baku, Quba, Shemakha, Oguz/Wartashen, Krasnaya Sloboda, and Mudzhi village); in Kabardino-Balkaria (Nalchik); in North Ossetia (Vladikavkaz and Mozdok), as well as in Moscow, St. Petersburg and Pyatigorsk.

Mountain Jews are believed to be descendants of ancient Jews captured and displaced from Israel and Judea to Mesopotamia, which later became an integral part of Achaemenid Persia, where they adopted the ancient Persian language. In the late Sassanian period (V-VI centuries), part of the Mesopotamian Jews were resettled in the Caucasus, in Caucasian Albania – in the territory of modern Northern Azerbaijan and Southern Dagestan. Judging by the epigraphic and other data, the bulk of the modern Mountain Jews of the East Caucasus are descendants of Jewish refugees and immigrants from Persia during the colonial policy of the Safavid shahs in the XVI-XVII centuries. A number of scholars such as R. Magomedov, M. Matatov and L. Avshalumova [1] claimed without evidence that Mountain Jews are Tats, that is, Persians by origin, some of whom were allegedly converted to Judaism during the period (VIII-X centuries) when the rulers adopted the Khazar Kaganate's religion.

According to General A. V. Komarov, "Mountain Jews in Dagestan began to settle in the late VIII- early IX centuries, and their first settlements were in Salah near the village of Khuchni in Tabasaran, and in Kaitag in a gorge near Kala-Koreish, now known as Zhiut-Katta, the Jewish Gorge. According to legend, about 300 years

DOI: 10.4324/9781003388579-22

184   *Dagestan – History, Culture, Identity*

ago Mountain Jews went from here to Majalis, and later some of them moved to Yangikent. Jews living in Temir-Khan-Shura district preserved the legend that their ancestors came from Jerusalem after the first destruction via Baghdad, where they lived for a very long time. Avoiding persecution and destruction from the Muslims, they gradually began to move to Tehran, Hamadan, Rasht, Quba, Derbent, Madzhalis, Karabudahkent and Targu and often they settled permanently" [2].

The first Mountain Jewish graduate of Moscow University wrote: "The history of the relocation of Mountain Jews to the Caucasus is not reliably known, and no texts have been preserved for the time of this relocation; but based on folk traditions, these Jews are descended from the Israelites, who were withdrawn from Palestine and settled in Media by Assyrian and Babylonian kings. Thus, their ancestors belonged to the times of the first temple and did not participate in the killing of Jesus Christ, as the Mountain Jews themselves say, no matter what village or city you come to, saying that it's tradition passed to them from their grandfathers and fathers. Even in Persia, the Jews mixed with the Persian tribe of the Tats, and some adopted the dominant pagan religion of the Persians, as a result of which, firstly, the present language of the Jews belongs to the group of Iranian languages, i.e. it is closely related to Persian, Kurdish, Ossetian, and Talysh (according to Professor V. Miller), and secondly, some pagan beliefs still remain in the religion of Mountain Jews. Then, in the Middle Ages, according to legend, the Tat Jews mixed with the Khazars who lived on the western shore of the Caspian Sea, so they consider the Khazar kings of these times to be their own. And, finally, during the Arab invasion of the Caucasus, whole villages of Jewish Tats accepted Mohammedanism, while the rest remained faithful to the religion of Moses and received the name Dag-Chufut, i.e. Mountain Jews" [3].

Yehuda Chernyi and Ilya Anasimov were the first Jewish ethnographers to write on Mountain Jews. As Chernyi wrote in 1870, "In Derbent, Quba, Temir-Khan-Shura, Khasavyurt and Grozny I saw decent European houses among the Mountain Jews, but they belong, of course, to the rich, who go to the Nizhny-Novgorod fair every year. Such Jews have one part of their home neat in Asian style, where they live with their families with an additional room for *kunakskaya* mountain guests, and another set of rooms in European style only for European guests . . . Every Muslim has his kunaks in Jewish villages, and every Jew has his close friends in Muslim villages . . . the Jews have completely assimilated into a Muslim character and much of the customs and lifestyle of Muslims: but their language remained the same, Farsi-Tat . . . they read prayers or the Talmud in Aramaic with a Farsi-Tat translation chanted with a Tatar melody" [4]. He also inaccurately created an image of Mountain Jews as both 'savage Asians' and 'primordial Jews' that fuelled anti-Semitism.

There were 2,500 non-Mountain Jewish Tats in Dagestan in 1866, living near Derbent in Zhalgan, Mitagi, Kemakh, Zidyan, Bilgadi, Gimeidi and Rukel villages. Over time, the Tats changed to speaking Azeri, keeping Tat in the family, and began to self-identify as Azerbaijanis.

About Mountain Jews 185

Mountain Jews were traditionally involved in agriculture, craft and trade. They cultivated vines and vegetables, and more profitably sericulture, madder cultivation and tobacco growing. They prepared sheepskins including Morocco, textiles, knitting, and dyeing, for tailoring and millinery. Mountain Jewish townspeople were merchants or craftsmen or petty traders in needles, threads and paints and other small hardware goods. They delivered their own wares and stocks to the villages, which developed their role as multilingual agents between highlanders, plainsmen and foreign merchants.

From medieval times travellers and later field ethnographers recorded the numerous Jewish quarters that existed until the end of the XIX century, in Azerbaijani, Lezgin, Tabasaran, Tat, Kumyk, Dargin and Avar villages, further evidenced by the toponymy throughout Dagestan including Juvudag, (*Juv-* and *Dzhu-* mean Jewish) Dzhugut-aul, Dzhugut-bulak, Dzhugut-kuche, Dzhufut-katta, Dzhugut Iazul-roso, Dzhugut kaburlar and Dzhugut. Mountain-Jewish communities assimilated closely with the majority populations of Akhti, Rutul, Karchag, Usukhchay, Usug, Ubra, Ruguja, Arakany, Salta, Muni, Mekegi, Deshlagar, Rukel, Mugatyr, Gimeidi, Zidyan, Maraga, Majalis, Yangikent, Dorgeli, Buinaksk, Karakudak, Kafir-Kumukh, Chiryurt, Zubutli, Andiri, Khasavyurt, Aksay and Kostek, where they were original members of many tukkhums created after they had assimilated. Traditional material culture of the Mountain Jews was similar to their neighbours in Dagestan and Azerbaijan, living in stone buildings with two or three rooms for guests, tools for building, crafts and agriculture, traditional types of clothing, utensils and jewellery. Their delicious food was similar to their neighbours with different ritual dishes (chapter 23).

Up to the 1930s, Mountain Jewish families mostly lived around a common yard with up to four generations of 10 to 40 people, where each family had its own house or private rooms. The father whom everyone should obey was head, in charge of the family economy and religion that regulated social life and ethical behaviour.

Marriages were often arranged between cousins in this extended family cluster. Girls were usually only 12–15 years old when married, boys 17–18. Levirate and sororate were not uncommon. Kalym was paid to her parents and to purchase her dowry. Matchmaking, betrothal and especially the wedding were celebrated with solemnity (chapter 17) in the synagogue's front courtyard, followed by the wedding feast and presentation of gifts. Bride kidnapping occurred which sometimes was consensual. Judaism allowed polygamy, but in practice bigamy was only observed among the wealthy and rabbis, if the first wife was childless. Women could not divorce and did not have an equal share of the inheritance. Marriage to Gentiles was forbidden because it involved converting to another religion and leaving the community. It was seen as a transition to another people.

Religious rites *numaz* were performed in the synagogue led by the Rabbi. Children were taught the basics of Judaism and educated in synagogue schools or occasionally privately. In the 1850s there were 27 synagogues and 36 schools *nubo*

186   Dagestan – History, Culture, Identity

hunde. The chief rabbi of the city, the chairman of the religious court and the head *dayan* of the higher religious school *yeshiva*, were elected by the community. Traditional rituals included circumcision, the bar mitzvah confirmation, *klub* (kosher) restrictions on food and the preparation of *matzah.* The High Holiday celebrations included Niesonu/ Passover, Aselt Shavuot, Rush gyo-Shone Rosh Hashana/ New Year, Aravoi Kushey, Yom Kippur/ Judgement Day and Gyomunu Purim feast of carnival and forgiving insults.

In Soviet times pre-1930s, the 'flowering and rapprochement of socialist nations and national cultures' allocated CPSU funds to develop 'Tat socialist literature and culture.' Mountain Jews were represented in the party and government, which gave them a sense of equality, reflected in their well-being. A newspaper was published in the Mountain Jews' language, also books, radio and television broadcasts and live performances in the municipal theatre in Derbent. Newspapers and magazines for and by Tats were published in Russia, Israel, and the USA. The *Vatan* newspaper was published in Dagestan in local Hebrew and Russian.

Mountain Jewish literature grew from their folklore and the rich imagery of their language transmitted through *ashugs* (singers), to include poets, writers, journalists and artists, composers, musicians and choreographers. Several were academicians and doctors and candidates of science in Nauka SSR. Others were CPSU politicians and heroes.

Most of the Ashkenazis arrived in Dagestan during 1941–1945 as war evacuees from Ukraine, Belarus and Leningrad. Many represented Soviet intelligentsia, scientists, physicians, academics and creative people, whose considerable talents helped their adopted country flourish.

In post-Soviet years, Mountain Jews occupied the following posts: a Minister of Energy of the Russian Federation, a deputy of the Russian Federation Duma, a President of the Guild of Russian Lawyers, Academicians of Natural Sciences, Chemistry, Cosmonautics and Cybernetics and History, an architect laureate and a Shakespeare authority, as well as several businessmen and philanthropists. In Azerbaijan there was a National Hero, a deputy of the Milli Majlis parliament and a chess master.

From the late 1980s the majority of Mountain Jews emigrated to Israel, the USA, and Germany. Of about 100,000 Mountain Jews worldwide 20,000 remain in the Russian Federation, 10,000 in Azerbaijan and about 1,000 in Dagestan. The remainders preserve their ethno-cultural, linguistic, confessional and food identity, but their fallen numbers has undermined the vitality of these traditions. Nevertheless mutual assistance and hospitality are practised seriously. The anti-Semitic repression against their ethnic identity was finally resolved in 2013 (chapter 11). In 2003 our OSCE election mission in north Azerbaijan drove past Qirmizi Qesebe (Russian name Krasnaya Svoboda) a beautifully kept Mountain Jewish village with a decreasing population and stopped at its walled cemetery that was in current use.

The tombstones have etched photos or statues of the deceased, images condemned by the local Rabbi. The émigré villagers returned home from outside Russia to enjoy their summer holidays.

References

[1] Semenov I.G. Mountain Jews. Some aspects of ethnic identification, end of XIX- beginning of XX century. Central Asia and Caucasus Journal. No. 3. 2003.
[2] Komarov A.V. Ethnic population of Dagestan oblast. Caucasian Dept. of Imperial Russian Geographical Society. Bk. VIII. 1873. p25.
[3] Anisimov I.S. Antiquities of the Mountain Jews. 1895.
[4] Chernyi I.Y. Mountain Jews. SSKG Bk. III. Pt. 1. 1870. pp4–6.

Additional Bibliography

Minorsky V.F. History of Shirvan and Darband X-XI centuries. 1963.
Eds. Kosven M.O. and Khashaev K.M. History geography and ethnography of Dagestan XVIII-XIX centuries. Archival Materials. 1958. p86.
Chenciner R. Madder Red: A history of luxury and trade. 2000.
Ibragimov M.R.A. and Magomedkhanov M.M. Ethno-demographic aspects of the formation of the urban population of Dagestan (end of XIX- beginning of XX century). Vestnik Istoriya. Vol. l. 2009. pp247–59.
Ikhilov M.M. Mountain Jews. Peoples of Dagestan. 1955.
Murzakhanov Y.I. Mountain Jews. Annotated Bibliographic Index Pt1. 1994.
Murzakhanov Y.I. Essay on the history of ethnographic study of highland Jews (XVIII-beginning XX century). 1994.
Eds. Begun I., Dymshitz V., Muradov Y., and Shlenov M. Mountain Jews: History ethnography culture. 1999.
Semenov I.G. On the origin of Mountain Jews. 1997.
Chlenov M.A. Between the Scylla of Judaization and the Charybdis of Zionism: Mountain Jews in XX Century. Diaspory. No. 3. 2000.
Ibragimov M.R.A. Mountain Jews in Dagestan. Peoples of Dagestan, No. 1. 2002. pp15–18.

23 Meat and Fish of the Mountain Jews

Traditional food and its preparation has always been a much-loved aspect of the ethnic identity of all Jews, including Mountain Jews. Having lived for some 1,500 years among other Dagestani peoples they assimilated Caucasian manners, behavioural norms, traditional methods of agriculture and trade, as well as house-building, clothing. And of course food.

The economy of Mountain Jews was based on trade, crafts and agriculture. As farmers they eschewed pastoral in favour of arable, and mainly concentrated on grapes and vegetables, though in Derbent and Kaitag regions every family had one or two cows or buffalos, a few sheep and as many chickens as possible. They eat more lamb than chicken or fish. Near and about Derbent, dried *kutum* a deep burgundy-coloured fibrous estuary fish from where the Sulak and Samur deltas meet the Caspian is a ritual wedding food or a snack with drinks. Otherwise fresh fish, even with the nearby Caspian, is unpopular; the Dagestanis dislike the mess of cleaning it. The exception is easier-to-clean sturgeon, dried or fried, which is an especial delicacy [1, 2].

Also sometimes eaten by Mountain Jews is a cooked fish dish *bugleme* using kutum or *sazan* a freshwater Caucasian carp or bream. The cleaned fish is cut into pieces and put into a glazed earthenware bowl with the prepared onions. For one kg of fish you need 1.5 kg of small pieces of onion rubbed with salt and glazed in a ceramic pot over a slow fire for one hour. The onions lose both weight and size. Add several whole potatoes, sour berberis berries, or if not available, *alicha* plums or *kuraga* apricots, dried mint, salt, pepper and enough boiling water to cover the fish. Then the pot is placed in a covered copper cauldron filled with water and the dish is cooked for 40 minutes as in a bain-marie.

Mountain Jews eat both fresh and dried meat [3] but do not buy fresh meat until their dried meat is finished. For one family on average four to five sheep and half a cow (shared with another family) last for the winter-spring period, except for religious feasts, *shashlik* for important guests, or for funeral ritual food. Ritual food is the same as daily food but is served ceremonially. *Tara, inhvara, ingara pol, plov* and chudu were used in *Peysach* (Passover) and for weddings.

DOI: 10.4324/9781003388579-23

Meat and Fish of the Mountain Jews 189

Tara is made of roasted onion, forcemeat, *myasnoifarsh* (meat stuffing in Russian), spices, sorrel and a little water cooked over a slow fire. When the forcemeat is almost ready, add rice and fennel and *kindza* a bitter minty leaf herb. The consistency is something in between soup and porridge and is eaten with fingers, dipping in pieces of bread.

Ingara pol is a sort of khinkal, but the dough consists of over 50% wild garlic and is bound with eggs, not water. The dough is cut into two-inch-long pieces, boiled and served on a separate large plate. The lamb is boiled separately and served on its own large plate. There are four garnish cups of crushed walnuts, boiled eggs, stewed dried apricots and garlic mixed with bouillon.

Chudu is made with fat meat cut into small pieces with a special knife. With roasted onion, a lot of pepper and *zelen'* mountain greens, the meal is put into the centre of a thick pancake, the ends of which are sealed, with a hole in the middle for the steam to escape.

The successful preservation of meat in autumn for winter and spring is celebrated by *Sugum*. The respected hausfrau invited the *Ravvin* (Rabbi), neighbours, relatives and other local worthies to participate in 'drawing out the sinews from the meat' and making sausages. Unmarried young people were invited to cut up the meat, make sausages, peel onions and garlic and cook shashlik for the feast. They also sang and danced (chapter 27).

The hostess cooked pieces of liver and meat, and sent her daughters with plates on their heads to distribute them to neighbours, relatives and poor widows. The beneficiaries 'gave back' a symbolic egg, or a clove of garlic or an onion. Mountain Jews' tradition was to share any non-staple food with their relatives and community. For example, after a cow or buffalo was born it was good manners to send their neighbours a plate of boiled milk and eggs. The plate was duly returned with water in it, as a symbolic wish that the cow would not be dry, and give a lot of milk.

The technique of preparing and drying meats in a shaded and slightly windy place is the same throughout Dagestan. Sausages are prepared from carefully washed and salted *kishki* intestines, filled with cut meat spiced by *tmin* mountain caraway, *chabrets* mountain thyme, some flour, garlic and pepper. Men friends would visit to congratulate the household for preparing an ample reserve for winter and for having shashlik and wine. Meantime the women worked at preserving meat, 'drawing out the sinews', and making sausages and *kaurma* (fried pieces of meat covered by fat and preserved in a ceramic jar in a cool, fresh and dark place). Kaurma and *bakl'* dried sausages were chopped as a filling for kurze, for chudu, for pies, and for soups.

Sausages are boiled for khinkal and soup, or roasted with potato and spices. A special type of sausage made immediately after an animal was slaughtered consisted of liver, very small pieces of potato, offal fat, salt, red and black pepper and a little wheat or corn grits.

190   *Dagestan – History, Culture, Identity*

Throughout Dagestan every balcony was festooned with a range of ageing dried fat-tailed sheep fat-tails, one of the best reserve foods in case of hunger and it was believed that the older the dried fat-tail, the better its medicinal value. In 2020 it was taken against Covid.

Offal fat was roasted and poorer fat preserved in ceramic jars. Roasted fat was used for deep-frying or as a sauce for soups, khinkal and other porridge dishes, like these three more variants of stew-soups:

- *Khoye-gusht* is made from one-inch cubes of fat meat, potato, roasted onion and spices, over which water is poured just covering the ingredients. It is then cooked on a slow fire. When the dish is ready, chopped fennel and/or kindza are added as garnish and eaten with a spoon.
- *Boz-bash* is made from fat meat cut into very small pieces, boiled with a lot of onion added, red and black pepper and pieces of 'sour bread' made of dried alicha.
- *Yagni* is made of meat, potato, zelen,', black and red pepper, and a little kuraga, boiled in water, eaten by dipping in bread with fingers.

Rice was added to a soup called *dyush-pere* made of beans with less-than-one-inch raviolis, stuffed with minced lamb or beef, as available.

The best time for meat preservation is in the first cold days of late autumn. Good quality fresh lamb is available only in summer and autumn, because the quantity of lambs from spring lambing makes them affordable, rather than their pasture location in the high mountains. In winter and springtime mutton decreases in quality, so Dagestanis switch then to dried meat.

Autumn days happily spent preserving meat were filled with social visiting, as there was more than enough delicious food such as shashlik, dolma (or *dulma*) and of course khinkal. Poor members of the community were always grateful for a piece of liver or offal.

Chicken was considered to be very delicious, though not essential for family well-being. As Professor Mikhail Ikhilov obm, a Mountain Jewish ethnographer and colleague, used to say: "one chicken is not enough for a family, two is expensive" [4, 5, 6].

Chetirma is eaten with rice – plov/ *hermeosh*, and the chicken is stewed separately. When small pieces of chicken meat are almost cooked they are sprinkled with flour, vinegar, green herbs and egg-yolk. Chicken was also used in different types of soups. Mountain Jews characteristically added egg-yolk or whole eggs to chicken dishes.

Slaughtering is a very important part of Jewish food culture. For kosher food the animal must be slaughtered by a special butcher at the synagogue or by the Rabbi.

Some animals are not kosher in themselves such as pork or horse; others have to be killed and prepared in specific ways, for example bones must not be broken when cutting up carcasses.

Meat prepared other than by kosher customs is *trephine/ harum* (forbidden). There were certain days when meat was forbidden, for example in the fast-period before *Peysakh* (Russian *Paskha*). Meat and milk foods could not be eaten at the same time.

Meat food is prepared by four methods of cooking – boiled: khinkal, kurze, boz-bash, yagni; roasted: shashlik or shish-kebab, *lulya-kebab*; stewed: *yapragi* or dolma, tara, bugleme, khoye-gusht; and baked: chudu.

While Mountain Jews' food culture has many similarities with other Dagestani traditional foods, the Mountain Jews preserved a number of traditional dishes and their distinct ways of using spices in other dishes – a family secret.

References

[1] Chenciner R.B. Dying for caviar. Oxford Food Symposium. 1997.
[2] Chenciner R.B. and Salmanov E. Little known aspects of north east Caucasian mountain ram and other dishes. Oxford Food Symposium. 1987.
[3] Ramazanova Z., Magomedkhanov M.M. and Ed. Chenciner R.B. Meat food of mountain Jews of Dagestan. Oxford Food Symposium. 2005.
[4] Ikhilov M.M. Mountain Jews. Nauka dissertation. 1949.
[5] Ikhilov M.M. Mountain Jews. Peoples of the Caucasus. Vol. 1. 1960. pp554–61.
[6] Ikhilov M.M. Peoples of the Lezgin ethnic family: Ethnographic research on past and present Lezgins, Tabasarans, Rutuls, Tsakhurs and Aguls. 1967.

24 Heroes of sport and finance

Picture postcards of Shamil and even Stalin for sale in Market No 2 in Makhachkala in 1984 symbolized the cult of the strongman in repressed Soviet Dagestan. The fighter-champions were the rare winners in the Soviet system and when I met a few retired toughies for a drink I noticed that they had an unusual look of freedom in their smiling eyes.

"In the quiet before dusk, high on a deserted valley between two mountain ridges, where the greens and sepias were turning into blues and violets to the sound of a burbling stream, there was a distant movement. I peered closer and made out three young men, who were silently practicing the karate reverse foot drop-kick. Was this the significance of the modern Olympic Latin motto, *citius, altius, fortius*, meaning 'faster, higher, stronger,' painted on the Spartak gym wall in Makhachkala?" [1]

Wrestling was even more popular than spectacular tightrope-walking. As in Ancient Greece, a dance was performed before the start of a wrestling match, but this custom disappeared in the 1850s, dourly banned by Iman Shamil because it was 'a time of danger for their land'. The fighters' technique was similar to Cumberland wrestling, the aim being to flip the opponent onto the ground, using only hands or knees, while remaining standing. The fights were umpired strictly by the Elders or *aksakal* white-beards, a tradition which reappeared in a different form in 2019 when a potentially nasty conflict was avoided by the sudden appearance of the elders who ordered the young bloods to go home, which they promptly did.

But forget those stories of the weak but cunning fighters beating their heavier opponents. It is the epic tales of the strong men of Dagestan forged in the wrestling or circus rings which are the currency of oral tradition from the 1900s.

Here, for example is the tale of Kochap Mamma (Magomed), a Kumyk-Avar, later known as Sali-Suleiman of international fame. Incalculable physical strength and an iron will made him the invincible king of wrestling, having fought in Poland, Iran, India, Turkey, Denmark and Sweden. He was honoured as Champion of Champions in his native town, Buinaksk, and lived until 1972 when he was over ninety. Mamma was born into a poor highland family, and laboured from childhood. At sixteen, he went to work as a loader for a wine merchant who was impressed and promoted demonstrations of Mamma's strength. When a circus came to Buinaksk,

DOI: 10.4324/9781003388579-24

Mamma went to watch the wrestling. A Turk had defeated all corners, and the crowd demanded that Mamma have a go. He lifted the Turk off the ground and threw him down. Back came the well-known 131 kg wrestler to teach the boy a lesson, but Mamma dropped him harder and broke his nose.

Once, on his way home, he came upon two men with daggers at each other's throats. Mamma snatched the blades and broke them as if they were wood and held the two men apart. He could easily break a chain, make a knot in a steel rod, or bend a train rail over his shoulders.

When Mamma won the championship of Azerbaijan, he became known as the Lion of Dagestan. Next he beat the Persian champion and was invited to Turkey to fight the Sultan's gladiator. The two men, smeared with oil (as is the local custom), had a hard contest but finally Mamma caught the Turk around the torso in a vice-grip and squeezed him into submission. The Sultan pronounced Mamma champion and renamed him Sali-Suleiman after an historic hero. Sali-Suleiman toured with the famed circus 'Maksa'. Once, in Rostov, he saw and was fascinated by classical wrestling, but when he asked advice from Le Bushe, the French champion, he was invited to a teaching demonstration and derisively thrown, by surprise. In St Petersburg, Mamma took the opportunity to train professionally. After a contest in the Zoological Gardens a defeated Spaniard, in revenge, opened the cage of a Bengal tiger which leapt on Mamma, who grabbed it by the throat and killed it, despite his wounds.

At the regional Mini-Olympic games in Odessa (c. 1900), the circus was packed to see the greatest wrestlers in the world. First in the ring was Mamma. His opponent was the elegant Le Bushe, who was still smiling when Mamma lunged forward and threw him with his own hold. Le Bushe had to be carried out. At the World Championships in Florence, Sali-Suleiman defeated his remaining rival, the world champion Pederson the Dane, and the following year in Paris he defended his title. He also won in Chicago, Washington, Rome, Madrid, Stockholm, Warsaw and even London. Dr Paruk Debirov, a huge laughing Avar, and one of my wonderful colleagues at the Academy of Sciences, had once met him and said that he was a fine figure of a man, but utterly mad.

I once saw a venerable long-haired straggling-moustachioed strongman in Baku lift twenty men standing on both ends of a length of railway track and then bend the track with his neck, as is he were being crucified. He had turned grey as he staggered away exhausted, the fat rippling over his corset-truss. Other strongmen threw donkeys, held revving cars immobile and twisted rail track with their bare hands. The most bizarre act I saw was a Lezgin who began by lifting three 16 kg iron balls, tied together with cloth, in his teeth. He then twisted four-inch nails with his hands. Next, he lifted another man sitting on a chair, taking the back of the seat in his teeth. Finally, he lay on his back and a worn rug was placed over his body with his head and feet protruding. Three assistants then manoeuvred a large rock onto his torso. The strongest assistant then took a sledge-hammer and mashed the rock like an energized convict. As it was going slowly, another helper got to work with a second

194   *Dagestan – History, Culture, Identity*

sledge-hammer. I was barely able to lift some of the smaller fragments of rock. There was no trick involved. The crowd loved it, particularly the boys.

Wrestling was taken seriously by the State too. The entrance to Makhachkala wrestling school, built in 1935, may be flanked by giant social-realist Soviet-style statues of revealingly-clad well-endowed Russian youth and girl athletes, but inside the hard transformation of boys into men was in progress.

International coaches instructed 8- to 16-year-olds, sometimes with their little brothers. Even the disabled son of one of the coaches had been helped to walk through wrestling. The nine pairs of older youths and 20 younger boys trained obsessively five times a week for one hour in the morning and from 3.30 till 5 in the afternoon. They all danced as well. Next, the senior class started with a line-up and the Muslim greeting *salaam aleikum* 'peace to you' from the coach, followed by a roar of *aleikum salaam* 'and peace to you!' from the class. There were two small and wiry champions in the senior group. "Why are they so tough?" I asked the coach. It was obvious. "Because they eat khinkal!"

The Russian wrestling team invited to Manchester for the 1994 British open championships was entirely made up of nine Dagestanis. Their local sponsor was Gamid Gamidov a retired champion and also president of the national savings bank and director of the Dagestan Central bank, who was later assassinated in a bomb attack in 1997. The wrestling school is named in his memory. Many of the bank staff were ex-wrestlers. But they never arrived – airfares had been hit by inflation and were unaffordable.

Nowadays, alongside the physical strong men, Dagestan's financial heavyweights are celebrities, as is shown by the following examples of Ziyavudin Magomedov and Suleiman Kerimov. Khabib Nurmagomedov the MMA champion and rugby star Tagir Gadzhiev are equally famous, where sport and finance meet to promote Dagestan.

Ziyavudin Magomedov

An Avar, he was chairman of the Summa Group, a conglomerate of about 11,000 employees providing port logistics, engineering, construction, telecommunications, and oil and gas services. His Peri Charitable Foundation was established in 2012. His fortune, held jointly with his brother Magomed, was estimated at $US 1.4 bn by Russian Forbes in early 2018.

Peri worked with leading British digital innovator Adam Lowe of Factum Arte on the digitalization and printing of inscriptions. The first inscriptions were from the mihrab and tombstones of Kala-Koreish, one of the oldest surviving mosques in Dagestan; the aim was to make the mountain site an accessible part of the Dagestan national heritage, as promoted by an exhibition at the Victoria and Albert Museum in London in December 2017. A more ambitious project is the scanning and restoring all the ancient manuscripts in Dagestan at the Academy of Sciences archive.

Other achievements include digitalizing some 400 objects in the Patimat Saidovna Gamzatova museum of fine art in Dagestan and rebuilding the museum with a new wing; and in 2015 in Derbent funding the creation of a museum and a creative technologies training centre for young people. On 9 November 2015 Peri began construction of the largest mosque in Europe near Makhachkala.

From 2016, Magomedov supported mixed martial arts, acquiring Russian MMA promoters, Fight Nights Global, and began wide-scale construction of new fight clubs. He established 'Eagles MMA', now home to some of the top Russian talents. Magomedov also financially supported several fighters, including Khabib Nurmagomedov (more below). In 2017 he paid for the fighter's back surgery in Germany.

The FT reported that he was unexpectedly arrested on 1 April 2018 for fraud linked to the construction of Kaliningrad Stadium, built for the FIFA World Cup in Moscow. The fate of Ziyavudin Magomedov may be linked to that of the prime minister [2]. *The Art Newspaper* reported on 14 May 2018: 'It is business as usual, says Peri's director, as its founder, Ziyavudin Magomedov, remains in custody awaiting trial' [3].

In August 2019 an ex-financier convict was rumoured to be preparing to implicate the brothers in a banker's murder, in exchange for a reduction of his 19-year sentence [4]. As of May 2021 Magomedov and his brother continued to be detained with more extensions likely. Assets worth nearly $600 million were seized from them as part of the Summa Group case. On 19 March 2021 the Moscow

Figure 24.1 Magomedov (right) with Khabib Nurmagomedov

Meshchansky District Court were to proceed with an alleged embezzlement case against the brothers [5].

Peri animated the cultural and educational life of the region. Any reduction of funding "would be a serious blow to prospects for the development of science, culture and education in Dagestan." Makhach Musaev, the director of the history and archaeology institute in Makhachkala fears for the state-of-the-art laboratory for conserving and restoring historic manuscripts opened last year.

Suleiman Kerimov

a Lezgi from Dagestan is Russia's richest man according to the Forbes list of August 2020 with US $24.7 billion [6].

His story reads like a film script of triumph over adversity. In 1999 Kerimov bought bankrupt oil trader Nafta Moskva and raised loans against its hugely revalued assets. Later that year he entered politics as a deputy from the Liberal Democratic party. Since 2008 he has been a senator in Russia's upper house, representing Dagestan.

In 2004, Nafta began buying strategic stakes in state-owned gas giant Gazprom and Sberbank. By the beginning of 2008, Kerimov had liquidated his Russian assets for some $20 billion. He reinvested in BP, Boeing and Deutsche Bank, and became the largest shareholder in financial giant Morgan Stanley. After the 2008 financial crisis, he continued to buy, convinced of a rebound. He lost almost everything, reduced to his last houses, cars and private jet. He soon returned with Russian investments, in 2009 buying almost 40% (later increased to 77 percent) of Polyus Gold, Russia's

Figure 24.2 Suleiman Kerimov, Russian Federation Council member, at work on 9 November 2011

(Photo ITAR-TASS/ Stanislav Krasilnikov)

largest gold-mining company, financed by state-owned bank VTB. It was his star investment. In 2018 he was personally sanctioned by the U.S. Since the beginning of the pandemic, Kerimov's fortune has increased by $14.7 billion to make him the richest person in Russia.

Khabib Nurmagomedov

He was nearly nine when his father Abdulmanap, a Red Army veteran and a USSR fight champion and coach, as a test told his son to wrestle a young unmuzzled bear that they had captured. He filmed a six-minute video of his son who repeatedly attacked the bear even though the bear put up a good fight [7].

An Avar, Khabib was about to catch a flight in January 2012 to Nashville Tennessee for his Ultimate Fighting Championship debut when he noticed a kiosk selling souvenirs [8]. His manager had asked him to bring something to catch the attention of the U.S. audience. His friends suggested that true to his Dagestani cultural heritage he should wear a white curly sheepskin papakha, the traditional male headdress for shepherds and warriors. It seemed like he was just wasting $50 for a hat. But it became a tangible part of his identity. When people hear his name now, the first thing they think of is the hat. "It's an honour to me to wear my papakha round the world, representing my culture, my history . . . If I have opportunity, why not? Why not?"

Nurmagomedov's fans in Dagestan wore papakhas to celebrate his win over Conor McGregor in 2018 [9]. In Nurmagomedov's village of Sildi in Tsumadinsky District the papakha-makers have never been so busy.

Twelve consecutive wins later, on 8 September 2019 Nurmagomedov remained the UFC lightweight champion, having defended his title against Dustin Poirier in Abu Dhabi. When he walked into the Octagon ring, he wore the same papakha he had bought years before. The thought of an arena full of fans wearing papakhas while cheering him on against Poirier made Nurmagomedov chuckle: "It's gonna be cool . . ." White papakhas are available on Amazon for only $34.99, and replicas are being sold in Abu Dhabi from customized snack vending machines.

A then 12-year-old girl in San Diego named Kylie Meade built a social-media campaign around Nurmagomedov and his hat. In Las Vegas in March 2017, where Meade asked him why he wore the papakha, Nurmagomedov gave her an authentic papakha of her own. Meade, who uses the social media handle 'Mini Khabib', attended all UFC events with her father. Fighters and other notables in MMA posed with her wearing her papakha. Meade posts all the photos and videos on social media for more than 96,000 followers on Instagram and more than 10,000 YouTube subscribers.

The history of the papakha in the Caucasus could stem from Greek mythology. Hercules wore a lion hide as a hat which is a possible origin of the sheepskin papakha. He was a principal actor in the west Caucasian myth about Prometheus, who was punished by the gods and chained to a rock, where his liver was eaten daily by

Figure 24.3 Khabib Nurmagomedov alongside his father Abdulmanap at the opening of a martial arts school in their native Dagestan in December 2019. His father died on 3 July 2020 of Covid that exacerbated his existing heart condition.

Zeus, in the form of an eagle. Hercules duly slew the eagle and freed Prometheus. Nurmagomedov's sobriquet 'The Eagle' is because the bird features prominently on Dagestan's coat of arms. The papakha, like the lion skin, was 'scare armour' to terrify the opposition. Nurmagomedov is descended from Nur Magomed a naib commander of Shamil (chapter 9).

Nurmagomedov revealed more than 20 relatives had spent time in intensive care during the Covid outbreak, with several dying.

In memory of his father, UFC lightweight champion Nurmagomedov retired unbeaten in all his 29 fights after stopping Justin Gaethje early in the second round at UFC 254 on Saturday night 24 October 2020. He was overcome by tears in the cage moments after triangle-choking Gaethje unconscious. "This was my last fight, there's no way I'm going to be back without my father. I spoke to my mother. She don't know how I fight without father, but I promised it's going to be my last fight, and if I give my word, I have to follow it" [10].

There are 13 UFC acclaimed MMA fighters who were born in Dagestan, though Nurmagomedov was the only one to wear a papakha. His popularity and reach with nearly 16 million Instagram followers has opened doors to meet several world leaders, starting with Russian president Putin.

Tagir Gadziev

Former MMA and sambo champion Tagir Gadziev, also a Dagestani Avar, caught the international media's attention as Russia's best rugby player in the 2019 World

Heroes of sport and finance 199

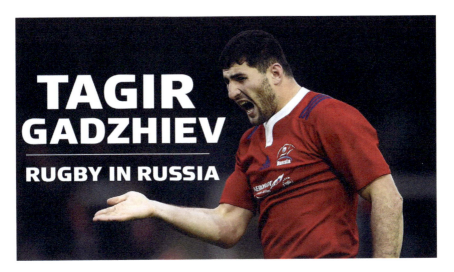

Figure 24.4 Tagir Gadzhiev

Cup. Even though Russia was beaten 61–0 by Scotland, the most admired player on the Russian side was the 6'2" flanker who switched to rugby from MMA. His play has been the one redeeming feature in all of Russia's games.

Ethnographers understand how important it is to be accurate about people's origins, in this case Dagestani, especially when giving praise in many Olympic games and world championships of wrestling, MMA, judo, weight-lifting and other martial arts especially when they come from what might otherwise appear as an homogenous union to the outside world. As professionals Dagestanis also fight in the colours of many other post-Soviet countries. In 2019 it was different. The British ITV commentators described him as from Dagestan, part of Russia, so it was a proud day for Dagestan's identity that the words rugby and Dagestan appeared together in admiration. In October 2019 when Tagir played in New Zealand, he brought Nurmagomedov Avar papakhas as gifts for delighted fellow Muslim All-Blacks Sonny Bill Williams and Ofa Tuungafasi.

References

[1] Chenciner R.B. Daghestan Tradition and Survival. Curzon Press, GB. 1997. pp13–38.
[2] Seddon M. and Hille K. Billionaire's arrest points to Kremlin power struggle. FT. 31 March 2018.
[3] Kishkovsky S. Russian billionaire's Peri foundation will keep paying for culture after arrest. The Art Newspaper. 14 May 2018.
[4] Magomedov brothers' defence treats their involvement in murder as fake Caucasian Knot. 6 August 2019.
[5] Burnov V. Summa Group owners charged with embezzlement to go on trial. Russian Legal Information Agency (RAPSI). 16 March 2021.

200 *Dagestan – History, Culture, Identity*

[6] Stognei A. How did Suleiman Kerimov amass a $25 bln fortune? thebell.io. 8 August 2020.

[7] Zidan K. Khabib Nurmagomedov Wrestled a Bear, Became a National Hero, and Is Ready To Smash Conor McGregor. Deadspin. Video of young Khabib wrestling a bear. https://deadspin.com/khabib-nurmagomedov-wrestled-a-bear-became-a-national-1829501029. 10 April 2018.

[8] Raimondi M. UFC 242: Inside the hat that helped shape Khabib's identity. ESPN. 4 September 2019.

[9] Salgereyev M. Photo. TASS via Getty images. 2018.

[10] Bleacher Report. Khabib Nurmagomedov announces retirement after defending lightweight title at #UFC254. 24 October 2020. https://twitter.com/BleacherReporthttps://twitter.com/bleacherreport/status/1320108241708224512?lang=en.

25 Monetizing the Mountains

Proposals for economic and tourism development have been monopolized by theoreticians, who have ignored what might be called 'ethno-entrepreneurism', that is to say, cultural geography, traditional environmental management, sustainability and the economic specialisation of ethnic groups.

As background, Dagestan has been repeatedly ruined from 1930s to the present. The country, with its abundant alpine pastures and mountain valley gardens, with vast winter pastures on the plain and fertile coastal lands, has always had the capacity to produce sufficient food for its inhabitants. Any imbalance between alpine grazing and cropland was minimized by mountains-plains and international trade, using ancient mountain terraced farming and mountain-valley gardening. High standards were maintained where land tenure and communal land use accorded with social justice and where the community was more important than the individual (chapter 21).

Soviet power eliminated private ownership of land and turned communal land into pseudo-public land under the kolkhoz/*Sovkhoz* collective farm system which radically changed the economy. The disastrous consequences of Collectivization and the savage elimination of the kulaks as a class are well-known (chapter 11).

The transition from *zastoy* stagnation and incomplete *perestroika* to the final destruction of the old political and community system affected all of society. Quality of life statistics in Dagestan were worse than other depressed regions in Russia. In spite of rich natural and labour resources, Moscow funded up to 90% of the state budget. The average per capita income was and is one third of that for Russian Federal republics. Of more than 800,000 economically active people one in five did not, and as of 2020, still do not have permanent jobs, excluding the grey economy.

In the 1990s more than 40% of the population lived in rural areas with scant agricultural mechanization and seasonal employment. About 700,000 Dagestanis lived outside the Republic, mainly in Russia. During the USSR, every March to November, more than 300,000 Dagestan men in brigades needed to migrate to work throughout the Union. Since then, aggravated interethnic relations in the Commonwealth of Independent States (CIS) and discrimination against 'people of

DOI: 10.4324/9781003388579-25

202 *Dagestan – History, Culture, Identity*

Caucasian nationality' have become a serious obstacle to labour and educational migration. For example, thousands of families of Dagestanis who worked for decades as sheep farmers in Kalmykia, the Stavropol Territory, Volgograd and Rostov regions, had to return with their families to Dagestan due to inter-ethnic tension, often provoked by the municipal authorities.

Returnees had no option but to resettle in the lowlands because only the cities and adjacent rich agricultural regions offered work and there was no will to restart the highland villages. The population of highland villages decreased below 1,000 – Joanna Nicholls' critical level for survival along the west coast of America [1]. Some 200 'ghost villages' appeared in the mountains. More than 90,000 hectares of mountain terraced fields were abandoned. Many local varieties of agricultural crops and livestock breeds adapted to local conditions disappeared (chapter 21).

In the 1990s privatizations, some 200 rich family-clans including supposedly pious nationalist extremists and former KPSS members who had appropriated state funds for some years, acquired the state farms and textile and other light industries. They started banks that failed, bought conspicuous consumer goods, built luxury fortified houses and drove about in expensive high status cars. In contrast workers, engineers and office workers were summarily sacked at the run-down factory gates.

Eighty-five percent of consumer goods were imports from Turkey, China, the United Arab Emirates, Iran, the Czech Republic and Poland. Ordinary families devised 'shuttle' trading. Contrary to Islamic prescriptions forbidding women to travel unaccompanied by husbands or close relatives, the majority of the shuttles were women who were also the majority of traders in markets and bazaars, cutting out intermediaries. Urban dwellers were also fed by products from their village relatives. Dagestan's leading independent commentator described the climate of shuttle trading: "The rapid growth in independent economic activity amongst the populace served as another motive for acquiring arms. Shuttle trading (where individuals travel back and forth purchasing small amounts of goods) was increasing, commercial shops and stores were being established, and innumerable cash transactions were being carried out directly, outside of the banking system. All this required reliable physical protection, which the state was not able to provide" [2].

Studies of mountain territories are related to Russian strategic priorities. A state program "Social and Economic Development of Mountain Territories of the Republic of Dagestan for 2014–2018" was announced, though implementation mechanisms were not defined, nor specific measures for sustainable development. Socio-economic and environmental development of the mountain regions and the country as a whole is urgent, especially after Covid.

It seems sensible to address the economic rehabilitation of abandoned mountain terraced arable lands and garden plots, backing 'Small and Medium-sized Enterprises' (SMEs) with hypothecated loans for mini tractors, tillers or mowing machines. Traditional animal husbandry should be restored, complemented by traditional crafts. Consumer cooperatives should be established with a subsidized pricing policy for 'mountain products', taking into account social profit and ecological factors.

To make this happen, a road network, communications, transportation, gas and other energy supplies are needed. The aim is to level-up the quality of life of the mountaineers to that of the plainsmen, overcome negative attitudes, slow down the depopulation of alpine regions and attract young Dagestani mountaineers to participate in a socio-economic and cultural revival [3, 4].

Ethno-entrepreneurship tries to preserve ethnic self-identification and traditional culture [5], even if it does not always succeed. When we visited the Navajo reservation in Arizona in 1998 in their boxed small modern terraces we found that they had lost their traditional foods, while the nearby Zuni stone fetish carvers had experienced an artistic renaissance [6]. In pre-Revolutionary Dagestan ethnic economic activity was transformed under state policy, particularly in the development of mineral spas, resorts, jewellery shops in Kubachi and in Soviet times incongruous isolated sports tourism *baz* and KPSS sanitoria [7, 8].

The best-known product of local entrepreneurship was Kubachi's decorative weapons and silver niello masterwork which since the 1870s were regular participants in international exhibitions, representing Russia.

The best results came when local communities were involved in the implementation of tourism, as in the German school teacher Harald Bohmer's natural dye carpet weaving DOBAG project in Ayvacuk Western Anatolia in Turkey. Both material heritage and state-stimulated ethnic entrepreneurship form an ethnic brand, marketing sustainable tourism. As a cultural addition, folklore may be exploited commercially for the tourism industry, as in popular theatre accompanied by the sale of bespoke multimedia memorabilia. In the UK there is the example of Taffy Thomas the professional storyteller of Grasmere in Cumbria who wore his cloak illustrating 300 folktales. His performances were not only entertaining but by repetition kept folklore alive [9].

Another example is the revival of vibrant decorative Kaitag embroideries by the Kaitag regional government and local embroiderer Zubaidat Gasanova who has established a workshop in Gapshima which also acts a school for future embroiderers. Before embroidery, raw silk, some of which is produced locally, is spun and plied into a thread and then dyed using local dyes, where available. Videos on Facebook have informed the whole of Dagestan about these products, creating the internal market selling the embroideries directly to homes. The videos also feature traditional music, song, dance and other handicrafts, promoting all these former exports during the Soviet period. It is a model of how village SMEs can revive the handicraft tradition in Dagestan and market their products first in Dagestan and then in the Russian Federation (chapter 25) [10–14].

Continuing degradation of landscapes, historical, cultural and natural heritage, traditional life support systems, economic specialization, handicraft centres, art and gastronomy reflect a weakened village society in Dagestan today. The mountaineers refused to adapt to the slow modernization of pre-Revolutionary Russia, initially out of stubbornness and then when they saw that it was not beneficial to them.

204 Dagestan – History, Culture, Identity

The formation and feebly attempted implementation of the National Policy Strategy (NPS), aimed at ensuring political stability in the region, was cosmetically based on the UN Sustainable Development Goals of 2015 [15]. Dagestan's treatment of the Highlanders was comparable to Brazil driving out Amazonian indigents and destroying the rain forests, while cynically signed up to the UN goals. The NPS in theory allows investing in the new social, cultural and landscape environment subject to existing limitations. Traditional ethno-economic and environmental traditions were to be taken into account with current natural and artificial changes in environment. However, demographic issues were rarely considered, neither were the challenges of progressive depopulation of the mountains. Dagestan's pluralist state faces similar challenges to other subsets of larger nations regarding their spiritualized historical memory and mother tongue, compound patriotisms and consciousness of belonging to a political nation.

At the Russian Investment Forum in Sochi on 14–15 February 2019, the Minister of the Russian Federation for North Caucasus Affairs Sergey V. Chebotarev proposed a model law [16] that "in this special economic zone, what is located above 1,500 meters, what is registered there as above 1,500 meters and what is produced there should receive benefits . . . About 60% of the North Caucasus Federal District is highland and therefore, we see the need for its additional legal representation." He added that "the development of the mountains should not affect the traditional North Caucasian highland culture and way of life. The cost of production on mountain pastures is known to be higher than on the plains, since the harsher winter conditions mean that livestock are fed in stalls for a longer period. Extreme examples are Archi and Bezhta which are snowed off between October and March. Be warned that since the collapse of USSR several development programs of mountain territories have failed through lack of political will, corruption and incompetence."

"A special feature of the alpine landscapes of Dagestan is that the Main Caucasus Range, 300 km long, is eroded by large rivers into a range of environments from mountain valleys to basins of exceptional ecological and ethno-cultural diversity, favouring cattle breeding and irrigated agriculture in the plains beneath. Sea level in the Caspian Sea is projected to fall by 9–18 m in medium to high emissions scenarios until the end of this century, caused by a substantial increase in lake evaporation that is not balanced by increasing river discharge or precipitation" [17]. That should increase the importance of highland ethno-tourism as described in the next chapter.

References

[1] Nichols J. Linguistic diversity and the first settlement of the new world. Language. Vol. 66. No. 3. 1990. pp475–521.

[2] Kisriev E. Dagestan: Power in the balance. The Caucasus armed and divided: Dagestan. Chapter 7. 2003.

[3] Poddubikov V.V., Sadovoi A.N. and Belozerova M.V. Expertise and monitoring traditional forms of environmental management of indigenous small ethnic groups. 2014.

Monetizing the Mountains 205

[4] Sadovoi A.N. Methodological aspects of analysis of traditional forms of ethnic entrepreneurship. Scientific Dialogue. No. 8. 2019. pp345–59.

[5] Sadovoi A.N. and Belozerova M.V. Ethnic economy in mountain ecosystems. Karachay Conference. 2019. pp213–18.

[6] Bahti M. Spirit in the stone. 1999.

[7] Magomedkhanov M.M. Dagestanis: Milestones in ethno-social history. 2007.

[8] Magomedkhanov M.M., Bakanov A.V. and Garunova S.M. Changes in social relations during the period of military people's administration of the Dagestan region of the Russian Empire. Klio. No. 7. 2019. pp91–7.

[9] Herman B. Intercultural demands and cultural identity. Language & Cultural Contact. 1999. pp11–23.

[10] Gasanova Z. Director. Municipal budgetary institution centre for traditional culture of the peoples of Russia (MBU TsTKNR): Video 'Kaitag ancient and forever young. Interviews. Part 1.' 35.10m. 25 September 2017. www.facebook.com/Kaitagi/videos/1643839749010855/.

[11] MBU TsTKNR video, Mountain women meeting at the spring. 1.00m. 16 April 2018. Original film. ND. c. 1970. www.facebook.com/Kaitagi/videos/1856461867748641/.

[12] MBU TsTKNR video, Kaitag region old traditions. 14.45m 18 September 2017. www.facebook.com/Kaitagi/videos/1637723952955768/.

[13] MBU TsTKNR stills with lively traditional music and dance; mainly of lots of embroiderers and Kaitags. 8.24m. 4 May 2017. www.facebookcom/Kaitagi/videos/1505283546199810/.

[14] MBU TsTKNR stills with commentary. International exhibition. 1.31m. 7 July 2017. www.facebook.com/Kaitagi/videos/1568752733186224/.

[15] UN Sustainable Development Goals. UN. 2015. www.un.org/sustainabledevelopment/sustainable-development-goals/.

[16] Chebotarev S.V. On development for the protection of mountain territories. 14–15 February 2019. https://vestikavkaza.ru/news/CHebotarev-zakon-o-gornykh-territoriyakh-pomozhet-sokratit-ottok-naseleniya.html.

[17] Prange M., Wilke T. and Wesselingh F.P. The other side of sea level change. Communications Earth & Environment. Vol. 1. Article No. 69. 23 December 2020. www.nature.com/articles/s43247-020-00075-6.

26 A virtual tour to Archi

The Tour hopes to show guests highland hospitality, staying in Archi homes and participating in everyday life, including traditional food and cooking and the opportunity to explore, walk and trek in the stunning alpine surroundings. Conservation challenges will be evident during their stay.

Dagestan has one of the richest glacial water resources in the world. Its 1,800 rivers, including the great rivers Terek, Sulak and Samur, are widely used for hydropower and irrigation. The effects of global warming are noticeable in the past five years when formerly year-long snowy mountains of the Great Caucasian chain disappear in the summer and glaciers shrink. In the near future this may reduce the sea level of the Caspian. Polluting the rivers and Caspian with waste and fertilizer run-off affects the fish and wildlife stocks, and the contaminated water, when used for irrigation, affects the crops too. The potential for tourism clearly suffers when the main selling point, the landscape, deteriorates – as it does aesthetically, as well, when unsympathetic new buildings are permitted.

The Ris-Or river (becoming the Khatar in Archi) is a natural treasure which has largely retained its pristine charm and purity. It was always treated very carefully by Archi ancestors. They did not throw animal corpses, manure, human excrement or household waste, nor do they now dispose of washing powder, plastic bottles and

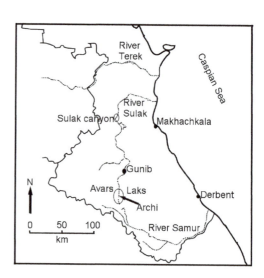

Map 26.1 Getting to Archi – and Dagestan's major rivers

DOI: 10.4324/9781003388579-26

A *virtual tour to Archi* 207

other garbage into the rivers, as in today's larger villages such as Akusha, Akhty and Bezhta, where there is no education about keeping their villages beautiful or it is ignored. As the Archi saying has it, 'put a ladle on the shore of the sea', enough is enough.

After the flight from Moscow, this ten-day virtual tour starts in Makhachkala city, near the airport, for sightseeing in the old centre and its village suburbs, which include Tarki (chapter 6).

Day two is filled with a day's drive (some 200 km, but slow and scenic roads) to Archi through the Sulak canyon, the Salta waterfall and past the volcanic formations of Upper Gunib.

The third day is a rest in a home in Archi to acclimatize to the altitude of 2,200 m, the direct unfiltered sunlight, the heat and the cold and the alpine winds.

Day four is spent visiting the Archi hamlets Khilikh, Keserib and Khitab (leaving Kalib and Alchunib for a return visit).

Next day is horse trekking from Kubatl village to the headwaters of Mount Taklik, as marked on map 26.2.

The sixth day offers workshops on cutting mutton for drying, making *khuyurma*, *milin-khitin*, *khalai*, *andargi*, and *gamgi*. As an alternative, various walks to explore the beautiful locality.

The seventh is the last full day in Archi and is devoted to gastronomy followed by the Farewell Dinner.

The drive back to Makhachkala fills most of the eighth day. It is broken for a picnic lunch in the Charodino forest.

On the nineth day the guest may either wander about Makhachkala and visit museums or join a trip to Derbent with its ancient history (and walls, chapter 3), 130 km to the south on the highway.

Transfer to the airport to catch return flights the next morning.

The following notes give some additional background and highlight some features of the area, though there won't be time to take in all these specifically in a single visit.

Topography

Archi is a mountain area with a community of seven villages inhabited by one of the 30 indigenous peoples of Dagestan. In 1866 the Russians counted 600 Archi people; in 1886, 800; in 1926, 900 and nowadays (pre-Covid) about 2,000, against the wasting trend described in previous chapters and, apparently, the Russian census of 2010.

208 *Dagestan – History, Culture, Identity*

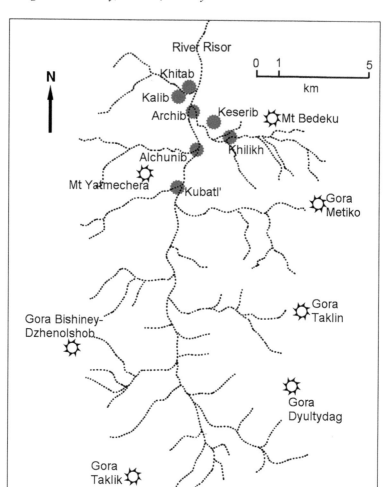

Map 26.2 Archi's villages, mountains and rivers

Archi (Arsha the name of the locality and people, Ruchi in Avar) is a union of seven self-governing villages (Khere, Khashilla, Kala, Lhatta, Alshuna, Kubatl, Keser, Khilikh) with a single administrative centre and a single cemetery (both in Khere). Archi is historically allied with neighbouring Avars and Laks, whose languages they speak as well as their own. The Archi perceive their Little Homeland firstly through elemental water, as the beginning and the final destination of the planet Earth because the Kara-Koysu River rises in front of their eyes. Secondly, through the element stone, because in southern Arsha there is a powerful outcrop of the

A *virtual tour to Archi* 209

Main Caucasian Range, through which passes neither foot- nor horse-track, except for experienced climbers. They revere their own sacred mount called Bedeku, like the Japanese Fuji.

Nature

Archi's hamlets occupy the floodplain of the Khatar-Ris Or river, which grows into the largest tributary of the Kara-Koysu River, which in turn merges with Kazi-Kumukh Koysu, Avar Koysu and Andi Koysu, to form the great Sulak River, that flows into the Caspian Sea. The highest surrounding mountain peaks are Dyul-tydag altitude 4,127 m, Bishiney 4,106 m, Taklik 4,046 m, Bedeku 3,997 m and Yatmechera 3,963 m. At the bottom of Bedeku's glacier there is a small lake called Basallahara, 3,276 m high in the floodplain of the river Tlirgankra, which flows into the Khatar. Fifteen glaciers flow from these five peaks, one of them feeding the Ris-Or; the largest stretches 3 km along Taklik ridge. It is confusing for sometimes more than one river flows from the same large glacier and the rivers merge downstream.

The flora of the Ris-Or valley is rich, with slopes of varied alpine and subalpine pastures, meadows and rhododendrons and pine birch and aspen forests along the side valleys and gorges, but little arable land.

Dagestan Tours, the state agency, helped preserve the local fauna by creating the Charodinsky reserve (*zapovednik'*) including Archi home to the wild Dagestan great spiral-horned mountain goat, in Russian *tur*, in Archi *bokh* and in Avar *chan*, also alpine mouflon, chamois, wolf, fox, hare, Caucasian *ular* (mountain turkey) locally called *mussal* and partridge. The Khatar is rich in alpine small-spotted trout.

The river features several 10 m high waterfalls on its middle reaches; other impressive waterfalls can be seen on its tributaries. The river's source in the Bishinei Range is beautiful and believed to have healing properties. From the Bedeku River gorge you can climb to the sheer walls of nearby Mount Metiko, also revered by the highlanders.

The Ris-Or valley has long been scattered with Avar and Lak villages, joined by the climbing 25 km Magar-Kubatl highway where a unique ancient horse-drawn trail led to the Archi pass 3,335 m and on to Rutul district. Some passes are cattle trails, and others are accessible to tourists and climbers.

Climate

Archi typically has cold but sunny winters, while summer is warm in the daytime cooling in the evening, interspersed with short, strong showers or hail, and occasional gentle drizzles on hot days when there are almost no clouds in the sky.

People

Archi has not been excavated by archaeologists. However, burial grounds have yielded ceramic and metal fragments with solar signs, suggesting Early Bronze Age (III – II millennium BCE) pagan settlement. Later finds suggest Christian influence before Islam was adopted by the X century.

During the Caucasian war (chapter 7), the Russian troops of Adjutant General Argutinsky "went to Archi aul . . . and after spending the night [of 25 July 1849] there, they burned the aul at dawn and marched back to the Shali Pass [towards modern Chechnya]. Aul Shali suffered the same fate, so the local wheat and flour supply was mostly destroyed."

The current nature of their close-knit community is friendly but sometimes wary towards both Dagestani and rare foreign visitors. There are also many rituals connected with their traditional hospitality which foreign guests may not be used to. Guests are accompanied everywhere as a mark of respect and as protection because they are often disoriented in the mountains where a small rock can appear to be a distant mountain. Women visitors are likely to be quickly accepted into the intricacies of Archi women's lives. There is a rule among mountaineers that they never ask any questions of their male or honorary guests for the first three days. They are proud people.

Economy

The economy is mainly based on sheep breeding. What little arable land there is derives from terraced fields on mountain and upland slopes. Wool weaving, wood carving and blacksmithing were commercially developed. Characteristic habitations are hamlets and settlements near grazing. Traditional dwellings are multi-storey stone buildings containing both living rooms and stabling.

Houses

'Houses in which is everything and anything extra' is an epigram of plenty that applies to the family (tukkhum) house of Magomedkhan in Khere the central village of Archi, built on a steep mountain slope. His house is on five floors with three street exits. The first two floors, the lower of which is a cattle barn and the upper for sheep, have separate exits to the lower street. The third floor consists of two large adjacent rooms under one roof, made of wooden beams with ceilings of stone tiles. The roof of these rooms serves as a courtyard on the next level; made of adobe, it is renewed after snow or rain by being sprinkled with clay and compacted with a wooden float or roller. There is an opening between the sleeping room and the room above which can be locked, for security. The passage way leads to the upper part of the village so you can escape in case of danger. Two windows of the first room face the lower street, so one can swiftly get from the lower street to upper floors via the sheep stable, or vice versa.

The second room on the third floor is cut from the living rock and its only window is on the roof. The village court of Archi was located in this room, before and after the accession to Russia, right up to the 1917 revolution. There is a staircase in it that leads to a small L-shaped covered courtyard (3 m wide with the 'L' 12 m long). In the northern part of the courtyard there is a small winter room (3 m by 4 m), and on the south side there is a low massive door with iron fittings leading to the pitch-black medieval dungeon drilled into the rock to the height of a man and 3 m long. These two rooms make up the fourth floor. There are two exits from the covered courtyard which is walled on the sides away from the rooms: the first on the right or north side leads to the lane connecting the upper and lower streets of the village.

The second exit is from the centre of the courtyard straight up more wooden stairs, through a manhole with a lockable door to the landing and the fifth floor, consisting of a front room and kunaks' room, above the courtyard and rooms of the 4th floor. These two large living rooms are built on the living rock.

Other houses in the area would have some if not all these local features.

In Soviet times, new houses were built, and old houses added to with an innovative long gallery on the front, and on steep slopes part of the roof of the lower floor served as a courtyard for the upper floor, leaving the rear part as an indoor floor.

Costume

Traditional costume for Archi women has distinctive cut details, colour preferences, and is worn in their special way as can be seen from the photograph. The asymmetric coin-coated patch on the *chukhta* (women's headdress) has survived in Archi, in combination with the headscarf, long straight pants, brightly coloured belts and sheepskin coats and hats.

Food

Archi food is mainly cooked from flour, meat and dairy products. The sheep's cheese and *bakhI* (dried sausage) have a unique taste. Unleavened bread is baked from flour every day, and fermented bread is used for weddings, funerals and sadaka (alms). Pies with meat or curd filling and corn flour cakes made from fresh milk are favourites. The most common dish is khinkal with meat, cheese, sour cream, or sour milk with garlic seasoning. Kurze raviolis are also prepared at home as are pies filled with meat, or with internal mutton fat and liver, or cottage cheese, eggs, nettles and wild garlic. For a khinkal soup small pieces of unleavened dough and crumbled cottage cheese are added to boiling milk, and seasoned with garlic and melted mutton or lamb tail fat, which is also used in meat soups.

212   Dagestan – History, Culture, Identity

Local cumin and thyme and traded pepper are widely used as spices. Dairy products include fresh and boiled milk, feta cheese, curdled milk, whey and kefir.

Summer and autumn meat dishes are made with fresh meat, and the rest of the year from dried meat. Sweet *buza* made of fermented hops or crushed bearberry flour with malt are traditional drinks at weddings and holidays.

For dessert, urbech paste is made from flax seeds or apricot kernels, and halva from flour, butter and sugar, or from hemp seeds, apricot kernels and nuts.

Pregnant women, women in childbirth, exhausted patients and the elderly are fed malt and oatmeal baked cakes or boiled porridge of manually-milled wheat or corn *khulurkhus* and many more dishes.

Social & family life

Archi social structure was based on one jamaat of seven villages that resolved the order of land ownership, the use of mountain pastures and hayfields and other local economic issues, under adat and sharia.

There is a clear separation of male and female responsibilities in parenting, housekeeping and family roles. Traditional family relationships are based on honouring elders and clan-based mutual assistance to pay for ritual celebrations of weddings and funerals.

A registration marriage is considered sinful without a religious service *nikah* where precautions against harmful magic are followed. If at the moment of conclusion of the nikah an ill-wisher ties a knot, closes the entrance, opens and closes a knife and takes out his dagger and puts it back wrong side up, this can negatively affect the groom. Wedding gifts are only brought by women, and are put on display. Men go to the wedding with mascara-lined eyes or a half carcass of ram, depending on the degree of relationship, or contribute a fixed amount of money.

Funeral rites are performed according to sharia. The peculiarities of observance of mourning and the funeral feast reflect pre-Islamic beliefs.

Many Archi customs are associated with the agronomic cycle. On 5 July the 15th day of summer, they celebrate driving the sheep to summer pastures with sports, wrestling, weight lifting, and a communal feast centred around a fresh sheep's cheese. At the end of October the autumn holiday celebrates the improvement of livestock breeds and is concluded as their children leave, singing their wishes to increase the number of sheep and their weight. Another holiday is dedicated to the safe wintering of livestock. In spring, they celebrate the First Furrow or the start of ploughing. The vernal equinox is celebrated with lighting of spectacular fires. If there is a drought, a ritual procession led by a rain-donkey Helmin Dogi passes through the village with him finally lying down covered from head to foot in grass by the celebrants.

As elsewhere in Dagestan, Archi hospitality is surrounded by customs. The house-owner may not sit while the guest is standing, or leave the guest alone without arranging for his relatives to take care of him, and not ask the guest about the purpose of the visit until he talks of the time of his departure.

Archi people's behaviour is based on pan-human values, recognizing good and evil, love and hatred and worthy and low deeds. Their honesty is associated with concepts of *yah* (will, conscience), *namus* (sense of duty, shyness), *bimushur* (real man) and *bitlonnol* (real woman), reinforced by strict, rigorous teaching of what is forbidden to the next generation (chapter 17).

Old literacy & education

Arab-Muslim culture influenced spiritual life where many Archi were prominent Alim scholars and, extraordinarily for such a small people, three sheikhs. Within the modern Lak, Kulinsky, Agulsky, Zakatalsky and Belokansky districts virtually every village had benefitted from an Archi mullah, kadi (judge) or madrasah teacher. Both in the past and today the Archi people use the Avar language as the lingua franca, and many additionally know Lak and Russian.

Some poems written in Archi are quoted in chapter 14 and there are also religious treatises and poems of the XIX century in the Archi language and others in Avar, Lak and Arabic written by the Archi authors.

Three of the greatest Dagestani teachers came from Archi: Arçibli Hacı Muhammed Efendi also known as Kazakilav the XVIII century astronomer, mathematician, doctor and author of several books and poems in Arabic. Kharda (or formally, Haji-Kharda ibn Muhammad-fakir al-Rochi) about 1800 was the author of "A torment-relieving elixir" (chapter 14), "Necklace of Pearls from the Depth of the Seas" and "On Logic for a Travelling Companion." Mamma-Dibir during the XIX century war was a *murshid*, successor to the Sufi sheikh Jamalutdin Kazikumukhsky and associate of Imam Shamil. Three future sheikhs of the Naqshbandi *tariqat* studied under them in Archi: Abdurahman Sogratlinsky under Kharda; and Shuayb al-Bagini and Sayfula-kadi Bashlarov under Mamma Dibir.

Even in Soviet times, Archi's children became academics, teachers, doctors, economists and cultural workers. Today there is one secondary school and three elementary schools, staffed by local teachers, served by Wi-Fi, cellular communications, wide-screen TVs, satellite broadcasts, personal computers, smart-phones and other tools of globalisation. However, the highlander still considers everything to be second to the Greatness of the Mountains, and that is that.

214 *Dagestan – History, Culture, Identity*

A photo tour

Figure 26.1 A view of Archi from the north

Figure 26.2 Archi village at the confluence of the Bidi and Klala rivers forming the Khatar River that becomes the Ris-Or

A virtual tour to Archi 215

Figure 26.3 The sacred mount Bedeku (on left)

Figure 26.4 Sheep and shepherd on summer pasture at the foot of Mount Taklik

216 *Dagestan – History, Culture, Identity*

Figure 26.5 The author (MM) checking wool and bargaining with a shepherd

Figure 26.6 Tasty dried meat and sausage with freshly made Gurkkimey sausage

A virtual tour to Archi 217

Figure 26.7 Archi felt mosaic carpets with natural dyes

Figure 26.8 Highland dancers – the folk ensemble 'Bedeku'

Figure 26.9 Highland singers – the folk ensemble 'Bedeku'

Figure 26.10 Men cooking the wedding feast

A virtual tour to Archi 219

Figure 26.11 Khvatli is a dish of oat flour – fast and satisfying

Figure 26.12 Showing gifts to the bride. The ceremony of showing gifts to the bride is not a man's affair: even watching from afar is frowned upon. After marriage, he would never open his wife's chest, or even look at it.

Figure 26.13 Flowers from Archi, with love

27 In Dagestan, as they say, everyone sings and everyone dances

My (Chenciner's) recordings made in the mid-1980s and early 1990s of languages included poetry, song and music, which complemented my photographic archive. At that time photographs were not considered to be serious academic evidence because they were biased, although of course the same objection might be made of the selection of textual evidence.

It was difficult to master a Marantz professional BBC recorder but in 1997 I was tutored by Tim Whewell and Andy Denton of the BBC while I helped them record *The Windy Sea – Caviar and Kalashnikovs*. For example, background noise needed to be recorded as fillers for later editing, because every location has its particular sound. In alpine villages over 2,000 metres altitude, recordings have a unique sound, in the thinner air or the mist or extreme cold; different both inside and outdoors. Similarly, recordings in the Caspian coastal cities of Makhachkala and Derbent in Dagestan and Baku in Azerbaijan have distinct Caspian sounds, perhaps because of the summer heat up to 40 degrees, or near unbearable humidity, or the unexpected flaws caused by coastal winds [1].

The *Sounds of the Caucasus* conference at UCL in August 2015 was largely concerned with instrumental music and songs which form a significant part of my archive. In addition to music I recorded people telling stories, taking part in rituals, weddings and domestic life, and even animals and ambient noises. Decades later, they evoke the last days of the USSR. I took for granted recording many unique sounds of the north and east Caucasus and North Ossetia which would otherwise have been forgotten. The archetypal sounds of the ancient local cultures in conjunction with the sounds of mountain nature or the Caspian Sea were fused into an oral-musical tradition, transmitted by local gifted folklorists, singers, musicians and dancers. They inherited a small local range of instruments, and others borrowed from Russia or Iran, to produce their particular sound.

My recordings were gathered on expeditions with my co-author or with my friend the late Dr Ramazan Khappoulaev during 1989. Magomedkhan's friend Dr Hasan Dzutsev in North Ossetia made possible the first and apparently only recordings of the rituals, chants and prayers of the pagan festival of St George called *Wastyrdjy* in 1991 [2].

DOI: 10.4324/9781003388579-27

222 *Dagestan – History, Culture, Identity*

The ever-present natural sounds of the mountains are a thorough-bass redolent of pagan nature-worship. It cloaks the listener with the closeness of thunder and wind, the echoing of surrounding rock masses, the rushing of ice-water and deadly stones down the ravines, and even the absence of insects at dusk. In addition, the muffling of sounds with dust occurs in both mountains and plains.

The oral tradition that transmitted folklore and epics has even greater longevity than the long multilingual poetic traditions in Dagestan written in Arabic/Persian script (chapter 14).

With regard to making music, Caucasian villagers individually specialized in one masterly skill of story-telling, dancing and singing as well as instrumental music. Performances are charged at a professional fee. Although village musicians earned a fee, this was for respect; they would labour with their fellows during the day, so they were different from state-employed 'national' troupes in the cities, many of whom toured Russia and the USSR. My musicologist colleague Stefan Williamson-Fa was easily able to distinguish between my domestic recordings, recordings at festivals and studio recordings. He found the domestic and some festival recordings to be more exciting because they have an intensity which resounds to an ancient tradition.

A perhaps unexpected aspect of 'sounds' are the silent languages of apotropaic symbols found in tattoos, textiles, tombstones, carved wood, and architecture. The ancient messages are frequently transmitted through the portrayal of fantastic animals such as dragons, eagles, horses and tur (mountain goats). Recognition of such a rich heritage amplifies the context of the recordings. The omnipresence of these symbols in the musicians' daily lives permeate their performances, their patterned significance being woven into the music.

Moreover, it seems that in the north Caucasus a much larger proportion of people played or sang as an essential part of their lives compared to contemporary Europe.

Wind reeded instruments

There is some confusion with the identification of Dagestani folk instruments which are unfamiliar in Europe. Thanks to Gamzat Izudinov's photograph of the Avar music festival (Дни аварского языка) in Makhachkala on 22 to 23 February 2015, it is now possible to identify some of the villagers' instruments. The apricot wood zurna is a double-reed pipe or conical oboe – a sort of trumpet-shaped flute. The *yasti balaban* is a short oboe, a cylindrical double-reed aerophone known as *balaban* in Azerbaijan, Iran and Uzbekistan, *duduki* in Georgia; *duduk* in Armenia; and *mey* or *ney/nay* in Turkey.

Stringed instruments

The Dagestani pandur is a 5-fret 2-stringed long-necked lute. Mammadibir Abdura-khmanov is a renowned maker. He was born in Maali village of Gergebil rayon

In Dagestan, as they say, everyone sings and everyone dances   223

and since 1970 lives in Shamkhal village, Kumtorkalinski rayon. He is additionally known as a folk musician and Master (a high Soviet award for achievement) of Dagestan traditional stringed instruments (pandur, chagana, komuz) which he learned from his father, who was similarly a great Master of pandur and a professional woodworker. His instruments are exhibited in CIS: in Glinka Museum in Moscow, in Sheremetevsky Palace Music Museum in St. Petersburg and in Azerbaijan State Museum of Musical Culture in Baku. He belongs to a musical family, one of five brothers, four of whom are singers. The Avar Theatre poster on his wall in the photo is for their family concert in the largest theatre in Makhachkala. Mammadibir won several competitions for the best pandur player and he is also the author of verses in his native Avar language. His art will carry on through his elder son Taimaz who is learning the secrets of pandur instrument-making.

As photographed at the Avar Festival, two komuz – eight-fret four-stringed lutes – were played by Abusufyan Alikaraev awarded Honoured art worker of the Republic of Dagestan, and Abdula Magomedmirzayev awarded National artist of Dagestan, employee of the Avar theatre. Our colleague S. Williamson-Fa observed that the komuz with its eight frets and four strings appears to be a Russianized version of the pandur with its five frets and two strings, which was suited to the traditional local pentatonic music.

The chagana a four-stringed bowed instrument with a circular drum-like body covered with hide (similar to a *kemenche*) is played by Mutay Khadulaev awarded Honoured artist of Russia.

Mutay Khadulaev is the last Dagestani maker of chaganas and the foremost chagana player. He is a 78-year-old Avar from Khakhita, *Zasluzhennii* (Deserved) artist of Russian Federation. In 2015 he said that he was too old to make any more. He wrote two pages of instructions on tuning the chagana. He recalled his participation in the *Den Pobedi* (Victory Day) concert at Kremlin palace of Congresses on 8th of May 1965, in front of Brezhnev and Malenkov. The vast audience applauded him generously though he remembered that his reception was dwarfed by the 15 minute standing ovation for Marshal Zhukov. In 1992 Mutay was honoured as an international 'virtuoso of the world'.

Percussion

The *baraban* drummer Shamil Nazhmudinov is also employed by the Avar theatre. The baraban is a 30–40 cm diameter squarish cylindrical double-headed drum either hung from the shoulder, if played when dancing, or wedged between the forearm and the knee. It is usually played just under the chin, on the top edge with both hands.

When the pandur is not being strummed it is also played by tapping the wood sounding board direct with fingers or enhanced by flicks of the outside fingers, as a drum.

Percussion is often simply with fingers on any objects to hand on the table.

224 *Dagestan – History, Culture, Identity*

Accordion

The *garmon* accordion a bellows-driven hand-held box instrument was introduced by the Russians during the mid-XIX century. The north Caucasus variant komuz is a piano keyboard diatonic accordion, based on the Vyatka garmon.

As S. Williamson-Fa noted, the most authentic songs are unaccompanied chants, often repetitive, which appear to be narrative; next are songs accompanied by traditional local instruments – the pandur, the chagana, the zurna, and baraban drum. Songs with komuz accompaniment appear to have been restructured to fit into a Russianized vocabulary of songs, or simply copied, as Russian songs with local lyrics [3].

S. Williamson-Fa has selected 29 of my 1989 recordings of songs and music made in Dagestan, now accessible on Soundcloud [4].

With the opportunity for wider access through the internet, new digital technology has encouraged more music and poetry festivals. Here are some evocative examples:

i. *Цамаури. Конкурс исполнителей на пандуре и чагане 'Играй, душа!'* (Tsamauri Competition of pandur and chagana 'Play, soul!'), 26 August 2013. 30 mins 16 secs. Much pandur playing; and a chagana at min. 20. www.youtube.com/watch?v=gyD3Lf8iRsw

ii. *'ГӀаданги гӀамалги заманги'* (Avar) ('Person, Behaviour and Time') Botlich. 16 August 2018.3.00 hours www.youtube.com/watch?v=wN_LDDcpAB4

iii. *Патимат Нажмудинова* (Patimat Nakhmudinova's), *Гьале доб унго-унгояб магӀарул кечӀги бакъанги* – Avar song with three women in Alice-in-Wonderland Red Queen headdresses. 9 January 2015 https://issuu.com/artsterritory/docs/fos2

iv. Avar Songs. 11 November 2019.27 mins www.youtube.com/watch?v=ZgrMbnP10yw

Dance has traditionally accompanied music and song. The ever-popular famed Lezginka is a very old Dagestani dance that has spread throughout the Caucasus and beyond, symbolizing the male warrior spirit, telling of a young man's ardent but respectful interest for a young woman. It is performed by a solo man or group of men, on point, with fast clear sharp movements, in a dazzling show of strength with courageous virtuoso leaps, often brandishing a *shashka* sabre. She tries to escape him through delicate flowing movements while he blocks her but never touches her. Her quieter movements emulate a wedding dance and are never performed alone.

Authenticity is the holy grail of the ethno-musicologist, so why is the dance called Lezginka as Lezgins are only one of the 31 ethnic groups in Dagestan and the numerous other ethnicities of north Caucasus and Transcaucasus, who all dance it?

In the Caucasus and under the Ottoman empire, all Dagestanis were called Lezgins, and today Turks and Azerbaijanis still call them '*Lyazgi*'.

The Lezginka dance [5], arguably best interpreted in Dagestan and in Azerbaijan – Lezgins live on both sides of their border – has become a symbol of the Caucasus. The first professional Dagestan dance ensemble 'Lezginka' was created by Tanho Izrailov, a Mountain Jew; and the children's dance ensemble 'Happy childhood' was created by Shalumi Matatov another Mountain Jew. Mountain Jews in Israel are legally entitled to dance their national dance, the Lezginka, wearing their kinjal (dagger). The full man's costume is a valuable *karakul* hat, a cherkess flared jacket in black or white with a row of bandoliers for powder charges, a thin silver encased belt with a kinjal, black hunting breeches and knee high Morocco-leather boots. The Lezginka is a most widespread export of the Caucasus. The dance can stand high with any of the dances from China to North Africa. It is almost non-existent in Iran and Turkey except among the North Caucasian Diaspora.

Figure 27.1 Lezginka dancers

References

[1] Magomedkhanov M. and Chenciner R. Foreignness of sound arts territory. 30 June 2015. pp25–47. https://issuu.com/artsterritory/docs/fos2.
[2] Chenciner R. 20. Notes on the pagan feast of St. George in North Ossetia. 19–26 November 1991.

226 *Dagestan – History, Culture, Identity*

[3] Abdullaeva E.B. and Magomedov A.D. Traditional musical instruments of Dagestan: Modern production practices. Questions of Theory and Practice. No. 11–12 (73). 2016. pp13–17.

[4] Williamson-Fa S. and Chenciner R.B. Dagestan music. 29 recordings. Soundcloud. 1989. https://soundcloud.com/caucasusallfrequency/sets/dagestan-unmastered-tape/s-VPyi2Zt6Jgg?fbclid=IwAR3GZdKwnqi_cRQBPi56e-iXCFXipxDAMcsw4NkffTpkilP62 gzy0auV8o0.

[5] Lezginka at wedding in Israel. 2.50-minute video. 2017. www.youtube.com/watch?v=6 LHAHSBCK5I&feature=youtu.be&fbclid=IwAR0PKB5JSUnOXtE8hPz7MPcd4kXX KCsSQttMACzdw3S4PYSoTM9RaFJzqV0.

Index

Note: Numbers in *italics* indicate figures on the corresponding page.

Abakarhaji (Qadi Muhammad
　　Akushi son) 63
'Abd al-Mutallib, 'ho (song) 110–11
abreks (raiding system) 55
Absally 6
Abubakarov, Said Muhammad Haji 123
Abu Bakr (sacrifices) 61
accordion (Dagestan) 224–5
'Actual Problems of Combating Religious-
　　Political Extremism (All-Russian
　　Conference) 120
adat, impact 74, 77
ad-Din, Rashid 2
a'dlu, commitment 75
advice *(nasiha)* 114
Afanasy Nikitin of Tver 24
afterlife *(akhirah)* 68
agach-komuz (lute) 141
agl (group of people) 70
Aglarov, Mamaykhan 109
Aglu-Dagistan, humanity 121
Agularin Khabarar (Agulskiye Vesti) 97
Agul language, dialects 96
Aguls, education 97
Ahvakh Edin (rural community) 148
Aimaki, Abubakar 67
ajamī (Arabic texts) 109
Ajam literature 116–17
Akaev, Abusufyan 69
Akavov, Rashid 145
akhirah (afterlife) 68
aksakal (white-bearded elders), embracing
　　155, 192
Akusha Confederation 43
Akushi, Qadi Muhammad 63
al-Baghdadi, Muhammad 67
al-Baghini, 'Mar-Apandi 109

al-Baghini, shu'aybAfandi 109
al-Bagini, Sheikh Shuayb 64
al-Bagini, Shuayb 213
Albasty 6
al-Bukhti, Ramadan-hajji 109
al-Doroni, Muhammad 'Umar 109
aleikum salaam (peace to you) 194
al-ghachadi, hajji-Muhammad 109
al-Ghazighumuqi, Jamal al-Din 111
al-ghumuqi, Budaychi-hajji 109
al-Ghumuqi, Jamal al-Din 112
al-Hakim, Lukman 165
Alham (Koran sura) 10
al-Hamahi, Muhammad 67
Alibekova, Raisa 146
Alikaraev, Abusufyan 223
Alikhanov-Avarsky, A.M. 56
Alikhanov, M. 81
alim: attitudes 64–5; 'Islamic scholar' 64
Aliyev, M.G. 123
al-Khurukhi, Da'ud 109
Allah Almighty, equality 70
al-Lekzi, Suleiman Sadreddin (Lak) 23–4
All-Russian Centre for Spiritual
　　Administration, creation 120
All-Russian Congresses of Muslims 95
All-Russian Islamic Cultural Centre,
　　creation 120
All-Russian Social and Political Movement
　　(Nur), creation 120
All-Union Census of 1926 100
All-Union Communist Party (VKP:
　　bolsheviks): property confiscation
　　85; resolution 84
al-Mazandarani, Muhammad al-Dailami
　　(Tukhfatal-Muminin) 165
al-Nitsovkri, Sayfullah-Qadi 109

228　*Index*

Alpab 6
Al-Qaida, links (denial) 123
al-Rochi, Kharda 110, 113
al-Rochi, Muhammad 113
al-Rochi, Sheikh Kharda 70
al-Rochi, Sheikh Mamma-Dibir 109
al-Suguri, Sheikh Abdurahman-Haji 72
al-'Uradi, 'Undal-hajji 109
amal (characters) 70
amal (habit/behaviour) 65–6
amanat (hostages): execution 56; taking 44
amanat (loyalty) 60
amirul'mu'minin (Shamil name) 56
Ananias of Shirak (Pseudo-Moses of
　　Khorene) 16
Anasimov, Ilya 184
Andalal (rural community) 148
andargi, making 207
Andi Koysu river 209
Andiyskiy, Umakhan 149
Andreusi, Labazan 61
Andyreusi, Idris (Effendi) 63, 64
animal products, usage 169–70
anti-*kolkhoz* (state farm) uprisings 82
anti-Semitism, impact 90
apotropaic metal amulets, usage 158
apotropaic symbols 222
Arabic, literary language 108
Arab-Muslim transnational cultural
　　tradition 128
AravoiKushey 186
arba (transportation) 75
arbabash (ox-cart covers) 118–19
arbabashs (felt-carpets), confiscation 76
arbakesh (driver) 75
Archi: Bedeku (folk ensemble) *217, 218*;
　　Bedeku (sacred mount) *215*; Bidi/
　　Klala river (confluence) *214*; bride,
　　gifts (display) *219*; climate 209;
　　costumes 211; customs, agronomic
　　cycle (association) 212; dried
　　meat/sausage *216*; economy 210;
　　education 213; family life 212–13;
　　felt mosaic carpets *217*; flowers
　　220; folk ensemble (Bedeku) *217,
　　218*; food 211–12; Gurkkimey
　　sausage *216*; highland dancers
　　217; houses 210–11; Khvatli *219*;
　　language, usage 108; Mount Kaklik
　　(sheep/shepherd) 215; nature
　　209; old literacy 213; people 210;
　　photo tour 214–20; self-governing
　　villages 208–9; social life 212–13;

topography 207–9; travel *206*;
　　villages/mountains/rivers *208*;
　　virtual tour 206; wedding feast
　　218; wool shepherd, checking/
　　bargaining *216*
Archib (rural community) 148
artel (cooperative), dissolution 83
artisans (social class) 71
Aselt Shavuot 186
Ashkenazi Jews, cradling process 161
Ashkharatsuyts 16
associated spirits 5–13
Astrakhan: conquest 30; settlement 39–40
Astrakhan Khanate, subordination 27
auctoritas 42
autochthonous languages 127–8
Avar grammar, creation 109
Avari, Hadji Murat 62
Avar Khanate, acceptance 42–3
Avar Khan, resistance 45–6
Avar Koysu river 209
Avar language, usage 108
Avar *Magals* (rural communities) 54
Avars: Avar Kolkhoz woman/baby *181*;
　　Facebook *(Maglarul matzI, tarikh
　　wa madaniyat)* 148; healers 165;
　　helmets 20; ruler 42
Avicenna 165
Avshalumova, L. 183
Ayuli 6
Azhdaha (serpent/dragon) 7
Azov, Don Cossacks capture 36

Baanov, Alexander 1
Badarkhan (ambassador) 37–8
Bailey, Harold 5
Bakhchisaray, Don Cossacks (impact) 36
bakhI (dried sausage) 211
Baktlukhi, Muhammad 63, 64
bakъ'il zaman ('adat time') 93
balaban (aerophone) 222
Balakhani, Musa 61
barakat (blessedness) 69
Barrow, Christopher 32
Basdyryk 6
Bashlarov, Sheikh Sayfullah 68
Bashlarov, Sheikh Sayfullah-kadi 69
Batak 63
batrakkom (landless seasonal agricultural
　　hired workers) 82
Batsadi, Kurbanalimuhammed 62
Batsadi, Muhammad 62
batsI (speed of the wolf) 12

Index 229

Bayrambekov, Ali 147
beauty, description 156
Bedeku: folk ensemble (Archi) *217, 218*;
    sacred mount *215*
bedkom (poor peasants) 82
beekeeping 169
beggars (fukara), social class 71
Bela Anchaba Tlo Gyini 6
Bezhta *udarnaya* shock group,
    counterattack 84
Bidi/Klala river (confluence) *214*
big bosses (social class) 70–1
bimushur (real man) 213
Bin Laden, links (denial) 123
birthing room, family (gathering) 158
bitlonnol (real woman) 213
black balaclavas, wearing 153
blessedness *(barakat)* 69
blood feud 65; *krovomoscheniya*, cessation
    74; Soviet response 78; trivial
    reasons 74–5
Bohmer, Harald 203
boklo (norm/rule/permission) 93
Bolshevism, fall 82
book of table etiquette *(Qilik kitap)* 64
Botlikhsy, military operations 122–3
Boz-bash, components 190
Brezhnev, Leonid 78
bride: choice, parental initiative 133;
    gifts, display *219*; kidnapping
    185; wedding obligations 141–2;
    wedding preparations, differences
    138; wedding salon visits 139
bride/groom, collusion 133–4
bridegroom, female mentor (meeting) 142
bride-price *(kalym)* 119
brigands, impact 75
Budallaba 6
bugleme (cooked fish dish) 188
Burkikhan (Agul language dialect) 95
Burnaya (Stormy) fortress 45
businesses, development 95
Bustan Avaristan/Rim, versification 116
Byzantium, bilateral treaty 15–16

"Canon of Medicine, The" (Avicenna) 165
caravanserais, presence 30
Caspian-Moscow, Volga route *27*
Caucasian defensive line, Left Flank
    command 48
Caucasian identity, concept 130
Caucasian nationality, discrimination
    201–2

Caucasus: ethnic situation 127; history,
    shaping 127–8
Caucasus Committee, governing body
    (creation) 50
Caucasus Emirate, terrorism 124–5
Caucasus Mountain Range, defensive line
    44–5
Caucasus Mountains, silver/copper
    search 40
cell phones (mobiles) 145; range 144–5
Central State Archive of Republic of
    Dagestan, materials (usage) 89
cereals, disappearance 174–5
ceremonial bread, apotropaic powers 11
Chabanmakhi, military operations 122–3
chabrets mountain thyme, impact 189
chagana (lute) 141
challah (mattress), usage 157
Chancellor, Richard 31
Charbili, Naib Giada 61
Charodinsky reserve *(zapovednik')* 209
chauvinism, increase 103
Chebotarev, Sergey V. 204
Chechen-Ingush ASSR, multi-
    nationality 89
Chechen rebels, impact 124
Chechen Republic, broadband
    connection 146
Chechnya, Shamil governance 65
Chenciner, Robert 40, 221
Cheremisinov, impact 27
Cherkhal Gyarulele Giamalal 66
Chernyi, Yehuda 184
chiecken, preparation 190
children: character traits, fear 156; physical
    deformity, fear 156; protection
    9–10; soul, belief 155
Chirkeyi, Miklik Murutazali 62
Chirkeyi, Shahmandaril Hajiyav 64
Chirkeyi, Sheikh Jamal 61
Chokhi, Abdullah 69
Chokhi, Musahadzhiyav 61
chudu, creation 189
chudu (pizza), serving 140
chungur (lute) 141
Chursin, G.F. 4
cIadulhIam (cIdudiIma) (cIudlhIam) 11
Ciscaucasia, silver/copper search 40
city weddings, cost 142
Civil War (1918–1921) 77, 179
clean places, medicinal/edible herbs
    (storage) 167
clergy, public life (relationship) 81

230 *Index*

climate (Archi) 209
clinical medicine, impact 155
clothes (traditional material) 67
clubs, development 95
collective dances 141
Commonwealth of Independent States
(CIS), interethnic relations 201–2
Communist Party of Society Union (CPSU)
78, 102, 103, 129
companions/commanders (naibs) 60–4
Constantinople: conquest 26; English
hostile ally (perception) 32
contemporary cultures 127
cornelian twigs *(bilikly)* 8
Cossack Mountain Republic, creation 82
Cossack villages, exclusion 34
costumes (Archi) 211
cough, usage 159–61
Council of People's Commissars of
Dagestan (CPCD), establishment 82
Council of People's Commissars (CEC),
resolution 85
courses, network (supply/development) 95
Covid-19 153–5; levels *154*; surviving,
traditional medicine (usage) 152
crime, crackdown 77–8
crushed stone, usage 170
culture: contemporary culture 127;
homogenisation 104; pre-Soviet
cultures 127

Dagestan: accordion 224–5; agricultural/
manufactured products, trading 20;
animal products, usage 169–70;
beekeeping 169; clothes (traditional
material) 67; conquest 49; cultural
sphere 128; dancing 221; defining
1, 2; description (IX-XIV centuries)
2; digital ethnography 146; eating,
proper method 69; economy,
interdependence 66; ethnic lands
47; Facebook, impact 203; free
societies, attraction 44; fruit trees,
planting 179; grooms, European
tradition (adoption) 138; healers,
ethnoecological perspective
165; herbs, selection/avoidance
168–9; horticultural cultivation
180–1; industrial production,
increase 180; infectious diseases,
transmission 166; insects, cures
170; Islamic identity, assessments
125; Islamization 123; knotted pile

carpets 50–1; large-scale orchards,
rarity 177; Lezginka dancers *225*;
life statistics, quality 201; literacy
106; location 4–5; major rivers
206; marriage, heterosexual alliance
132; minerals, usage/importance
171; mountain Dagestan, traditional
medicine (usage) 164; mountain-
valley horticulture 174; non-
Mountain Jewish Tats, presence
184; paradoxical treatments
165–6; people, ethno-cultural/
ethno-psychological characteristics,
suppression 121; percussion 223;
plants, supernatural properties
166–8; public life 68–9; rebels,
impact 124; regions *(nahiya)*
2; rulers, attraction 44; secular
republic 122; singing 221; social
classes 70–2; social structure,
tribal/patriarchal nature 80; Soviet
rule, repression 118; stringed
instruments 222–3; surgeons,
treatment 164; terracing *176*;
territory, perception 2; topography
180; unification 57; unusual
recipes, usage 170–1; war region
(dar al-harb) 2; water, private
ownership (absence) 178; wind
reeded instruments, usage 222;
wormwood, heat treatment 169
Dagestan Autonomous Soviet Socialist
Republic (ASSR) (DASSR) 87–8;
districts, annexation 88; ethnic
population, literacy **105**; rulers,
impact 80
Dagestan Commissars, farm resettling 88
Dagestan Khans, loyalty 48
Dagestan Regional Party Conference 86
Dagestan Region, Russia establishment 55
Dagestan Scientific Centre Russian
Academy of Sciences 1
Dagestanskaya oblast' (administration) 73
Dagh bari (mountain wall) 16
DagTelecom 145
Dargins, healers 165
Daryal pass 14
dayan, impact 186
Day of Judgement 162
death cult 10
Debirov, Paruk 193
Declaration of the Rights of Peopls of
Russia 81

Index 231

Decree of the People's Commissariat (RSFSR) 102
decrees *(firmans)* 53
Deep packet inspection (DPI) technology, requirement 150
demons 5–13; Kumyk demonic female character 6
Den Pobedi (Victory Day) concert 223
Denton, Andy 221
deportees, origin 77
Derbent (program launch) 50
Derbent Gate 14
Derbent walls *15*
derkhap 11
dhimmi 114
dialectical materialism 53
disadvantaged (zugIafa), social class 71
diseases, children (protection) 9–10
disinterested protector *(zuhd auliya)* 68
'divide and rule' policy, adat/sharia (impact) 74
diyat (ransom) 74
djin-kapura (infidels) 7
Djinss, representation 7
Djuhurum, classification 90
DOBAG project (Ayvacuk Western Anatolia) 203
dolma, serving 137
dragon: stylized dragon (Kaitag silk embroidery, detail) *9*; woollen knotted carpet (detail) *9*
dried meat/sausage (Archi) *216*
dum tapestry-woven carpets 28
dyes, Great Russian merchant purchases 32
dyush-pere, rice (addition) 190
Dzutsev, Hasan 222
Dzutsev, Valery 126

Early Bronze Age, pagan settlement 210
eating, proper method 69
echelons (military groups), impact 85
economy (Archi) 210
education (Archi) 213
Eid al-Adha 132
Eid Uraza Bayram, performing 155
engagement, differentiation 135
English transport ship, value (estimation) 32
enjoyment *(keyf)* 69
equals, self-rule 81
estate-land commission 53–4
ethnic culture sites 148
ethnicity, suppression 103

ethnic languages, erosion 104
ethnic (national) self-consciousness, growth 129
ethnic self-identification, preservation 203
ethno-cultures, cross-generational transmission (decrease) 103
ethno-entrepreneurship 203
ethno-religious Imamate (Shamil) 60
Europe, gendarme 44
evil eye: children, protection 9–10; impact 159
evil spirits: habitats 6; impact 166

fajiruna 2
false sheikhs, damnation 65
family life (Archi) 212–13
farsh, performing 70
Farsi-Tat translation, usage 184
fatal reality, enforcement (perception) 76–7
fate 67–8
Federal Information Resource Government of Russia, comparisons 153
Federal Service for Supervision of Consumer Rights Protection and Human Welfare 153
Federal Veterinary and Phytosanitary Oversight Service *(Rosselkhoznadzor)* 175
felt mosaic carpets (Archi) *217*
Fight Nights Global 195
finance, heroes 192
fire, spring festival (relationship) 12
firmans (decrees) 53
First Furrow, celebration 212–13
fish, consumption 188
Fitinsky (Agul language dialect) 95
flowers (Archi) *220*
folk ensemble (Bedeku) (Archi) *217, 218*
folk medicine, usage 155–62
food (Archi) 211–12
free people *(Uzden)* 54
free societies *(vol'nye obshchestva)* 42
Free Society 39
free will 67–8
fruit trees, planting 179

Gadzhiev, Murtazali 1
Gadzhiibragimov, Dzhamaludin 154
Gadziev, Tagir 198–9, *199*
Gaethjue, Justin 198
gamgi, making 207
Gammer, Moshe 1
Gamzatov, G.G. 102

232 Index

Gamzatov, Rasul 89–90, 128, 130
Garunova, Saida 1
Gazikumukhi, Bukmammad 61
Gazimuhammad (Imam) 61; innovations 66; Shamil ally 66
Genibikh (pear-cutter-in-half) 62
Genovese e dunque mercato 23
Georgian Military Highway, construction 18
Ghan, P.V. 49; program, implementation 50
Ghilghilchay (defensive long wall) 14–16
glabid (pilgrim) 62
gladlu (society) 70–1
Giamal kvesh 66
giavam (society) 64
Gielmu lalel glalimal glodoreglanlun gari 64
Gilmu-l-Basharia (socio-ethnology) 68
godekan (bench), meeting 155
God, fear 70
Godunov, Boris (reign) 29–30
Golden Horde: diplomacy 23; trade 18
good character, Shamil promotion 65–6
goods, accumulation 66
Goryana-coat 119
Goryanka: emancipation 120; liberation 119
Grand Princes of Kiev, dominance 20
Great Russian merchants, Constantinople ban 34
Great Russia, survival 21
Great Silk Road (GSR) 18, *22*; access 26, 34–5
groom: gift-giving, delay 136; party, preparation 138–9; presentation 137; wedding preparations, differences 138
Guducl 6
Gulistan Peace Treaty (1813) 44
Gumbet district, deportee origin 77
guofer (rocking cradle), usage 157
Gurkkimey sausage (Archi) *216*
Gurzhistan mountains 3
Gusatu-l-mutatlavvigati-Allagase glolo gazavat gabulel chagli rugo (veteran fighters) 68
Gyomunu Purim 186

hadiths 65
Hannal Murad (Damadan) medical guide 165
Harahi, Muhammadamin 61, 63
hasiyat (character) 65–6

Hawa 'Iech (Apple of Eve) 167
healers: ethnoecological perspective 165; impact 165; recipes, control 168
heat treatment 169
herbal medicines, administration 168
herbs/spices: selection/avoidance 168–9; trading 212
hermeosh, preparation 190
Hiamal klodoli 66
highland dancers (Archi) *217, 218*
Highland feudalism 53
hijab, wearing 135
hirs (gluttony) treatment 69
historical consciousness (XIX century) 53
hnafarush (Persian title) 50
holy buildings, destruction 76
homogeneous Socialism 102
honey, beekeeping 169
honey-derived wax, usage 169
horticultural cultivation 180–1
horticulture, small mechanization 180–1
horticulture/winemaking, jamaat regulation 176
hostages *(amanat):* execution 56; taking 44
houbal (supernatural beings) 5
'ho, untamed body' (Qasida) 115–16
houses (Archi) 210–1
humanity, supreme values 94, 128
human rights, Russian regulation 149–51
Human Rights Watch (HRW) report 149
Huns, Sasanian wall protection 14

Ibn Rushd 10
ibn Sina, Abu Ali (Avicenna) 165
Ibnu-sabil (traveller on his journey) 68
Ibragimov, Magomed-Rasul 1
Ichkeria, secession 125
igbi (seeing off winter) 12
ignorant (social class) 71
Igor (Grand Prince) 20
Ikhilov, Mikhail 190
Ilisui, Daniyalbek 62
Ilyasova, Elmira 147
Imamate: ethno-religious Imamate (Shamil) 60; fall 65
imams, political trustworthiness 119
industrial production, increase 180
infectious diseases, transmission 166
Ingara pol 189
Ingushetia, broadband connection 146
Inholi, Aligaji 66–8
insects, cures 170

Index   233

Institutionalized lying, repression
(comparison) 90
interethnic mixing 104
inter-ethnic relations, risk 130
internal self-government/status,
recognition 44
Internet Protocol (IP) addresses, RKN
blockage 150
Internet, usage 146–149
Iranian languages, Jewish language
(relationship) 184
irrigation system, self-regulation 178–9
Isfahan: encroachment 40; flourishing,
reforms 36
Ish al-yavma ka annaka tamutu gadan 68
Islam: Puritans of Islam, denials 121–2;
religion, comparison 118;
revival 120
'Islamic scholar' 64
Israel, Mountain Jews emigration 186–7
'I was enchanted by this transient world'
(Qasida) 115
Izudinov, Gamzat 222

jamaat 42
jamaats: horticulture/winemaking
regulation 176; permission,
absence 178
jamaats, split 56–7
Jenkinson, Anthony 31
Jewish food culture, slaughtering (usage)
190–1
Jewish refugees/immigrants,
descendants 183
Jewish-Tat 90
Joint State Political Directorate (OGPU) 83

kachaglar 75
Kadinaylo, Abdurahman 147
Kadis 65
Kadis, nominal subjects 43
Kadiyate, abolishment 43
Kaitago-Tabasaran District 77
Kaitag silk embroideries 8
Kaitag Utsmi: agent 40; nominal subjects 43
Kakabadze, Zurab 129
Kaliningrad Stadium, construction 195
kalym (bride-price) 119
Karachay-Cherkessia (Klaukhorsky/
Sapcharsky passes) 18
Kara-Koysu River 209
Karamakhi, military operations 122–3
Karati, Galbatsdiber 62

Kartlis Tskhovreba (compilation) 130
kaurma (fried meat pieces) 189
Kazan, conquest 30
Kazan Khanate, conquest 27
Kazikumukh, Aslan-khan (power
transfer) 46
Kazikumukh Khan, nominal subjects 43
Kazi-Kumukh Koysu river 209
Kazikumukhsky, Jamalutdin 213
kekul (one strand), preservation 161–2
kemenche 223
Kerimov, Suleiman 194, *196*, 196–7
keyf (enjoyment) 69
Khabib (The Eagle) Nurmagomedov 154
Khachaburov, Ruslan 123
khachag'al 75
khachagatal 75
Khadzhimuhammad-Musalav 67
Khal 6
khalai, making 207
Khalilov, Minkail 77
Khan, Abu Sultan-Nutsal (power
transfer) 46
Khanate of Derbent, income usage 43
Khanate of Mehtuli, natural rulers
(jurisdiction) 49–50
khanates, split 55–6
Khans: alliance 48; reciprocal rights 39;
social class 70–1
Khappoulaev, Ramazan 221
kharakter (temperament) 66
Khasavyurt district party committee,
responsible officers *(ovetstvennie
rabotniki)* impact 87–8
Khasavyurt *raion*, convening 83
Khatar-Ris Or river 209
Khilmi, Sheikh Hassan 68
khinkal 19
khinkal (four dumping) 137
Khoye-gusht, components 190
KhuduchI 6
khulurkhus 212
Khunzakhi, Akhberdilmuhammad 61, 63
Khushtadi, Musalav 61
Khushtadi, Zakariyahadzhiyav 61
khuyurma, making 207
Khvarshin spirits 5–6
Khvatli (Archi) *219*
Kievan Rus: collapse 21; contacts 18–19;
influence 21
Kievan Russ, trade 18
kings (social class) 70–1
kinjal (silver-mounted daggers) 28

234 *Index*

kinjals (daggers), usage 49
kinship, degree 136
Kish Kaftar 6
kishki intestines, preparation 189
Kizilov (Cornelian cherry dogwood) 8
Kizilyurt fortification, completion 45
Klaukhorsky pass 18
klub (kosher) restrictions 186
Klyuchevsky, Vasily Osipovich 1
Kochap Mamma (Magomed) (Sali-
    Suleiman), fame 192–3
kolkhoz: collective farm system 201;
    dissolution 84
Kolupaev, impact 27
Köppen-Geiger CSA 177
Koshan (Agul language dialect) 95
Kosven, M.O. 125
Kovalevsky, M.M. 125
KPSS members, state fund
    appropriation 202
krai 132
Krasnaya Svoboda 186–7
krestkom (peasant committees), land
    transfer 82
krovomoscheniya (blood feud), cessation 74
Krygyzstan, relatives (transportation) 87
Kudali, Hassan 67
Kudutli, MaxIahIajiyav 62
Kudutli, Musa 67
kulaks: production, termination 85; rights,
    restoration 83
kulak, vilification 82
Kultsansturm (1928) *96*
Kultsansturm (cultural revolution
    slogan) 95
Kumyk demonic female character 6
kunakskaya 184
Kupriyanovich, Leonid Ivanovich 144–5
Kurakh-Kazikumukh Khanate, division 46
Kurakh Khanate, annex 43–4
Kurbanilali (Batsadi Muhammad son) 62
kurdyuk (fat tail sheep fat), usage 169
Kurze raviolis, preparation 211
kurze (dumplings), serving 140–1
kutum, usage 188

Laks, healers 165
landlords *(pomeshiki)* 82
Land of Mountains, inhabitants 29
land, privatization 174
language policy 93
large-scale orchards, rarity 177
Latin Crusader Empire, existence 22–3

layer of important people *(Tabakat
    al-hwajakan)* 64–5
layette, preparation (absence) 157
leeches, usage 170
leisure, Gazimuhammad innovations 66
Lekhi Mountains (kuh-i Leksi) 33
Lenin 53, 82, 152
Lezginka dancers *225*
Lezgin line, completion 45
Lezgin Sumak rungs 40
Lezistan, term (usage) 2
lichen, treatment usage 171
Limes Caspius 16
literacy, Tsar/Soviets (impact) 100
Livonian War 30
local ethnic language, omission 128
Lowe, Adam 194
loyalty *(amanat)* 60
Luguev, Sergey Abdulkhalikovich 11
lula (afterbirth), treatment 159

MagIarul matzI, tarikh wa madaniyat
    (Avars Facebook) 148
magic 5–13; wedding rites 10–11
magic places 5
magIishatI, social economics 66
Magomedkhan (Khere) 210
Magomedmirzayev, Abdula 223
Magomedova, Malvina 147
Magomedova, R. 183
Magomedov, Magomed
    Abdulgamidovich 174
Magomedov, M.M. 98
Magomedov, Ziyavudin 194–6, *195*
Makhachkala 192, 207; 'Actual Problems
    of Combating Religious-
    Political Extremism (All-Russian
    Conference) 120; hospital,
    quarantine 153; Javatkhan arrival
    78; land redistribution 89
Makhachklaa, Novoe Delo 1
Makhmudov, Rustam 148
malik 2
Mamma-Dibir al-Rochi 111–12
Manifesto of the Union of Farmers,
    founding 82–3
manti (kurze), serving 141
marriage: civil registration, fixation 137;
    collective dances 141; common
    ground, finding 135; conspiracy
    133; dance groups, invitation 141;
    religious weddings 137–8; ring,
    presentation 136

Marx, Karl 102
Matatov, M. 183
matchmaking: ceremony, initiation 137; engagement, differentiation 135–6
maternity rites, folk medicine (usage) 155–62
matzah, preparation 186
Mavraev, M. 101
МаГаруJI МаЦI ТарИх Ва МаДаНИЯТ (rural community) 148
McGregor, Conor 197
Meade, Kylie 197
meat: consumption 188; preservation 190
Megafon PJSC 145
Mehtulinsky, Akhmed Khan (power transfer) 46
Mengu-Timur: empire, collapse 26; privileges/attack 23–4
mental illness, sulphur (impact) 7
merchant Disaporas, emulation 91
merchants (social class) 71
Michael VIII Palaiologos 22–3
migrant Dagestanis, repression 91
migrants, bailiff charge 48
Mikailov, Mikail 148
Mikhailov, A.M. 101
milin-khitin, making 207
milo (circumcision) 160–1
minerals, usage/importance 171
mishiravi (hand of Moses), decoration 158
mobiles. *see* cell phones
monsters 4
moral social relations, decline 4
Moscow-Europe, trading routes *31*
Moscow Tsardom, trade (XV-XVI centuries) 26
Moskva, Nafta 196
Mountain Botanical Garden Institute 174
mountain Dagestan, traditional medicine (usage) 164
mountaineers, lifestyle 166
mountain gardening, tradition 175
Mountain Jews 140, 183; census 90; emigration 186; material culture 185; maternity rites 155; meat/fish, consumption 188; relocation, history 184; swaddled cradle, belief 161
Mountain Jews (Tats) 90
mountains, monetization 201
mountain-valley horticulture 174
mountain women, liberation 119
Mount Kaklik (sheep/shepherd) *215*
mudir (mystic) 62

Mudirs 65
Muftis 65
muftis, political trustworthiness 119
Muhammad-Paqir 110, 114
Mukhtasibs 65
Murat, Hadji (denunciation) 62
muridism (national liberation struggles) 57
murshids (presence) 65
Musaeva, Maysarat 1
Muscovy Company, foothold (attempt) 32
Muscovy, trade (XVII-XVIII centuries) 34
Muslim brotherhood, slogans 120
Muslim clergy, power (paralysis) 74
Muslim Russian Empire, religion (fate) 76
Muslim Spiritual Board 123
muta'allims, education 81
myarkushi 11

Nabiev, Khadzhimurad 147
nafs (egos): combatting 71; education 69
nā'ib (assistant, deputy head) 73
naibs (companions/commanders) 60–4
namaz, performing 167
namus (sense of dury, shyness) 213
narcotic plants, application 168
Narodniy vrach Dagestana' (Peoples' Doctor of Dagestan), title 152
narodnosti (nationality), *Djuhurum* classification 90
narzans (healing springs) 171
nasiha (advice) 114
national culture, writing 101
nationalism, increase 103
national languages/cultures, promotion 104
national liberation struggles *(muridism)* 57
National Policy Strategy (NPS), implementation 204
native language, developing/ strengthening 95
natsionalnost (ethnos), pejorative term 90
natural assimilation, phenomena 101–2
nature (Archi) 209
Nazhmudinov, Shamil 223
Nazim of Durghili 110
Nazm Kvanil adab-Sunnatab (Food Culture following Sunnah) (Sirazhudin) 69
"Necklace of Pearls from the Depth of the Seas" 213
newborns: birth, preparation 158; cradle, laying 161; hygiene 160–1; midwife examination 159; *milo* (circumcision) 160–1; mortality 159

236   *Index*

New Millennium banquet hall, usage 137
Niesonu/Passover 186
nikah (religious service) 212
nilfarush (Persiantitle) 50
nizam 60
NKGB secret police, impact 88
nof (umbilical cord), washing/drying 159
non-clipping tariff-free trade, conducting 36
non-Great Russian peoples: assistance 95;
    labouring masses, assistance 95
non-Mountain Jewish Tats, presence 184
North Caucasian caravans, arrival 37
North Caucasian republics, survival
    problems 120
North Caucasus, strategic positions
    (seizure) 35–6
Novolaksky, military operations 122–3
Novoye Dello Dagestan 153
nubo hunde, presence 185–6
numaz (religious rite), performing 185–6
Nurmagomedov, Abdulmanap 197, *198*
Nurmagomedov, Khabib 146, *195*, 197–8,
    1979
NVF Buinaksk, wanted poster 124

obedience, piety (association) 133
obkom (regional committee) 80
Oboda, Sirazhudin 116
Obodi, Sirazhudin 69
October Revolution (1917) 77
Odnoklassniki (OK), LinkedIn
    (comparison) 145–6
offal fat, roasting 190
official Islam 119
ointments, preparation 168
old literacy (Archi) 213
"On Logic for a Travelling
    Companion" 213
'On the Languages of the Peoles of the
    Russian Federation' law 97–8
Opera (anonymiser), usage 149–50
order, traditional commitment 75–76
Orthodox Georgia, annexation 42
Osmann, Murad 146
Ottomans: commerce, mastery 39–40
Ottomans, control 26–7
ovungez (gold jewellery) 158

Pankil kulgyu, kyolol bertin ('for a funeral
    a cake, for a wedding a toast') *sto
    gram* (Russian for a hundred grams
    i.e. a measure of vodka) 68
paradoxical treatments 165–6

Park, Robert Ezra 91
Parteigenosse (Member of the Party) 78
Paskevich-Erivansky (Governor Count),
    complaint 48
patronimiya 80
pear-cutter-in-half *(Genibikh)* 62
Pechenegs 20
people (Archi) 210
pepepai (peshepay) 11
percussion (Dagestan) 223
Persia, Caspitan traffic 32
personal vengeance, obligation 76
pervaya borozda (First Furrow) 12;
    watering, initiation 179
Peysach (Passover) 188
Peysakh (Paskha), fast-period 191
Pies, N.I. 164
piety, obedience (association) 133
pilaf, serving 141
plants, supernatural properties 166–8
Plenum of the Dagestan Regional
    Committee, Turkic (state
    language) 103
plov, preparation 190
poems, Avar/Archi languages (usage) 108
Poirier, Dustin 197
poisonous plants, application 168
political trustworthiness 119
Polovtsy, impact 20
polygamy, support 119
pomeshiki (landlords) 82
pood 38–9
poor *(miskin)*, social class 71
possessions, abolishing/redrawing 45–6
pregnant women: actions 156; contractions,
    ease 158; hygiene 160–1; isolation
    160; layette, preparation (absence)
    157; newborns, mortality 159;
    uncleanliness, consideration 157
pre-historical meaning 80
pre-Soviet cultures 127
press, development 95
prioritisation, compromise 130
procession circles 140
Prophet Muhammad (sacrifices) 61
propolis, usage 169
Pskov 21
public consciousness: poisoning 119;
    re-Islamization 118
public life 68–9
publishing, Tsar/Soviets (impact) 100
pupils (social class) 71
Puritans of Islam, denials 121–2

Qadi Ali 67
Qasidas: 'ho, untamed body' 115–16; 'I was enchanted by this transient world' 115; sheikh Mamma-Dibir al-Rochi 111–12; 'This transient universe' (Sulen Muhammad) 116
Qasvini, Hamdallah 3
Qazi 76
qiadrab gIamal 66
Qilik Kitap (Akaev) 69
Qilik kitap (book of table etiquette) 64
Qirmizi Qesebe (Krasnaya Svoboda) 186–7
Quba Uyezd (program launch) 50

Rafi, Muhammad 2
raiding system *(abreks)* 55
raikrestkom (regional citizens committee) 83
rain rituals 11
Ramazanova, Zoya 1
ranginfarush (Persian title) 50
ransom *(diyat)* 74
raw silk cost *(pood)* 38
Red Web, The (Soldatov) 150
re-Islamization 118
religion: fate 76; fight, relaxation 118–19
religious weddings 137–8
repression 80
RF Administrative Code 149
Richin (Agul language dialect) 95
ring, presentation 136
Risis (creature) 8
Ris-Or river 206
robbery 75
Rodrigue, B.H. 1
Romanov, Mikhail Fedorovich 34
Roskomnadzor (RKN) 149–50
royal jelly, usage 169
rural communities, ethnic pages 148–49
rural societies, civil self-government 76–7
Rush gyo-Shone Rosh Hashana/New Year 186
Russia: agreed obligations 36; Avar Khanate protection 42–3; governance (1801–1859) 42; prosody rules, deviations 109
Russian Empire, population (census) 94
Russian-European educated bourgeoisie 57–8
Russian government, legal systems 73
Russian language, cultural integration/political consolidation (full-scale functioning) 99

Russian painted boxes/caskets/sieves/dishes/chests, demand 37
Russian power, armed opposition 55
Russian Revolution (1905–1907) 77
Russian Social Democratic Workers' Party, Second Congress 81
Russian State, military-political alliance 35
Russian state xenophobia 145–6
Russia-Persia rout, protection (inability) 35
Russification 102–3
Rustam-kadi, support 46
Rustam Khan, Kaitag Utsmi 37

saadak 65
Saadullah 63
sacred trees 12
sadan (unclean forces) 158; hiding 160–1
Sadovoy, A.N. 1
Safat-Girey (Crimean Khan) 36
Safavid Persia, rtrade (re-establishment) 34
Safavids, ouster 30
saints *(GIubad, Zugiad, Mukhlis)*, social class 71
salaam aleikum (peace to you) 194
sala-uzden (class) 54
Salti, Umar 63
Samur Lezgins, social structure 54
Sapcharsky pass 18
Saray-Berke, destruction 24
Sasanian walls, protection 14
sausages, boiling 189
savdagars 37
Saypudinova, Zarema 147
sazan, usage 188
Schilling, E. 4
schools: Decree of the People's Commissariat (RSFSR) 102; network, supply/development 95; Tsar/Soviets, impact 100
scientific process, principles 155
scriptless languages, culture (absence) 109
scripts, creation 95–6
self-assimilation, objective necessity 97
self-determination, freeing 81
self-rule 81
selkhozarteli collective farm, demonstration 83
Sergei Posad, destruction 30
sericulture, usage 185
serif line 36
Shabbat (Saturday), cradle (laying) 161
Shah Abbas I the Great, reforms 36
Shahanshah Yazdegerd I 14–15

238   *Index*

Shaitans (negative spirits) 4
Shamil *57*; Chechnya governance 65;
  Dagestan unification 57; epidemics,
  combatting 166; ethno-religious
  Imamate 60; Gazimuhammad
  (Imam) ally 66; good character
  promotion 65–6; *maglishatl*, social
  economics 66; naibs (companions/
  commanders) 60–4; name 60;
  opponents 50; picture postcards,
  sale 192
Shamkhalstvo possessions, control 45
Shamkhalstvo Tarkovsky: natural rulers,
  jurisdiction 49–50; threat 45;
  transfer 43
Sharafutdinova, Rukiya 108
Sharh al-Muhazzaba 66
Shariah Council, impact 84
sharia, impact 74
sharia, Wahhabi introduction 122
shashki (sabres) 28
shashlik (religious feast) 188
shawls, gift 138
Sheikh Ali Khan: independence/
  sovereignty/ouster 43; removal
  43–4; support 46
Shikhsaidov, Amri 3
Shodrodi, Hajiyav 63
Shulani, Ismaildiber 117
shuttle trading 202
Siberia, exile 49
sipat (qualities) 70
Sistema Venture Capital 145
skin diseases, curing 171
Small and Medium-sized Enterprises
  (SMEs) 202–3
SMERSH, impact 88
"Social and Economic Development
  of Mountain Territories of
  the Republic of Dagestan for
  2014–2018" 202
social bloggers 147
social classes 70–2
social life (Archi) 212–13
social media (XXI century) 144
social networks, impact 136
social self-affirmation,
  encouragement 129
society *(gladlu)* 70–1
socio-ethnology *(Gilmu-l-Basharia)* 68
Sogratli, Khursh 62
Sogratlinsky, Abdurahman 213
Soldatov, Andrei 150

*Sordo-koyal kwanase kven rokob bougev
  chiyas, Chiyadasa jo gari, kurab jo
  badib chlvayi* 68
sore throat *(zhuzam baras)* 69
sorochene 37
Sounds of the Caucasus conference 221
sovereign bins, goods storage 38
sovereign feasts 38
sovereign service 36
Soviet ethnography, creation 53
Sovietization 80
Soviet Man, beliefs 103
Soviet people, collective 99
Soviet power: establishment 128–9;
  neutralization 84
Soviet Power, establishment 179
Soviet statehood, developing/
  strengthening 95
Sovkhoz collective farm system 201
spavochnik (directory) 144
spirits: associated spirits 5–13; evil spirits,
  habitats 6; evil spirits, impact 166;
  Khvarshin spirits 5–6
sport, heroes 192
spring festival, fire (relationship) 12
Stalin 83; picture postcards, sale 192
state language, Federal Law
  (superseding) 98
state-owned warehouses, goods storage 38
Stavropol Territory borders, interethnic
  mixing 104
stringed instruments (Dagestan) 222–3
strugs, usage 37
students (social class) 71
stylized dragon (Kaitag silk embroidery,
  detail) *9*
Sublime Porte 26; protest 29
substances 4
success, achievement 129
Sufis, Salafis (religious conflict) 123
Sugum (celebration) 189
Sukhayb 62
Sulag 6
Sullen Muhammad (Qasida) 116
sultans (social class) 70–1
sumakhs (weft-float brocades) 50–1
sunduk (chest) 138
sunna 69
supernatural beings *(houbal)* 5
Surkhab-bek Bek, support 46
Surkhay-khan: devotion, absence 45–6;
  nominal rule 46; possessions,
  deprivation 46

surroundings 5–13
Suv-anasy 6
Svyatoslav (Grand Prince) 20
Syutkatyn 6

Tabakat al-hwajakan (layers of important people) 64–5
Tabasaran Maysumate, abolishment 46
Tabasaran Maysum, nominal subjects 43
Tabasaran *rayon* (Soviet administrative unit), demonstration 83
Takho-Godi, Alibek 86–7, 119
Talhis al-maa'rif fi tahrib Muhammad 'Giarif (Khilmi) 68
tariqa (theological disputes) 103
Tarki, threatening 45
Tarkovsky, Ildar 37
Tarkovsky, Shamkhal 36
Tats 90; census 90–1
Taylor, George 164
Telegram Open Network (anonymiser) 149–50
Teletli, Kebdmuhammed 62, 64
Temir-Khan-Shura, judgements 73
Terki, securing 29–30
terracing *176*
Tersky, location *35*
Tersky Settlements, markets 30
textile symbols 8
'This transient universe' (Sulen Muhammad) 116
Tindi village (Risis) 8
titular peoples 99, 104
tmin (mountain caraway), impact 189
Tokhtamysh 23
topography 180
topography (Archi) 207–9
Tor (anonymiser) 149–50
'torment-relieving elixir, A' (Kharda al-Rochi) 112–15
Tpig (Agul language dialect) 95
traditional medicine, usage 152, 164
Transcaucasians, imprisonment 85
Transcaucasus, premature interference 29–30
tribal frameworks 125
tribunes (social class) 71
Tsar, Khan resistance/submittance 45
tsIugyaduleb gIamal 66
Tsubutli, Rajab 63
Tsumadinsky, military operations 122–3
tukkhum 80

tukkhum (clan), representative (actions) 11
Turkish-Crimean troops, free passage (ensuring) 35–6

udarnaya shock group, counterattack 84
Ulus Magal (program launch) 50
Uman (security services) AAG (social class) 71
umma, extoling 114
Ummah Khan of Avar, village taxation 176
Ummul Bayan (Old Lady) (Chokhi) 69
unhappy/sick (social class) 71
Union of Muslims of Russia 120
United State of North Caucasus Mountain Peoples, creation 81
Unkrak (rural community) 148
unusual recipes, usage 170–1
urban life, pressures 134
urban weddings, traditions 132
urbech (highland chocolate) 168
urtilunchov 11
USM 145
Usmanov, Alisher 145
USSR, language policy 93
Uzden (free people) 54

Vakhabism (Wahhabism transliteration) 124
vakuf (religious charitable foundation) property, appropriation 82
Vasilij, Abaev I. 130
Vasilyev, Vladimir 153
Vatan (newspaper) 186
Vechekhur 156
Veliky Novgorod 21, 24
Veon 145
vezirs (ministers), social class 71
videophones, usage 144
villages, life (peacefulness) 57
virtual private networks (VPNs): operation 150; usage 149–50
voenno-narodnoe upravleniye (military-national government) 73
voinstvuyushii ateizm (militant atheism) 90
Volga-Astrakhan-Shirvan route 27
Volga-Capsian trade artery, focus 31–2
Volga route *27*
vol'nye obshchestva (free societies) 42
Volozh, Arkady 145
von Uslar, Peter 109

Wahhabis: propaganda 121; sharia, introduction 122
waqfs 65

240 *Index*

Wastyrdjy (St George festival) 221
watering, initiation 179
water, private ownership (absence) 178
water rites, usage 11
websites, blocking 150
wedding: city weddings, cost 142; expenses, reduction 142–3; First Visit 142; preparations, differences 138; ritual songs 143; waiters, arrival 140
wedding banquet hall (interior) *138*
wedding feast (Archi) *218*
wedding-*mawlid* 137–8
Wedding Planner (TV program) 139
WhatsApp 150
Whewell, Tim 221
White Sea ports, opening 32–3
Williamson-Fa, Stefan 1, 223, 224
wind reeded instruments, usage (Dagestan) 222
wirds (mystic categories) 70
wisdom, seekers (social class) 71
witnesses, reluctance 76–7
wolves 12–13
women (social class) 71
wooden utensils, demand 37
wool shepherd, checking/bargaining (Archi) *216*
Words about Igor's Regiment (Vernadsky) 20
worker-peasant Union, destruction 82–3
worldly life, renunciation 70

worldly matters, transience 67–8
wormwood, heat treatment 169
wrestling, seriousness 192–4

Yagni, components 190
yah (will/conscience) 213
Yandex.ru search engine, usage 145
Yarovaya amendments 149
yasti balaban (oboe) 222
Yazdegerd I (Shahanshah) 14–15
Yeltsin, Boris N 97–8
yeshiva (religious school), presence 185
Yom Kippur/Judgement Day 186
Young Ahvakh (rural community) 148

zagyids 70
Zakatala okrug, deportee origin 77
zamzam 65
zastoy stagnation 201
Zasulak Kumyk possessions, internal management 42
Zhalki, Usman 63
Zhirinovsky 152
Zhiut-Katta (Jewish Gorge) 183–84
zhuzam baras (sore throat) 69
Zirichgeran 2
ziyarats (holy shrines) 119
Zubair ("Khusro") 63
zuhd auliya (disinterested protector) 68
Zulak Kumyk possessions 42
Zunsi, Ummah 63
zurna (reed instrument) 6